Environmental Crises in Central Asia

T0295732

Environmental conditions do not exist in a vacuum. They are influenced by science, politics, history, public policy, culture, economics, public attitudes, and competing priorities, as well as past human decisions. In the case of Central Asia, such Soviet-era decisions include irrigation systems and physical infrastructure that are now crumbling, mine tailings that leach pollutants into soil and groundwater, and abandoned factories that are physically decrepit and contaminated with toxic chemicals.

Environmental Crises in Central Asia highlights major environmental challenges confronting the region's former Soviet republics: Kazakhstan, Kyrgyzstan, Tajikistan, Turkmenistan, and Uzbekistan. They include threats to the Caspian and Aral seas, the impact of climate change on glaciers, desertification, deforestation, destruction of habitat and biodiversity, radioactive and hazardous wastes, water quality and supply, energy exploration and development, pesticides and food security, and environmental health. The ramifications of these challenges cross national borders and may affect economic, political, and cultural relationships on a vast geographic scale. At the same time, the region's five governments have demonstrated little resolve to address these complex challenges.

This book is a valuable multi-disciplinary resource for academics, scholars, and policymakers in environmental sciences, geography, political science, natural resources, mass communications, public health, and economics.

Eric Freedman, a Pulitzer Prize-winner, is Knight Chair and Director of the Knight Center for Environmental Journalism at Michigan State University, USA.

Mark Neuzil is a professor of communication and journalism at University of St. Thomas in St. Paul, Minn., USA, where he teaches environmental communication, multimedia reporting, communication history, and communication ethics.

Routledge Studies in Environmental Communication and Media

Environmental Crises in Central Asia

From steppes to seas, from deserts to glaciers

Edited by
Eric Freedman and Mark Neuzil

LONDON AND NEW YORK

First published 2016
by Routledge
2 Park Square, Milton Park, Abingdon, Oxon OX14 4RN

and by Routledge
711 Third Avenue, New York, NY 10017

First issued in paperback 2018

Routledge is an imprint of the Taylor & Francis Group, an informa business

British Library Cataloguing-in-Publication Data
A catalogue record for this book is available from the British Library

Library of Congress Cataloging-in-Publication Data
A catalog record for this book has been requested

ISBN 13: 978-1-138-59753-2 (pbk)
ISBN 13: 978-1-138-82484-3 (hbk)

Typeset in Goudy
by HWA Text and Data Management, London

Contents

Figures

Tables

Contributors

Murat Aitmatov – Professor at Kyrgyz National Agrarian University named after K.I. Skryabin in Kyrgyzstan, Director of its Center of Bio-cultural Diversity and project manager of 'Increasing Community Resilience to Climate Change Impacts in Mountain Areas of Kyrgyzstan' at the Aga Khan Foundation. Educated at Moscow Veterinary Academy, Kazakh National Agrarian University, he pursued his doctorate in environment and veterinary sanitation in Kazakhstan and confirmed his degree in Kyrgyzstan. Under his leadership, Michigan State University's Integrated Pest Management programme in Kyrgyzstan implemented Farmers Field Schools and created a Student Field School at Kyrgyz National Agrarian University.

Kazbek N. Apsalikov – Director of the National Research Institute for Radiation Medicine and Ecology in Semipalatinsk, Kazakhstan. He holds an MD and a PhD in Radiation Hygiene. He has participated in clinical and epidemiological research among the population in the Semipalatinsk region and has participated in a number of international projects related to health effects around the Semipalatinsk Nuclear Test Site.

George Bird – Professor of Nematology in the Department of Entomology at Michigan State University, U.S., and former Research Scientist with Agriculture Canada and Associate Professor at University of Georgia. He received his BS and MS degrees from Rutgers University and PhD from Cornell University. As a recipient of the MSU Distinguished Faculty Award and former Director of the U.S. Sustainable Agriculture Research and Education Program, he maintains bio-based agriculture, soil health biology and sustainable development programmes.

Tobias Bolch – Senior Researcher at the Department of Geography, University of Zurich, Switzerland, and Institute of Cartography, Dresden University of Technology, Germany. He studies the impact of climate change on glaciers and other elements of the cryosphere in different parts of the earth by remote sensing and field investigations. His main regional focuses are the high mountains of Asia, including Tian Shan and Pamir.

Allan Buras – Postdoctoral Fellow at the Institute of Botany and Landscape Ecology, Ernst-Moritz-Arndt University, Greifswald, Germany. He focuses on dendroecology of trees and shrubs in arctic, temperate, and arid regions. Further research activities comprise the development of statistical tools in terms of climate reconstructions.

Christine Carmichael – PhD candidate, Department of Forestry, Michigan State University, U.S. Her research interests include community engagement in forestry-related issues, urban political ecology, feminist approaches to research, environmental justice, and media coverage of environmental issues. She is collaborating with a non-profit environmental organization in Detroit, Michigan, to examine resident and organizational staff perspectives on street tree planting projects, emphasizing the role of heritage narratives and symbolic meaning of trees in constructing the urban landscape.

Mustapha El-Bouhssini – Earned his PhD in 1992 from Kansas State University, U.S. In 1996, he joined the International Center for Agricultural Research in the Dry Areas (ICARDA) in Aleppo, Syria. His research has been on integrated pest management of cereals and legume crops. As part of the decentralization strategy of ICARDA, he has been based in Morocco since 2012.

Jeanne Féaux de la Croix – Social anthropologist based at Tübingen University, Germany. She directs a Junior Research Group on the cultural history of water in Central Asia. She is also co-leader of a team researching the Naryn and Syr Darya rivers, supported by the Volkswagen Foundation and a project investigating salinization processes and effects. Recent fellowships at Zentrum Moderner Orient in Berlin focused on investigating aging in Central Asia, the impact of energy policies, and development projects such as dams on everyday life in the region. Together with David Gullette, she co-edited the *Central Asian Survey* special issue on everyday energy challenges in Central Asia and the Caucasus.

Eric Freedman – Knight Chair and Director of the Knight Center for Environmental Journalism at Michigan State University, U.S. He is a former Fulbright Scholar in Uzbekistan and Lithuania, and former International Scholar at American University of Central Asia through the Open Society Foundations Academic Fellowship Program. His books include *After the Czars and Commissars: Journalism in Authoritarian Post-Soviet Central Asia* (Michigan State University Press).

Tracey German – Senior Lecturer in the Defence Studies Department at the Joint Services Command and Staff College, King's College London. Her research focuses on conflict and security in the Caucasus and Caspian region, as well as energy issues in the region.

Bernd Grosche – Division Head, Effects and Risks from Ionizing and Non-Ionizing Radiation in the Department of Radiation Protection and Health of Germany's Federal Office for Radiation Protection (BfS). He holds a PhD in Epidemiology and an MSc in Sociology. He has lengthy experience in Kazakhstan-related projects on risk assessment, in particular in relation to nuclear weapons testing.

David Gullette – Social anthropologist and development expert focusing on Central Asia. He has worked extensively on examining challenges in the energy sector. He co-edited the *Central Asian Survey* special issue on everyday energy challenges in Central Asia and the Caucasus with Jeanne Féaux de la Croix. He also assists with international development activities focused on disaster risk reduction and resilience, and mining issues.

Wilfried Hagg – Heisenberg Fellow at the Università degli Studi di Milano-Bicocca, Milan, Italy. Hagg is a Physical Geographer with a research focus on runoff modelling in glacierized catchments. His PhD thesis compared the hydrological response of glacier retreat between Central Asia and the European Alps. After a postdoc position on Bavarian glaciers, he lectured at the Geography Department of the Ludwig-Maximilians-University in Munich. He now investigates glaciers in the Italian Alps and in Central Asia.

Megan Kennelly – Associate Professor of Plant Pathology at Kansas State University. She was involved in the IPM Innovation Lab project for Central Asia, providing expertise for plant diseases and diagnostics. In addition, she worked with Central Asian scientists through the U.S. Department of Agriculture's Cochran Fellowship programme. She is a board member of the Office of International Programs of the American Phytopathological Society.

Ausrele Kesminiene – Deputy Head of the Environment and Radiation Section at the International Agency for Research on Cancer (IARC), Lyon, France. She is a physician trained in radiation epidemiology and in cancer epidemiology and registration. She has long-running experience in studying health effects following the Chernobyl nuclear plant accident and coordinates the EU-funded SEMI-NUC project to assess the feasibility of further epidemiological cohort studies of health risks from nuclear weapons testing in Kazakhstan.

John P.A. Lamers – Senior Researcher at the Center for Development Research (ZEF), Bonn, Germany. Since 1997, he has worked in the former Soviet Union in research and development, and between 2002 and 2011 was resident research coordinator in Uzbekistan. He has authored or co-authored more than 220 contributions on sustainable intensification, farm forestry, resource management, technology transfer and local knowledge in Central Asia and West Africa.

Doug Landis – Professor of Entomology at Michigan State University, U.S. He received his BA degree in Biology from Goshen College and his MS and PhD degrees in Entomology from North Carolina State University, U.S. He has research and teaching responsibilities in insect ecology, with research focusing on the role of landscape structure in shaping insect–insect and insect–plant interactions in working landscapes. His awards include the Recognition Award in Entomology by the Entomological Society of America for outstanding contributions to agriculture and an MSU Distinguished Faculty Award.

Joy Landis – Assistant IPM Coordinator and Communications Manager for the Integrated Pest Management Program at Michigan State University, U.S. She has produced IPM websites, videos and publications for more than 25 years. Along with print communications, during 2008–2014, she established the Central Asia IPM Innovation Lab Project website and hosted a blog featuring the team's interactions at the 2009 Central Asia IPM Forum.

Karim Maredia – Professor and Senior Associate to the Dean of Agriculture and Natural Resources at Michigan State University, U.S. and Director of the World Technology Access Program. He has organized international training programmes on Integrated Pest Management, agricultural biotechnology, biosafety, food safety, intellectual property rights and technology transfer, and worked in international development projects funded by USAID, USDA-FAS, UN-FAO, the World Bank, Rockefeller Foundation, Winrock International, and the Bill and Melinda Gates Foundation. He is a former Research Scientist with the International Maize and Wheat Improvement Center in Mexico.

Christopher Martius – Principal Scientist Climate Change at the Center for International Forestry Research (CIFOR), Bogor, Indonesia. Also teaches agroecology and landscape management at the University of Bonn, Germany. He sits on the Advisory Board for DesertNet International with a background in ecology and has managed interdisciplinary research projects and programmes on climate change, land use, and biodiversity. He has co-authored about 130 articles on tropical ecology in rainforests and drylands, nutrient cycling, soil ecology, biodiversity, and climate change.

Mark Neuzil – Professor in the Department of Communication and Journalism at the University of St. Thomas in St. Paul, Minnesota, U.S. He is the author or co-author of six books and has worked as a reporter and editor for the Associated Press, the *Minneapolis Star Tribune*, and other news organizations.

Maik Rehnus – Former Scientific Assistant in the project ORECH-LES in the Groupe de foresterie pour le développement (GFD), Department of Environmental Sciences, ETH Zurich, Switzerland. His research focuses on silviculture, agroforestry, firewood use, and biodiversity in the walnut-fruit forests in Kyrgyzstan. He has used a bio-ecological perspective to address multifunctional sustainable management of these forests. Currently he is a scientific guest at the WSL Swiss Federal Research Institute, Switzerland, focusing on conservation of biodiversity in the Alps.

Shakhodat Saibnazarova – Teacher of environmental journalism at Russian–Tajik SlavonicUniversity in Dushanbe, Tajikistan. She has extensive experience in environmental journalism as a radio broadcaster, television reporter, and editor. She received a degree in Journalism and Communication from Rostov State University, Russia, and her PhD in journalism from Russian–Tajik Slavonic University. She conducts research on the problems of objective coverage of environmental issues in Tajikistan and follows environmental trends throughout Central Asia.

Nurali Saidov – In-country Project Coordinator of the Tajikistan Nutrition-Sensitive Vegetable Technologies Program of AVRDC – The World Vegetable Center. From 2006 to 2014, he was a Research Fellow with the CGIAR/ICARDA, coordinating programmes and activities of the Central Asia Regional IPM CRSP/I projects Ecologically Based Integrated Pest Management and Ecologically Based IPM Packages for Field and Vegetable Crop Systems in Central Asia. Previously, he was Agricultural Extension Coordinator for Food Security Programs with Counterpart International, U.S. and Oxfam G.B.

Venera Sakeeva – Master of Public Affairs with a focus on Human Security in crisis and post-crisis settings from L'Institute d'Etudes Politiques de Paris (Sciences Po. Paris). Her academic training includes evaluation of peace-building and conflict prevention programming, and she served as a researcher on Afghanistan's regional security complex and its impact on national minorities and neighbouring states. Her experience includes peace-building and gender, advocacy and empowerment of vulnerable groups, inter-ethnic dialogue, and platforms for inclusive policy and decision-making. She works as a Human Dimension Officer in the OSCE Mission in Kosovo.

Steven L. Simon – Head of the Dosimetry Unit in the Division of Cancer Epidemiology and Genetics, National Cancer Institute, National Institutes of Health, Bethesda, Maryland. He holds a PhD degree in Radiological Health Sciences and has many years' experience in estimating doses and health risks from nuclear weapons testing at nuclear test sites around the world, including Nevada, the Marshall Islands, and Kazakhstan.

Jean-Pierre Sorg – From 1977 to 1986 he worked with the Swiss Agency for Development and Cooperation and Intercooperation as project manager and scientist for projects in Rwanda and Madagascar. From 1986 until 2011, he was a lecturer in international forestry and agroforestry at the Department of Environmental Sciences at the ETH and head of the Groupe de foresterie pour le développement (GFD). He is now retired but conducts consultancies in applied research, education, project assessment, monitoring, and evaluation in Africa and Central Asia.

Bruno Takahashi – Assistant Professor at Michigan State University, U.S., with a joint appointment in the School of Journalism and the Department of Communication. He is also the Research Director of the Knight Center for Environmental Journalism. His research focuses on environmental and science communication, environmental journalism practices, and the links between media and policymaking.

Niels Thevs – Postdoctoral Fellow, Institute of Botany and Landscape Ecology, Ernst-Moritz-Arndt University, Greifswald, Germany. His research foci comprise ecological questions related to Central Asian ecosystems.

Kristopher D. White – Geographer and Associate Professor at KIMEP University in Almaty, Kazakhstan. The regional socio-economic impacts of the Aral Sea crisis and the ongoing human-nature interrelationships within the region guide his current research efforts. In addition to offering a university course titled 'The Aral Sea Crisis: A Geographical Perspective,' he has published studies on nature–society linkages and regional economy in the Aral Sea region.

Martin Wilmking – Professor for Landscape Ecology, Institute of Botany and Landscape Ecology, Ernst-Moritz-Arndt University, Greifswald, Germany. He focuses on ecosystem dynamics, forest ecology, and landscape evolution in mid-latitude, boreal and arctic systems. He is also interested in sustainable research and teaching organizations.

Amanda E. Wooden – David and Patricia Ekedahl Professor in Environmental Studies and Associate Professor of Environmental Politics and Policy at Bucknell University in Pennsylvania, U.S. She specializes in environmental discourses, protests and conflicts, and the politics of water, gold mining and shale gas drilling. Recent publications include 'Kyrgyzstan's dark ages: framing and the 2010 hydroelectric revolution' and 'Another way of saying enough: environmental concern and popular mobilization in Kyrgyzstan'.

Walter Wucherer – Postdoctoral Fellow at Succow Foundation, Greifswald, Germany. His research foci comprise ecological questions related to Central Asian ecosystems.

Aitmukhanbet Yesdauletov – Associate Professor, Journalism and Political Science Department, L.N. Gumilyov Eurasian National University, Kazakhstan. His research focuses on history and theories of communication/ journalism, mass media law in Kazakhstan, and coverage of environmental issues in the press. His academic interests include economic development and interrelations between audiences and mass media. His dissertation was about formation of print media (newspapers and journals) during *Perestroika* and the first years of Kazakhstan's independence (1986–2006).

Ardak Yesdauletova – Professor, Department of International Relations, L.N. Gumilyov Eurasian National University, Kazakhstan. She teaches in the areas of foreign policy of Kazakhstan, energy and water policies, and the role of mass media in diplomacy and international relations. Her publications include the themes of resource factors in foreign policy, Eurasian integration in post-Soviet countries, and challenges in the Central Asian countries.

Frank Zalom – Distinguished Professor of Entomology at University of California Davis, U.S. He served as Director of the UC Statewide IPM Program for 16 years. A Fellow of the California Academy of Sciences, Entomological Society of America (ESA), and American Association for the Advancement of Sciences, he received ESA's Achievement Award in Extension and Recognition Award, the Entomological Foundation's IPM Team Award and Excellence in IPM Award, the James H. Meyer Award from UC Davis for teaching, research, and service, a Fulbright Senior Research Fellowship, and the ESA's CW Woodworth Award.

Stefan Zerbe – Full Professor for Environment and Applied Botany at the Faculty of Science and Technology, Free University of Bozen-Bolzano, Italy. His research focus lies on landscape history, sustainable land use, biodiversity research, biological invasions, urban ecology and ecosystem restoration. He has published around 200 papers, chapters and monographs on vegetation ecology and interdisciplinary landscape ecology.

Acknowledgements

We deeply appreciate the intellectual contributions of our colleagues around the world who participated in this ambitious project, as well as the support of our faculty colleagues at Michigan State University and the University of St. Thomas. We also thank Professor Elira Turdubaeva of the Department of Journalism and Mass Communication at the American University of Central Asia in Bishkek, Kyrgyzstan, and Michigan State University students Sarah Anderson, Amanda Proscia, Katie Susko, Tatiana Voloshina, and Caroline White for their valuable assistance.

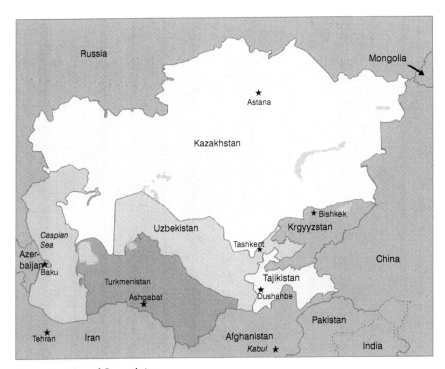

Figure 1.1 Map of Central Asia

1   Examining the terrain

Eric Freedman and Mark Neuzil

The hauntingly iconic images of rusting merchant and fishing ships abandoned in the heavily polluted sands of what was once the bottom of the Aral Sea still capture media attention around the world. Once teeming with the fish that kept canneries humming and drew tourists from across the Soviet Union, the southern portion of the Aral is dead, dried up—a ghost of an inland sea. During World War I, fish were so plentiful that Russian train engines were adapted to burn fish that had been caught and dried for fuel (Bailey, 1946). But central planners in distant Moscow decided that it made economic and political sense to divert water from the two rivers that fed the Aral to irrigate the expanded cotton farming in the desert.

Figure 1.2 Ghost fishing ship *Karakalpakstan* on the Aral seabed (photo: Eric Freedman)

The legacy of that devastatingly short-sighted policy relegated what was Uzbekistan's portion of the Aral to ghost sea status, home to a ghost fleet and one of the world's highest rates of respiratory illnesses from wind-borne pesticides and fertilizers. Its eastern basin became the world's newest desert, and it is now known as the Aralkum.

When the English rock band Pink Floyd sought a location to record the video for its song "Louder than Words," it chose a site near the Aral's once-thriving fishing village of Aralsk in Kazakhstan. In an interview with Radio Free Europe/Radio Liberty, band creative director Aubrey Powell attributed that seemingly peculiar decision to a combination of the media-driven image of stranded ships on the erstwhile seabed and a desire to deliver an environmental message. The video, Powell explained, is "not so much about the disaster—that's been written about endlessly—but more about a generational thing, more about what it means to the younger generation, the children of the impoverished and disenfranchised communities around the Aral Sea that have lost fishing and culture." Those children, he continued, will know about the Aral and what it represents only through their parents or grandparents (Pannier, 2014).

Efforts to revive the northern part of the Aral—the section in Kazakhstan—have been partly successful, but never again will this "Sea of Islands," once the world's fourth-largest inland body of water, rank among the largest lakes on the globe. Rather, it will symbolize another of history's most devastating human-induced environmental disasters, alongside the massively deadly chemical leak at Union Carbide's pesticide plant in Bhopal, India, and the meltdowns of the Chernobyl nuclear power plant in Ukraine and the Fukushima nuclear power plant in Japan.

Awareness of the Aral's dire situation or other environmental danger signals is not new.

In the delta of the Amu Darya River, the Turan tiger was hunted into extinction in the 1970s. The last known survivor, the ending of its species, was mounted and displayed in a museum in the dusty city of Nukus in western Uzbekistan, not far from where the waters of the Aral once lapped the shore.

In 1986, the Scientific Council on Problems of the Biosphere—an arm of the Soviet Academy of Sciences—held a fact-finding conference in Ashgabat, which is now the capital of Turkmenistan. As A.L. Yanshin wrote (1988, p. 9), "The council considered what should be done to improve the environment in this arid region, where many oil and gas fields have been discovered. It also examined health resorts in the piedmont and mountains of Central Asia, the stabilization of moving sands, control of desertification, and rational use of the limited water in this desert." At the time, planners were considering a scientifically far-fetched and unrealistic scheme to divert water from rivers in distant Siberia to replenish the Aral.

By 1991—the year the Soviet Union collapsed and the ex-republics of Central Asia achieved independence—the process of anthropogenic desertification had been going on for three decades, and as Kotlyakov (1991, pp. 4–5) noted, "these negative ecological changes" due to irrigated agriculture "have been

Figure 1.3 Entering the former fishing port of Muynak, Uzbekistan (photo: Eric Freedman)

accompanied by grave socioeconomic costs: deteriorating human health, increasing unemployment as resource-based economic activity declines, and decreasing production of cotton, rice, and other agricultural crops."

We cannot attribute all blame for the region's eco-crises to the policies of the Soviet Union. Even before the Bolsheviks occupied the region after the Russian Revolution, Kizel-Su[1] was nicknamed "the city of the red water" because the Kizel-Su River was "so dirty that only camel drivers were said to bathe in it" (Reiss, 2005, p. 51). And in 1917, when a Danish army officer arrived in the region then called Turkestan on a humanitarian mission to monitor the wellbeing of Russian-held prisoners of war from Austria-Hungary, he crossed the steppe by train on route to Tashkent. He later wrote, "The landscape was perfectly flat and barren; and assumed, if possible, an even more melancholy aspect from the large snow-white stretches of salt which appeared here and there on its desolate surface" (Brun, 1931, p. 39). However, he also acknowledged the natural beauty of the steppe, at least briefly in the spring when the ground remains moist from melting snow: "It is a vast carpet of flowers ... where the scarlet poppies in great multitude first of all delight the eyes of the beholder; and there too are the other hundred varieties of wild flowers, filling the air with colour and fragrance, doing their best to make us believe that the steppe is like a carpet of flowers all the year round" (Brun, 1931, p. 46).

Yet the megastory of the Aral Sea and the microstory of the extinction of a single species are only small episodes of a much larger saga, one that encompasses a wide range of environmental challenges in this remote yet ecologically, strategically, culturally, and economically crucial part of the world.

Other major environmental challenges confront the five former Soviet republics in Central Asia: Kazakhstan, Kyrgyzstan, Tajikistan, Turkmenistan, and Uzbekistan. They include threats to the Caspian Sea, the impact of climate change on glaciers, desertification, deforestation, destruction of habitat and biodiversity, overfishing, radioactive and hazardous wastes, water quality and supply, energy exploration, air pollution, pesticide pollution, food security, and environmental diseases. The region, which is already vulnerable to landslides and avalanches, is expected to undergo a large amount of seismic activity during the next decade, with a likelihood of earthquakes and related natural disasters. These challenges all carry implications that transcend national borders and influence economic, political, and cultural relationships on a vast geographic scale. At the same time, the region's governments—burdened by limited economic resources, weak civil society institutions, and political authoritarianism rooted in their Soviet past—have demonstrated little resolve or even an ability to address these complex challenges.

Not all these challenges are as high profile as the plight of the Aral. There are no hauntingly iconic photos of Semipalatinsk, the site in Kazakhstan where the Soviet Union carried out about 470 nuclear tests between 1949 and 1989, or of overgrazed pastures in Kyrgyzstan, or of the melting mountain glaciers in the Pamirs of Tajikistan. However, that does not minimize their environmental significance.

Environmental conditions don't exist in a vacuum. They are influenced by science, politics, history, public policy, culture, economics, public attitudes, and competing priorities. They are also shaped by past human decisions, actions, and inaction. In the case of Central Asia, such Soviet-era decisions and actions include irrigation systems and physical infrastructure that are now crumbling, mine tailings that leach pollutants into soil and groundwater, and abandoned factories that are both physically decrepit and contaminated with toxic chemicals.

The fact that Moscow-based central planners made megapolicy and mega-implementation mistakes with such mega-ramifications doesn't tell the full story, however.

That full story includes the devastating human impacts, and not just concerning the Aral. A EurasiaNet article (Igoe, 2012) illustrates the point. It recounts the situation of Orto Talaa, a remote village in Kyrgyzstan's Tien Shan mountains that the Soviet Union developed in 1988 for residents transplanted from a nearby community vulnerable to landslides. Infrastructure projects were promised but not completed. The Soviet-installed pumps that once irrigated the Orto Talaa's wheat fields failed and were scavenged, leaving residents with no water to grow vegetables. Post-independence administrations have failed to remedy the problems.

Other overarching factors contribute to these problems, regardless of country. All five countries are plagued by corruption and favoritism in government, business, and the nongovernmental organization sector. There is a shortage of scientists researching environmental issues and a shortage of practitioners developing and implementing plans to address the issues. There is a lack of will at the highest levels of national governments to act decisively.

Not surprisingly, Central Asia's overall environmental status is among the worst in the world. For evidence, one only has to look at the Environmental Performance Index (2014) from Yale University's Center for Environmental Law & Policy and Columbia University's Center for International Earth Science Information Network (in collaboration with the World Economic Forum). That study paints an independent, science-based portrait of the severity of the region's eco-problems. It ranks the performance of 178 countries on protection of ecosystems and protection of human health from environmental impacts. In Central Asia, Kazakhstan ranked the "healthiest" in 84th place, followed by Turkmenistan at 109th, Uzbekistan at 117th, Kyrgyzstan at 125th, and Tajikistan trailing in 154th place. Another study (Varis, 2014) highlights Central Asia's troubling status among the world's leading wasters of water resources, based on per capita use and water consumption per dollar of gross domestic product.

Admittedly, the price tag for comprehensive, effective environmental protection and remediation is daunting, even for countries such as Turkmenistan and Kazakhstan that are rich in oil, gas, and other natural resources—and even if regimes were willing to pay the price. Comparative national poverty magnifies the geographically imbalanced distribution of resources and the realistic amount of lead time required to move meaningfully toward more balance. As Middleton (2010, p. 5) wrote about Tajikistan, "In the long-term, abundant water resources can be harnessed for generation and export of power to neighbouring countries, but it will require very large investments."

Environmental projects in Central Asia must compete with projects in developing countries elsewhere for outside funding from donors and multinational agencies. Hostility to human rights means that organizations, environmental activists, and citizens critical of governmental environmental policies often are ignored at best and suppressed at worse. Constraints on the press—ranging from censorship and self-censorship to conflicts of interest and assaults on journalists—discourage fair and balanced coverage of environment-related events and controversies.

Overview of the book

This book takes a multidisciplinary approach. It highlights environmental challenges and their context through the lens of scholars, researchers, and practitioners representing a wide range of natural science and social science fields, such as environmental sciences, geography, political science, natural resources, mass communications, public health, and economics.

We organized the book by six intimately and intricately interwoven themes indicated by these headings: Climate change, Water, Energy, Public policy and mass media, Environmental health, and Ecology. Under Climate change, you'll read about the dire impact of melting glaciers in the Tien Shan and Pamir mountains. The Water section explores human security aspects of water-related conflicts in the Ferghana Valley. The Energy section examines controversy and public discourse about planned hydroelectric dam projects in Kyrgyzstan and the ecological consequences of energy exploration in the Caspian Sea. Chapters in the Public policy and mass media section address how to separate environmental myths from environmental realities, the need to holistically address a country's array of interrelated environmental challenges, Western press coverage of environmental news in Central Asia, and how newspapers in Kazakhstan reported on such issues during *perestroika* and now. In the Environmental health section, you'll read about the continuing adverse human health effects caused by exposure to radiation from nuclear testing in the Semipalatinsk region of Kazakhstan. The final themed section, Ecology, covers the partial resurrection of the commercial fishery in the Northern Aral Sea of Kazakhstan; the fate of the walnut forests of southern Kyrgyzstan; an integrated pest management project for cotton, wheat, and potato crops in Uzbekistan, Tajikistan, and Kyrgyzstan; and carbon stocks in the northern Karakum Desert.

One common thread woven through the book is that these environmental crises pay no mind to political borders, those artificial lines drawn on a map for historical or political reasons. Ecological systems do not heed such human-made markers. Air pollution drifts from one country to another. Melting glaciers drain into watersheds in more than one country. Many residents of Uzbekistan displaced by the Aral Sea's disappearance have immigrated to Kazakhstan.

Another common thread is the intersection of contemporary and historical values, lifestyles, legends, and beliefs with their natural and built environments. To illustrate, Middleton writes about a shrine in the Pamir Mountains of Tajikistan dedicated to Pir Yakhsuz: "According to local legend, Pir Yakhsuz freed the Roshtkala valley from glacier ice. ('Yakhsuz' means 'ice-flame' in Tajik and Shughni.)" A second shrine nearby is "dedicated to Bombomfail, who was reputed to be able to melt snow and ice with his prayers" (2010, p. 88).

Nowhere in Central Asia is that reality clearer than in the fertile, densely populated Ferghana Valley, checkerboard-like parts of which belong to Uzbekistan, Kyrgyzstan, and Tajikistan. Here are serious and contentious transboundary environmental problems, especially ones involving energy and water. Violent confrontations occur. Writing about the Ferghana Valley, Bichsel described water as a "mobile, fluid and fugitive natural resource with an inherent uncertainty about its quantity and location" (2009, p. 49). Here, as in the nearby Isfara and Sokh valleys, "ecology, lived geography and political formations" intersect, according to Reeves. For example, "[a]ppropriating water to a private garden plot through illicit outfalls from an uncared-for public canal can be interpreted as a source of domestic survival, an index of disregard for the commons, and a provocation to downstream communities" (2014, p. 19).

It is essential to consider current environmental crises in a broad context and with eyes wide open to the future. "Global climate change looms here as the umbrella problem under which water and energy conflicts threaten to worsen and natural disasters imperil dams, irrigation networks, villages, and industrial sites" (Freedman, 2014, p. 48). And the United Nations Environmental Programme/ GRID-Arendal listed such effects of climate change in the Ferghana Valley as desertification, lower agricultural productivity, faster melting of ice caps and glaciers, elevational shifts in biodiversity, changes in permafrost and snow cover, and reduced river flow (Rekacewicz, 2006). Meanwhile, ethnic rivalries, corruption, national security concerns, national identity disputes, migration, weak central government control, Islamist militancy, and trade further complicate the ecological problems.

A similar transborder situation exists in the eastern Caspian Sea region of Kazakhstan and Turkmenistan, the site of massive energy extraction, environmental problems, security conflicts, and rural–urban economic disparities. "The quality and availability of freshwater in the arid eastern Caspian region is a key factor for rural development and public health. While urban centres located on the seacoast can afford expensive desalinization plants and/or the delivery of water via regional pipelines, access to reliable freshwater sources for the hinterland remains difficult and the vulnerability of these regions could increase with rising problems of environmental pollution and degradation" (De Martino and Novikov, 2008, p. 9). And such human-induced ramifications come on top of nature-driven vulnerabilities that ignore national borders. As De Martino and Novikov point out, "The Caspian Sea coast is highly vulnerable to rapid and destructive fluctuations in sea level. The latter, together with other natural hazards, including storm surges, earthquakes and regional epidemics, presents a serious risk to human security and loss of livelihoods for the whole Caspian Sea region" (2008, p. 12).

Yet another environmental conflict area exists where Kazakhstan and China's Xinjiang Uyghur Autonomous Region meet, a border crossed by more than twenty rivers. Both sides express grievances about what Baizakova describes as "two fundamental issues" between the two countries: a "'rational and equitable' water allocation and pollution prevention" (2015, p. 1). Her study says that bilateral agreements between China and Kazakhstan don't address environmental damage or include institutional mechanisms to address such damage and warns, "The risk appears very high that without any sustainable bilateral policy to protect transboundary water resources, industrial development upstream will have detrimental impact on societies, communities, and ecosystems downstream," referring to Kazakhstan (2015, p. 8).

Of course, it is impossible for a single volume to cover every major environmental crisis confronting Central Asia in depth, so this book can provide only a sampling of those issues. As editors, we sometimes found it difficult to decide what to include and what to omit. For example, there also is important research underway on such eco-questions as mining-related pollution; coal supplies and fossil fuel dependency; repurposing of vacant factories and other industrial facilities; de-collectivization of Soviet-era collective farms; overexploitation of forest resources; rehabilitation of abandoned irrigated croplands; invasive species; waste management; animal diseases; overgrazing; and urban air quality, including emissions from coal-fired power plants.

Conclusions

As this book illustrates, there are few absolute black-and-white answers and much gray for citizens, scientists, decision-makers, and decision-shapers. As scholars, practitioners, scientists, citizens, or activists, we can criticize lack of enforcement of environmental laws but must recognize that cash-strapped countries such as Kyrgyzstan and Tajikistan also lack enough money to pay for public health and education programs. We can criticize individuals who poach wildlife or overgraze their livestock but must recognize that subsistence hunting and fishing are traditional and that they lack viable economic alternatives to feed their families. We certainly can identify some "good guys" and some "bad guys," but the picture is not always clear.

Note

1   The city of Kizel-Su in what is now Turkmenistan was renamed Turkmenbashi after independence.

References

Bailey, F.M. (1946). *Mission to Tashkent*. (London: J. Cape).

Baizakova, Z. (2015). The Irtysh and Ili transboundary rivers: The Kazakh–Chinese path to compromise. George Washington University Institute for European, Russian, and Eurasian Studies.

Bichsel, C. (2009). *Conflict Transformation in Central Asia: Irrigation Disputes in the Ferghana Valley*. (Abingdon, UK: Routledge).

Brun, A.H. (1931). *Troublous Times: Adventures in Bolshevik Russia and Turkestan*. (London: Constable & Company).

De Martino, L. and Novikov, V. (2008). Environment and security: Transforming risks into cooperation. The case of the Eastern Caspian region. United Nations Environment Programme, United Nations Development Programme, United Nations Economic Commission for Europe, Organization for Security and Co-operation in Europe, Regional Environmental Centre for Central and Eastern Europe North Atlantic Treaty Organization. Available at http://www.grida.no/files/publications/envsec/envsec-caspian2-eng_scr.pdf.

Environmental Performance Index. (2014). Available at http://epi.yale.edu.

Freedman, E. (2014). Barriers to coverage of transborder environmental issues in the Ferghana Valley of Central Asia. *Applied Environmental Education and Communication*, 13(1), pp. 48–55.

Igoe, M. (2012). Kyrgyzstan: Peak living has many languishing in valley of despair. EurasiaNet. Available at http://www.eurasianet.org/node/64821.

Kotlyakov, V.M. (1991). The Aral Sea basin: A critical environmental zone. *Environment*, 33(1), pp. 4–9, 36–39.

Middleton, R. (2010). *The Pamirs—History, Archaeology and Culture*. (Bishkek: University of Central Asia).

Pannier, B. (2014). Pink Floyd and the Aral Sea. Radio Free Europe/Radio Liberty. Available at http://www.rferl.org/content/pink-floyd-video-aral-sea-kazakhstan-uzbekistan/26690106.html.

Reeves, M. (2014). *Border Work: Spatial Lives of the State in Rural Central Asia*. (Ithaca, NY: Cornell University Press).

Reiss, T. (2005). *The Orientalist: Solving the Mystery of a Strange and Dangerous Life*. (New York: Random House).

Rekacewicz, P. (2006). Water issues in the Ferghana Valley. GRID-Arendal. Available at http://www.grida.no/graphicslib/detail/water-issues-in-the-ferghana-valley_108d .

Varis, O. (2014). Resources: Curb vast water use in central Asia. *Nature*, 514(7520), pp. 27–29.

Yanshin, A.L. (1988). Reviving Vernadsky's legacy: Ecological advances in the Soviet Union. *Environment*, 30(10), pp. 6–9, 26–27.

Part I
Climate change

2 Less water from the mountains?

Consequences of glacier changes in Central Asia

Wilfried Hagg and Tobias Bolch

Introduction

Rivers originating in the Tien Shan and Pamir mountains do not reach the ocean but belong to closed inland watersheds, common in arid climates where evapotranspiration exceeds precipitation. The largest of these catchments are the basins of the Aral Sea (1.2 million square kilometers; 463,000 square miles), Tarim River (530,000 square kilometers; 205,000 square miles), and Ili-Balkhash (413,000 square kilometers; 160,000 square miles). The Aral has two inflows that do not reach the lake every year due to intense water consumption. The Amu Darya River (465,000 square kilometers; 180,000 square miles) drains the largest part of the Pamirs and is the main tributary of the Aral; about 68 percent of total runoff in the Aral Sea Basin is formed in its catchment (United Nations Environment Programme, 2006). The remaining 32 percent is provided by the Syr Darya River (777,000 square kilometers; 300,000 square miles) that originates in the Central Tien Shan. The Tarim River is formed at the confluence of three rivers from Inner and Central Tien Shan, Eastern Pamir, and Kunlun Shan. The Ili River, which flows into Lake Balkhash, drains the northeastern part of the Tien Shan.

These mountain chains force an uplift of air masses that leads to condensation of water vapor and eventually to precipitation and runoff. Due to low temperatures at high elevations, a large fraction of this precipitation falls in solid form. If the terrain is high enough, the snow pack does not entirely melt in summer and slowly compacts into glacial ice.

Most of this precipitation falls during winter in Western Pamir, while maximum precipitation shifts to late spring in most parts of Northern Tien Shan. The greatest precipitation in Central and Eastern Tien Shan and Eastern Pamir occurs in the summer, but in a much lower total amount than in the outer ranges (Sorg et al., 2012).

The mountain cryosphere delays seasonal runoff because melting occurs in spring to early summer in the case of snow, and in summer to early autumn in the case of glacial ice. This effect is essential for water to be available during the main growing season. Since melt occurs mainly during hot and dry weather and is reduced during cool and wet periods, glaciers have a compensating effect on stream flow. That is because rivers with glaciers in their catchment have a guaranteed water yield from either rainfall or from melt. Therefore, such rivers vary less from year to year than those depending on rainfall exclusively and that can undergo severe low flow events during dry weather. Especially in dry lowlands, glaciers' storage capacity and their seasonal delay of runoff are vital for the socioeconomic wellbeing of downstream users.

Statement of the problem

The share of glacial melt in total runoff increases with glacierization and aridity and is exceptionally high in Central Asia. Dikich et al. (1995) estimated that 15 percent of runoff in Kyrgyzstan originates from glaciers, with that proportion significantly higher during summer. Kaser et al. (2010) found that in the Aral Sea Basin, the contribution of glacier meltwater to total runoff is the highest among eighteen large river catchments investigated around the globe. They concluded that a population of more than 10 million would suffer from water shortages if the glaciers disappear.

The glaciers' share of the total runoff in the Tarim River is about 40 percent (Sorg et al., 2012), while up to 20 percent could be attributed to an increase in glacial melt in recent decades (Pieczonka and Bolch, 2014). In the lowlands, the flow is reduced through evaporation, infiltration, and withdrawal for irrigation. In 2010, 58 cubic kilometers (14 cubic miles) of water were withdrawn from the Amu Darya in Uzbekistan and Turkmenistan. Of that, 92 percent was for irrigation (United Nations Environment Programme, 2011). It was this type of nonsustainable water use that caused the Aral Sea to shrink by 84 percent from 1960 through 2013 and separated the sea into three individual lakes (United Nations Environment Programme, 2014). In 2014, the eastern part completely dried up (National Aeronautics and Space Administration, 2014).

There are complex interrelations among changing climate, reliance on glacial melt to supply water for agricultural irrigation and hydropower, transborder river flows, and national political, security and economic rivalries. Thus, what does science predict will happen to the glaciers of Central Asia?

Findings

Observed glacier changes

As in many other parts of the globe, glaciers in the Tien Shan have retreated significantly since their maximum extent during the Little Ice Age (1350–1850), with only a few years of advance in between (Solomina et al., 2004). Reported shrinkage in Northern Tien Shan (Ile, Kungöy, and Kyrgyz Alatau) varied around 20 percent during the last decades of the 20th century (Aizen et al., 2006; Bolch, 2007; Niederer et al., 2008; Narama et al., 2010). Similar area losses occurred in the Naryn Basin in Inner Tian Shan draining into the Syr Darya (Hagg et al., 2013a). In contrast, glaciers in Central Tian Shan around the highest peaks and in the Kokshaal-Too showed more modest shrinkage rates of 5 percent or less during the same period (Osmonov et al., 2013; Pieczonka and Bolch, 2014). Most glacial melt here drains into the Aksu River and subsequently into the Tarim. Similarly low area losses occurred in the Chinese part of the Tarim catchment (Shangguan et al., 2009), while shrinkage was more pronounced in Eastern Tian Shan in China where Li et al. (2006) reported a 13 percent loss between 1962 and 2000. Hence, glacial shrinkage was higher in the more humid outer mountain ranges than in the drier inner ranges of Tian Shan (Sorg et al., 2012; Aizen and Aizen, 2014).

In Pamir, the rate of glacial shrinkage was similar or slightly lower than in Tian Shan. For example, Chevalier et al. (2014) reported the loss for the Vaksh and Pyandj catchments in west central Pamir of between 5 and 25 percent between 1980 and 2000. A complete assessment of the entire glacial coverage (1,500 square kilometres; 580 square miles) of the Lake Karakul Basin showed a 9 percent area loss between 2000 and 2011 (Holzer et al., forthcoming). Aizen and Aizen (2014) found glacier shrinkage of 5 percent for the entire Pamir between 1970 and 2009, mostly affecting small glaciers, while larger ones were almost stable. Fedchenko Glacier, by far the largest in Pamir, shrank by only 1.4 percent between 1928 and 2007 (Lambrecht et al., 2014). Hence, the relative area of retreat, as in most parts of the world (Bolch et al., 2010; Paul et al., 2004), depends significantly on glacier size. This makes direct comparisons of area changes difficult because glacier size can vary widely throughout the mountain ranges. In addition, area and length changes provide a delayed signal about climate fluctuations and also depend on nonclimatic, topographic factors. A more direct, unfiltered, and undelayed response to climate offers glacier mass balance, which is defined as the difference between mass gains, mainly by snowfall, and mass losses, mainly by melt. This net balance is measured in meter water equivalent (m.w.e.) and represents the water column that is lost (negative sign) or gained (positive sign) over the entire glacier during a budget year (m.w.e. per year).

Since the 1980s, the mass balance of only a few glaciers in Central Asia has been measured in the field, providing sparse information (Figure 2.1). The collapse of the Soviet Union interrupted measurements of several glaciers, but some recently resumed. Continuous measurements are available for only two glaciers: Tuyuksu Glacier in northern Tian Shan in Kazakhstan, and Urumqi Glacier No. 1 in Eastern Tian Shan in Xinjiang, China. The only glacier with existing in situ measurements close to Pamir is Abramov Glacier in the Pamir-Alai range; results there show mass changes around zero in the 1960s and significant loss of mass from the 1970s until today.

Differencing of digital elevation models (DEMs) used to complement in situ data have allowed scientists to improve their knowledge about glacier mass changes. Comparing DEMs of glaciers in the Ala Archa catchment in Northern Tian Shan, Kyrgyzstan, that were generated from Corona (U.S. spy images acquired during the Cold War) with recent ASTER images from the SRTM (Shuttle Radar Topography Mission) revealed that conditions were likely balanced during the 1960s, followed by a strong loss of mass and then a slower

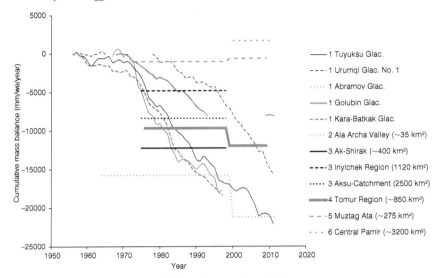

Figure 2.1 Selected glacier mass balance data in Central Asia

Data sources: 1 WGMS (in situ measurements), 2 Bolch (2015), 3 Pieczonka and Bolch (2015), 4 Pieczonka et al. (2013), 5 Holzer et al. (2015), 6 Gardelle et al. (2013).

loss of mass since 2000 (Bolch, 2015). Glaciers in the Aksu-Tarim catchment in Inner and Central Tian Shan lost mass at a rate of 0.35±0.34 m.w.e. per year from the mid-1970s until 2000 (Pieczonka and Bolch, 2014), which is similar to the global average for the same period. Mass loss likely decreased in this region between 2000 and 2010 (Shangguan et al., 2014; Pieczonka et al., 2013), as occurred in the Ala Archa valley. Results from Tian Shan using laser altimetry data of the Ice, Cloud, and Land Elevation Satellite (ICESat) revealed one of the highest mass losses in High Asia for 2003–2009.

DEMs for Central Pamir revealed likely positive glacier mass balances during the last decade (Gardelle et al., 2013). Results using ICESat laser altimetry data, however, showed slight (Gardner et al., 2013) or even larger mass losses (Kääb et al., 2012) for Pamir during a similar period. That difference can be attributed to both the low data coverage of ICESat measurements and the radar beams' likely underestimated penetration of SRTM C-band data into snow and ice (Gardelle et al., 2013). Glaciers at Muztagh Ata in Eastern Pamir have likely been in balance at least since the 1970s. In situ measurements confirm the slightly positive geodetically derived mass balanced estimates for 2003–2012 (Holzer et al., 2015).

Hence, at least parts of the glaciers in Pamir show normal behavior like those in the Karakoram south of Pamir (Gardelle et al., 2013) and Western Kunlun east of Pamir (Neckel et al., 2013). In addition, many surge-type glaciers—glaciers that regularly and rapidly advance due to strong mass relocation from the upper glacier reaches to the tongue—have been reported in Pamir (Kotlyakov et al., 2008; Gardelle et al., 2013; Holzer et al., 2015, forthcoming).

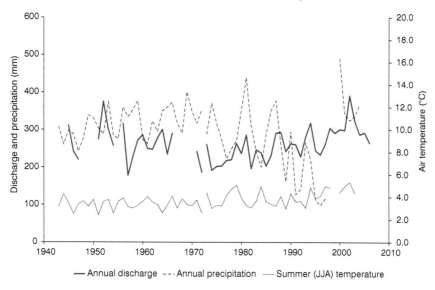

Figure 2.2 Annual precipitation, summer temperature of Tian Shan station

Observed runoff changes

The mass loss of glaciers also contributes to stream flow and causes more discharge than from balanced glaciers. For example, this can be observed at the Big Naryn River, the most heavily glacierized subcatchment of the Syr Darya. Runoff has increased there since 1972 despite a decrease in precipitation (Figure 2.2).

Finaev (2008) analyzed discharges from 1990 to 2005 and reported an average 13 percent runoff increase for the Syr Darya, Zeravshan, Varzob, Vanj, and Gunt rivers. Positive runoff trends suggest that these catchments are still in a phase where larger ablation zones (due to elevated snowlines) and/or increased melt rates (due to warming) overcompensate for the adverse effect of overall glacier shrinkage.

In Kyrgyzstan, annual runoff has increased from 47.1 cubic kilometers (11.3 cubic miles) from 1947 to 1972 to 50 cubic kilometers (12 cubic miles) between 1973 and 2000 (Mamatkanov et al., 2006), caused mainly by basins in the inner ranges. At the same time, catchments in the outer ranges showed stable behavior (Sorg et al., 2012). In the outer ranges, more winter rainfall compensates for reduced summer runoff, which could be due to prolonged glacial retreat. At least for the Ile Alatau in Northern Tian Shan, Vilesov and Uvarov (2001) reported negative runoff trends caused by glacier shrinkage.

In a literature review based on more than 100 studies and datasets, Unger-Shayesteh et al. (2013) concluded that basins with a distinct glacier coverage generally experienced positive runoff trends in the recent past. For the Aksu River in the Tarim catchment, Krysanova et al. (2014) confirmed positive trends in summer runoff due to increased temperatures and precipitation.

Future trends

After the prolonged reduction of glacial area that scientists anticipate in the future, there will be a tipping point after which the increased runoff from glacier wastage will turn into reduced meltwater flows. This effect will at first be observed in summer due to a shift toward earlier melt in the spring. However, as soon as the excess runoff is reduced, annual discharge will also decrease. Increased evapotranspiration in a warmer atmosphere will exacerbate this trend, further reducing water availability downstream.

Hagg et al. (2013b) assessed the hydrological response to climate change and glacier recession through 2050 in the Tanimas River, a 4,300-square-kilometer (1,660-square-mile) and 10 percent glacierized subcatchment of the upper Panj. They assumed temperature rises of 2.2°C (4°F) and 3.1°C (5.6°F), which mark the extreme values of regional climate scenarios (Agaltseva et al., 2005) and extrapolated future glacierization by a simple parameterization scheme. Modified climate and glacierization data provide input to a hydrological model to identify changes in water cycle and in seasonal water availability.

The results revealed that annual runoff will decrease only slightly—by 5 percent—through 2050 because the projected reduction in glacial area is almost offset by enhanced melt rates due to the warming atmosphere (Hagg et al., 2013b). One possible interpretation of the annual flow reduction is that the peak flow period, where excess runoff from glacier wastage is at its maximum, is already finished in this catchment, at least through 2050. In other words, the turning point—when total glacial area recession predominates over enlarged ablation zones and intensified melt in a warmer atmosphere—will happen between now and 2050 in this catchment. From the results of a watershed hydrological model applied in the whole Vakhsh River and Panj River catchments, Kure et al. (2013) predicted an increase in annual stream flow until 2060 and a decrease from 2080 on.

Future seasonal water availability at the Tanimas River is shifting toward the early melt season, creating a surplus of water (15–100 percent) in May–June and a shortage (18–34 percent) in July–September (Figure 2.3). Kure et al. (2013) confirmed this general pattern for the entire Pamir.

An earlier, more intense snowmelt has increased runoff in spring and early summer. In July, the glacial area depletion in the two scenarios overcompensates for enhanced melt rates due to warming, resulting in lower runoff values compared to the 1980s.

The mean shares of glacial runoff at the basin outlet, calculated as ice melt minus evapotranspiration of melted ice, are 21 percent (+2.2°C or +4.0°F) and 24 percent (+3.1°C or +5.6°F).

Sorg et al. (2014) simulated glacier retreat and hydrological response in a transient way in the Chon-Kemin Basin of Northern Tian Shan based on different climate scenarios. Even the most glacier-friendly scenario anticipates a 60 percent loss of area between 1955 and 2100. More pessimistic scenarios foresee the glaciers disappearing completely by 2080. The consequences for stream flow vary considerably among three scenario types: warm scenarios lead to runoff decreases

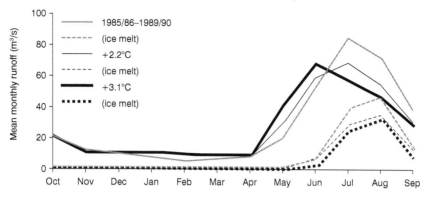

Figure 2.3 Baseline and future scenarios for Tanimas River

after a peak flow period in the 2020s, dry-cold scenarios cause a gradual decrease in runoff, and wet-cold scenarios show no considerable changes in annual discharge. However, all these scenarios predict water shortages during the summer (Sorg et al., 2014).

Because the retreat rate of glaciers depends on several topographic and local factors, it differs in individual parts of the mountains. Therefore, the timing of the hydrological consequences varies among mountain ranges and river catchments.

On a regional scale, current runoff is likely to remain stable or to increase slightly in the near future. By the end of the 21st century, the peak flow period is expected to be past, and total runoff will probably be smaller than today (Hagg et al., 2006; United Nations Framework Convention on Climate Change, 2009). Following a moderate (B1) and an aggressive (A1F1) greenhouse gas emission scenario, representing the lowest and highest temperature increases to be expected, according to the Intergovernmental Panel on Climate Change (2000), The United Nations Environment Programme (2009) predicts a runoff decline of 12–24 percent by 2050 and of 18–36 percent by 2100, mainly due to increasing evapotranspiration.

Conclusion and discussion

Prolonged glacier retreat will transform glacial-nival runoff regimes into nival-pluvial (snow-dominated and rain-dominated) regimes. This goes along with a loss of the compensating effect of glaciers on runoff and thus with increased year-to-year variability and extreme low flow events during dry periods.

Furthermore, evapotranspiration losses in downstream regions will be significantly higher than in the headwaters, which will further tighten water availability during the growing season.

Such hydrological changes intensify ecological problems such as the drying up of the Aral Sea and contribute to social and political instability in Central Asia.

High water consumption has transformed the downstream section of many major rivers and caused catastrophic changes such as the drying out of the Aral and Lake Balkhash (Kezer and Matsuyama, 2006). Also in the Tarim River Basin, downstream runoff has decreased, causing serious degradation of the riparian ecosystem (Hou et al., 2007), although stream flow from the tributaries leaving the mountains shows positive trends.

The transboundary character of many Central Asian rivers requires multilateral planning of adaption and impact mitigation strategies to secure the livelihood of the population.

Water shortages in summer will stress the region's agricultural system, further fueling tensions that have existed since the collapse of the Soviet Union (Malone et al., 2010).

Acknowledgements

Wilfried Hagg's research is financed by the Heisenberg Programme of the German Research Foundation (project HA 5061/3-1). Tobias Bolch acknowledges funding by the German Research Foundation (DFG, project BO 3199/2-1).

References

Agaltseva, N., Spectorman, T., White, C. and Tanton, T. (2005). Modelling the future climate of the Amu Darya Basin. In *Interstate Water Resource Risk Management: Towards a Sustainable Future for the Aral Basin*, eds Olsson, O. and Bauer, M. (London: IWA Publishing), pp. 9–36.

Aizen, V. B. and Aizen, E. M. (2014). The Central Asia climate and cryosphere/water resources changes. *Materials of the International Conference 'Remote- and Ground-based Earth Observations in Central Asia'*, Bishkek, Kyrgyzstan.

Aizen, V. B., Kuzmichenok, V. A., Surazakov, A. B. and Aizen, E. M. (2006). Glacier changes in the central and northern Tian Shan during the last 140 years based on surface and remote-sensing data. *Annals of Glaciology*, 43(1): 202–213.

Bolch, T. (2007). Climate change and glacier retreat in northern Tian Shan (Kazakhstan/Kyrgyzstan) using remote sensing data. *Global and Planetary Change*, 56(1–2): 1–12.

Bolch, T. (2015). Glacier area and mass changes since 1964 in the Ala Archa Valley, Kyrgyz Ala-Too, northern Tian Shan. *Лёд и Снег (Ice and Snow)*, 129(1): 28–39.

Bolch, T., Menounos, B. and Wheate, R. (2010). Landsat-based inventory of glaciers in western Canada, 1985–2005. *Remote Sensing of Environment*, 114(1): 127–137.

Chevallier, P., Pouyaud, B., Mojaïsky, M., Bolgov, M., Olsson, O., Bauer, M. and Froebrich, J. (2014). River flow regime and snow cover of the Pamir Alay (Central Asia) in a changing climate. *Hydrological Sciences Journal*, 59(8): 1491–1506.

Dikich, A. N., Sokalskaya, A. M. and Yan, S. (1995). Glacier runoff. In *Glaciation of the Tian Shan*, eds Dyurgerov, M. B., Lyu, S. and Se, Z. Moscow Vsesoyuznyy Institut Nauchnoy i Tekhnicheskoy Informatsii, pp. 131–168 [in Russian].

Finaev, A. (2008). Review of hydrometeorological observations in Tajikistan for the period of 1990–2005. In *Assessment of Snow, Glacier and Water Resources in Asia*, eds Braun, L., Hagg, W., Severskiy, I. and Young, G. IHP/HWRP-Berichte 8, pp. 73–88.

Gardelle, J., Berthier, E., Arnaud, Y. and Kääb, A. (2013). Region-wide glacier mass balances over the Pamir-Karakoram-Himalaya during 1999–2011. *The Cryosphere*, 7: 1263–1286.

Gardner, A. S., Moholdt, G., Cogley, J. G., Wouters, B., Arendt, A., Wahr, J., Berthier, E., Hock, R., Pfeffer, W. T., Kaser, G., Ligtenberg, S. R. M., Bolch, T., Sharp, M. J., Hagen, J. O., van den Broeke, M. R. and Paul, F. (2013). A reconciled estimate of glacier contributions to sea level rise: 2003 to 2009. *Science*, 340(6134): 852–857.

Hagg, W., Braun, L. N., Weber, M. and Becht, M. (2006). Runoff modelling in glacierized Central Asian catchments for present-day and future climate. *Nordic Hydrology*, 37(2): 93–105.

Hagg, W., Mayer, C., Lambrecht, A., Kriegel, D. and Azizov, E. (2013a). Glacier changes in the Big Naryn basin, Central Tian Shan. *Global and Planetary Change*, 110(A): 40–50.

Hagg, W., Hoelzle, M., Wagner, S., Mayr, E. and Klose, Z. (2013b). Glacier and runoff changes in the Rukhk catchment, upper Amu Darya basin until 2050. *Global and Planetary Change*, 110(A): 62–73.

Holzer, N., Golletz, T., Buchroithner, M. and Bolch, T. (forthcoming). Glacier variations at the Trans-Alai Massif and the Lake Karakul Catchment (Eastern Pamir) measured from space. In Singh, R. B., Schickhoff, U. and Mal, S. (eds), *Dynamics of Climate, Glaciers and Vegetation in the Himalaya: Contribution Towards Future Earth Initiatives*, Heidelberg: Springer.

Holzer, N., Vijay, S., Yao, T., Xu, B., Buchroithner, M. and Bolch, T. (2015). Four decades of glacier variations at Muztag Ata (Eastern Pamir): a multi-sensor study including Hexagon KH-9 and Pléiades data. *The Cryosphere Discussions*, 9: 1811–1856.

Hou, P., Beeton, R. J., Carter, R. W., Dong, X. G. and Li, X. (2007). Response to environmental flows in the Lower Tarim River, Xinjiang, China: an ecological interpretation of water-table dynamics. *Journal of Environmental Management*, 83(4): 383–391.

Intergovernmental Panel on Climate Change (2000). Emissions Scenarios: Summary for Policymakers. IPCCSpecial Report. Available at https://www.ipcc.ch/pdf/special-reports/spm/sres-en.pdf.

Kääb A., Berthier, E., Nuth, C., Gardelle, J. and Arnaud, Y. (2012). Contrasting patterns of early twenty-first-century glacier mass change in the Himalayas. *Nature*, 488(7412): 495–498.

Kaser, G., Großhauser, M. and Marzeion, B. (2010). Contribution potential of glaciers to water availability in different climate regimes. *Proceedings of the National Academy of Sciences of the United States of America*, 107(47): 20223–20227.

Kezer, K. and Matsuyama, H. (2006). Decrease of river runoff in the Lake Balkhash basin in Central Asia. *Hydrological Processes*, 20(6): 1407–1423.

Kotlyakov, V., Osipova, G. and Tsvetkov, D. G. (2008). Monitoring surging glaciers of the Pamirs, central Asia, from space. *Annals of Glaciology*, 48(1): 125–134.

Krysanova, V., Wortmann, M., Bolch, T., Merz, B., Duethmann, D., Walter, J., Huang, S., Tong, J., Buda, S. and Kundzewicz, Z. (2014). Analysis of current trends in climate parameters, river discharge and glaciers in the Aksu River basin (Central Asia). *Hydrological Sciences Journal*, 60(4): 566–590.

Kure, S., Jang, S., Ohara, N., Kavvas, M. L. and Chen, Z. Q. (2013). Hydrologic impact of regional climate change for the snowfed and glacierfed river basins in the Republic of Tajikistan: hydrological response of flow to climate change. *Hydrological Processes*, 27(26): 4057–4070.

Lambrecht, A., Mayer, C., Aizen, V., Floricioiu, D. and Surazarov, A. (2014). The evolution of Fedchenko glacier in the Pamir, Tajikistan, during the past eight decades. *Journal of Glaciology*, 60(220): 233–244. DOI: 10.3189/2014JoG13J110.

Li, B., Zhu, A. X., Zhang, Y., Pei, T., Qin, C. and Zhou, C. (2006). Glacier change over the past four decades in the middle Chinese Tian Shan. *Journal of Glaciolology*, 52(178): 425–432.

Malone, E. L. (2010). Changing glaciers and hydrology in Asia: addressing vulnerabilities to glacier melt impacts. Technical Report USAID.

Mamatkanov, D. M., Bazhanova, L. V. and Romanovskij, V. V. (2006). *Water Resources of Kyrgyzstan* (National Academy of Science of the Kyrgyz Republic, Institute of Water Problems and Hydropower) [in Russian].

Narama, C., Kääb, A., Duishonakunov, M. and Abdrakhmatov, K. (2010). Spatial variability of recent glacier area changes in the Tian Shan Mountains, Central Asia, using Corona (1970), Landsat (2000), and ALOS (2007) satellite data. *Global and Planetary Change*, 71(1–2): 42–54.

National Aeronautics and Space Administration (2014). The Aral Sea loses its eastern lobe: image of the day. Available at http://earthobservatory.nasa.gov/IOTD/view. php?id=84437.

Neckel, N., Kropáček, J., Bolch, T. and Hochschild, V. (2014). Glacier mass changes on the Tibetan Plateau 2003–2009 derived from ICESat laser altimetry measurements. *Environmental Research Letters*, 9(1): 14009–14015.

Niederer, P., Bilenko, V., Ershova, N., Hurni, H., Yerokhin, S. and Maselli, D. (2008). Tracing glacier wastage in the Northern Tian Shan (Kyrgyzstan/Central Asia) over the last 40 years. *Climatic Change*, 86(1–2): 227–234.

Osmonov, A., Bolch, T., Xi, C., Kurban, A. and Guo, W. (2013). Glacier characteristics and changes in the Sary-Jaz River Basin (Central Tian Shan, Kyrgyzstan) 1990–2010. *Remote Sensing Letters*, 4(8): 725–734.

Paul, F., Kääb, A., Maisch, M., Kellenberger, T. and Haeberli, W. (2004). Rapid disintegration of Alpine glaciers observed with satellite data. *Geophysical Research Letters*, 31(21): L21402.

Pieczonka, T. and Bolch, T. (2014). Region-wide glacier mass budgets and area changes for the Central Tian Shan between 1975 and 1999 using Hexagon KH-9 imagery. *Global and Planetary Change*, 128: 1–13.

Pieczonka, T., Bolch, T., Wei, J. and Liu, S. (2013). Heterogeneous mass loss of glaciers in the Aksu-Tarim catchment (Central Tian Shan) revealed by 1976 KH-9 Hexagon and 2009 SPOT-5 stereo imagery. *Remote Sensing of Environment*, 130: 233–244.

Shangguan, D., Liu, S., Ding, Y., Ding, L., Xu, J. and Jing, L. (2009). Glacier changes during the last forty years in the Tarim Interior River basin, northwest China. *Progress in Natural Science*, 19(6): 727–732.

Shangguan, D., Bolch, T., Ding, Y., Pieczonka, T., Kröhnert, M., Wetzel, H.-U. and Liu, S. (2014). Elevation changes of Inylchek Glacier during 1974–2007, Central Tian Shan, Kyrgyzstan derived from remote sensing data. *The Cryosphere Discussions*, 8(2014): 2573–2610.

Solomina, O., Barry, R. and Bodnya, M. (2004). The retreat of Tian Shan glaciers (Kyrgyzstan) since the Little Ice Age estimated from aerial photographs, lichenometric and historical data. *Geografiska Annaler Series A*, 86(2): 205–216.

Sorg, A., Huss, M., Rohrer, M. and Stoffel, M. (2014) The days of plenty might soon be over in glacierized Central Asian catchments. *Environmental Research Letters*, 9(10).

Sorg, A., Bolch, T., Stoffel, M., Solomina, O. and Beniston, M. (2012). Climate change impacts on glaciers and runoff in Tian Shan (Central Asia). *Nature Climate Change*, 2: 725–731.

Unger-Shayesteh, K., Vorogushyn, S., Farinotti, D., Gafurov, A., Duethmann, D., Mandychev, A. and Merz, B. (2013). What do we know about past changes in the water cycle of Central Asian headwaters? A review. *Global and Planetary Change*, 110(A): 4–25.

United Nations Economic Commission for Europe (2011). Second assessment of transboundary rivers, lakes and groundwaters. Available at http://www.unece.org/?id=26343.

United Nations Environment Programme (2006). Tajikistan: State of the Environment 2005. Available at http://ekh.unep.org/files/State%20of%20the%20Environment_1.pdf.

United Nations Environment Programme (2009) *Second National Communication of the Kyrgyz Republic to the United Nations Framework Convention on Climate Change*, Bishkek: UNEP.

United Nations Environment Programme (2011) *Second Assessment of Transboundary Rivers, Lakes and Groundwaters*. New York and Geneva: UNEP,

United Nations Environment Programme (2014). The future of the Aral Sea lies in transboundary co-operation. UNEP Global Environment Alert Service. Available at http://www.unep.org/pdf/UNEP_GEAS_JAN_2014.pdf.

United Nations Framework Convention on Climate Change (2009). *Second National Communication of the Kyrgyz Republic to the United Nations Framework Convention on Climate Change*. Available at http://unfccc.int/resource/docs/natc/uzbnc2e.pdf.

Vilesov, E. N. and Uvarov, V. N. (2001). *Evolution of the Recent Glaciation in the Zailyskiy Alatau in the 20th Century*. (Almaty: Kazakh State University) [in Russian].

Part II
Water

3 Increasing human security to avert water wars in the Ferghana Valley

Venera Sakeeva

Introduction

The Ferghana Valley extends across three countries—Kyrgyzstan, Tajikistan, and Uzbekistan—covering about 22,000 square kilometers (13,700 square miles) (Goudie, 1996, p. 12). Approximately three-quarters of Central Asia's water supply comes from its two main rivers: Amu Darya and Syr Darya. The Syr Darya runs through the heart of the Ferghana Valley (McKinney, 2004). The Ferghana Valley is situated in a semi-arid climate with minimum precipitation from April to October (Siegfried et al., 2011, p. 2). In addition to its dry climate, the changing climate pattern in recent years makes the amount and frequency of rainfall unpredictable (United Nations Development Programme, 2012, p. 13).

It is the most heavily populated region in Central Asia, with 11.3 million inhabitants representing about 20 percent of the region's total population. They account for 50 percent of Kyrgyzstan's residents, 31 percent of Tajikistan's, and 27 percent of Uzbekistan's (United Nations Development Programme, 2005, p. 26). The population is expected to increase by 33 percent by 2020 due to high birth rates (United Nations Development Programme, 2005, p. 27). The region is home to various ethnic and religious groups and is densely populated, particularly in Uzbekistan's territory. As a result, demand for water continues to escalate.

The Ferghana Valley is a cradle of complex, unsolved issues including demarcation and border disputes. The Soviet regime implemented a policy of imaginary borders so that none of these fraternal countries could take sole ownership and control of this highly productive and strategically important region. As a result of the Soviet breakup, current national borders do not correspond to the ethnic and language distributions of the populace. In addition, this causes ongoing tension among the three countries about territorial disputes and water management. Consequently, rivers cross borders as many as thirty times, making it difficult to formulate and adopt comprehensive and effective water management across the region.

The three states hold conflicting views on water use. For Uzbekistan, located downstream of the Syr Darya river, the priority is agriculture. A large amount of water is necessary for irrigation as the Uzbek government enforces mandated targets for cotton and wheat production on its farmers. For Kyrgyzstan and

Tajikistan, generating electricity from hydropower plants is the most crucial use of water. Approximately 93.3 percent of the electricity generated in Kyrgyzstan and 98.8 percent in Tajikistan comes from hydropower plants, and these two countries' electricity generation capacity has not yet been fully realized (World Bank, 2010, p. 87). This is a result of state policy initiated in the mid-1990s to switch to energy generation in winter rather than relying on volatile prices and counting on a stable supply of power and fuel from Kazakhstan and Uzbekistan (World Bank, 2014). Such divergent priorities and poorly timed water transfers exacerbate tensions among the countries.

Statement of the issue

These irreconcilable views on water use and management, together with the legacy of Soviet five-year plans, severely impact the environment and increase economic hardship in the area. The unique and complicated political, social, and economic contexts and history of the Ferghana Valley require solutions that are comprehensive rather than target-specific. This requires untangling multiple issues in different areas that are interrelated in both obvious and subtle ways.

Soviet five-year economic planning targeted high agricultural output, which led to changes in the natural course of the river flows to the Aral Sea and to the fields of Uzbekistan and Kazakhstan. In return, Uzbekistan and Kazakhstan compensated Tajikistan's and Kyrgyzstan's water loss by providing these largely mountainous countries with guaranteed supplies of energy. Since the disintegration of the Soviet Union, the Central Asian republics have not only inherited ecological and environmental consequences associated with the shrinking of the Aral Sea, but also face economic crises where a Soviet-style compensation system was unable to meet the realities of the capitalist market.

Water shortages and water mismanagement led to conflict not only at state levels, but also among communities. In particular, the region depends heavily on agriculture; most residents work in the agricultural sector. The high poverty rate indicates the region is vulnerable to economic slumps, and reduced agricultural outputs could create food insecurity. Border disputes, political tension among adjoining states, and lack of economic opportunities have prevented development of an effective water management mechanism at the state level. These differing priorities lead to poorly timed water transfer among communities, which adds to the complexity of the problem.

Generally speaking, water management is negotiated and arranged by the state as water is perceived as a transboundary resource. Kazakhstan, Kyrgyzstan, Uzbekistan, and Tajikistan attempted to develop a comprehensive water management plan based on bilateral, trilateral, and other international and regional agreements. These agreements address collective management of water resources for agriculture and electricity, as well as environmental problems associated with the shrinking Aral. However, water use is only one dimension of the problem. For example, the Syr Darya is the largest river that passes through four Central Asian republics and flows to the Aral. Approximately 95 percent of its waters are regulated by reservoirs, of which the Toktogul Reservoir in Kyrgyzstan—with a volume of 690 billion cubic feet—is the largest. It is considered a long-term regulated reservoir. To compare, the second-largest, the Andijan Reservoir in Uzbekistan, has a volume of approximately 62 billion cubic feet (Ministry of Agriculture of Kazakhstan, 2006). Hence, not only its use, but also its allocation becomes another problem. Parallel to this, while Kyrgyzstan controls the downstream Syr Darya through the Toktogul Reservoir, Tajikistan controls the Vakh River, an Amu Darya tributary, through its Nurek Reservoir ,and that is attracting investments to build the controversial Rogun Dam. These rivers make mostly impoverished Kyrgyzstan and Tajikistan potential world leaders in the renewable energy sector.

The 1992 Almaty Agreement assigned 51.7 percent of the river flow to Uzbekistan, 38.1 percent to Kazakhstan, and 10.2 percent to Kyrgyzstan and Tajikistan. Thus the upstream countries are subject to greater per capita water stress (Bichsel, 2011, p. 26). In addition, efficiency of water use should be highlighted. Statistics show that the main water loss occurs in the on-farm delivery networks and directly in the fields. According to the Water Use and Farm Management Survey, such losses alone may account for 37 percent of the total supply to farm users. On average, about 50 to 80 percent of irrigation water is wasted directly in the fields due to outdated irrigation systems (International Crisis Group, 2014; Human Rights Watch, 2013).

Since the Almaty Agreement, the countries have signed multiple agreements, made joint statements and declarations, and even created an International Foundation on Saving the Aral Sea. Finally in 1998, four countries reached the Bishkek Agreement, which outlined collective responsibilities and provided for the construction of new reservoirs (Agreement between the Government, 1998). The Bishkek Agreement was not ratified by Tajikistan, however. While both agreements envisaged the equality of all sides in using water resources, none of the documents envisaged the adversarial needs of countries regarding water use, and they failed to outline how to reinforce each country's responsibilities and liabilities.

In 2000 and 2001, Tajikistan and Uzbekistan started signing bilateral agreements on a compensatory mechanism in which upstream Tajikistan receives gas, coal, and fuel oil (*masut*) in exchange for releasing water for Uzbekistan's agriculture. Parallel to this, in 2004–05, Kyrgyzstan and Kazakhstan started signing bilateral agreements on common use of water and energy resources (Ministry of Agriculture of Kazakhstan, 2006, pp. 7–8). Although this was a step forward in an almost decade-long deadlock in negotiations, it addressed only the seasonal needs of each country and conflicted with agreements reached in 1992 and 1998. These bilateral agreements failed to address long-term strategy in regional and transboundary water management. The short-term nature of these agreements and lack of commitment to the agreements can be explained through a "win-lose" model contained in the regional approach to water management. Hence, we might ask about the real reasons for the shrinking of the Aral and what have been the excuses or bargaining chips in water management negotiations.

Findings

Abstracting themselves from the broader Central Asian context and refocusing on the realities of the Ferghana Valley, the three countries have failed to move from politicization of water to compromise on their differing priorities. Russia is another obstacle created by their irreconcilable approach to water use. If in the mid-1990s Russia positioned itself as a mediator, by 2013 Moscow actively supported Kyrgyzstan's hydropower ambitions through $1.7 billion in loan assistance for construction of the Kambar-Ata cascade reservoirs able to export electricity at 1,860MW (Cooley and Larelle, 2013). Russia also is considering funding the Rogun Dam in Tajikistan, although it has not made a solid offer of financial assistance. Such developments aggravate Uzbekistan, where 10 million people depend on water originating from these countries.

Distribution of water has become more or less regarded as a negotiation tool for the upstream countries to import natural gas at a more reasonable price from the downstream countries (Bichsel, 2011, p. 25). Downstream countries like Uzbekistan have an abundant supply of gas but a water scarcity. Such politicization of water negotiations causes deterioration in conditions at the community level. Less natural gas imported by the upstream countries from the downstream countries means the upstream countries will become more dependent on hydroelectric power plants. This means the upstream countries will have to discharge more water in the winter to meet the high demand for electricity. Subsequently, there will be less water for irrigation in downstream countries in spring and summer. As a result, a comprehensive water management mechanism has not been successfully developed at the state level.

Why human security is an alternative in the Ferghana Valley

The challenges in the Ferghana Valley are highly complex. Involved are myriad political, social, economic, and environmental issues with multiple causes and implications. Hence, this is potentially a pre-conflict situation, and if the issue is not addressed successfully and in a timely manner, it might set off a domino effect leading to a regional water war. These issues are interdependent and interrelated, and they require a holistic approach in understanding the problems. These complicated issues highlight the volatility of human security, particularly uncovering threats to freedom from fear, freedom from want, and freedom from indignities.[1]

Since this chapter is moving away from a traditional understanding of problems and threats, it will explain the nuts and bolts of a human security approach before presenting a detailed contextual analysis that justifies the use of this model in the Ferghana Valley. The concept of human security developed after the Soviet Union disintegrated. This meant a paradigm shift from recognizing *realpolitik*-type national security threats to recognizing a wide range of threats that affect international, regional, state, and human security. Transboundary problems, including those with environmental impacts and those threatening food, environmental, and economic security, have led to an expansion of the scope of security.

Human security is a framework and approach that addresses protection of the "vital core of all human lives in ways that enhance human freedoms and human fulfillment" (Commission on Human Security, 2003, p. 2). It addresses severe and widespread threats to survival, livelihoods, and dignity by protection of freedom from want, freedom from fear, and freedom from indignities (Tadjbakhsh and Chennoy, 2007, p. 13). To achieve these goals, the human security perspective advocates a mutually reinforcing approach—protection and empowerment—that provides a shield from dangers and enables people to develop an ability to exercise their choices and their capacities so they can fully participate in decision-making processes that directly affect their lives (United Nations Commission on Human Security, 2006).

In addressing an array of human insecurities such as food, economic, political, health, environmental, community, and personal, the concept encapsulates human elements of security and takes an interdisciplinary approach. Based on five main characteristics—people-centered, multi-sectored, comprehensive, context-specific, and prevention-oriented—it launches a critical approach in understanding a problem (United Nations Trust Fund for Human Security, 2009, p. 7). Hence, it designs policy interventions concentrated on diagnosis and treatment, rather than taking an ad hoc solution approach to the symptoms. Furthermore, it analyzes the interconnectedness of threats. The human security approach shows potential for a "domino effect" with chain reactions and spillover if well-designed policies are not introduced on time. It advocates equal weighing of threats, their interconnectedness, and setting priorities (Tadjbakhsh and Chennoy, 2007, pp. 16–17).

Looking at water issues and disputes in the Ferghana Valley through a human security lens is holistic. It combines traditional security, human rights, and human development, and interconnects peace, security, and sustainable development. It also focuses on the community and individual levels and adopts a "people-centered" approach. This establishes an effective framework, particularly in the Ferghana Valley, where state-to-state negotiation has stagnated while the same problems and pre-conflict conditions continue.

Aga Khan Planning and Building Services (AKPBS) used the human security approach to design community-level water management systems in northern Pakistan, illustrating a less politicized and non-state-led approach to water management.[2] Driven by a people-centered philosophy, the organization's development interventions targeted confidence-building within local communities that are at risk of water dispute; it aimed to empower communities to improve their own living conditions and economic opportunities. It took an integrated, community-based approach to sustainable development while its development programs addressed not only the immediate needs of clean water and adequate sanitation, but also the overall impact of these initiatives on economic, social, and environmental sustainability.

Similarly, a self-reliant community-based mechanism can be considered for the Ferghana Valley. However, such an alternative mechanism must mobilize people and infrastructure across sovereign states and form partnerships with authorities in each country. Moreover, allocation of water within a single country is fundamentally different in the Ferghana Valley, where inter-state resource allocation and differing economic priorities further complicate the situation. Thus, an alternative mechanism here would require intricate detail on the transfer of water resources across borders. Nevertheless, the mechanism implemented by AKPBS provides a good example of a community-led holistic effort.

Communities and the people-centered approach in the Ferghana Valley

As the end users of water, communities and individuals bear the consequences of its mismanagement. The impacts of ineffective state policies have had an equally negative effect on the people of Kyrgyzstan, Tajikistan, and Uzbekistan. Heavily dependent on income from agricultural production, households remain vulnerable to distribution of scarce water resources for irrigation. If a government shows reluctance or lack of discretion in implementing the Almaty and Bishkek agreements, communities suffer the most. Smaller harvests can trigger instability, and potential conflicts over water-sharing at the community level can create a "domino effect" with aggravated consequences at the regional level. In addition, the region already has a history of ethnic conflict over distribution of land following the collapse of the Soviet Union.

Just as the communities themselves can potentially serve as a disrupting power, they can also be agents of change in their own lives. By focusing on improved cooperation in better management of water resources at the community level, they can also increase their economic self-sufficiency and welfare. Therefore, by identifying communities as a target group, this chapter seeks to fulfill two mutually reinforcing tasks: uncovering the most acute needs of these communities and tackling insecurities that will lead to the communities themselves addressing those insecurities by ensuring cooperation. By focusing on communities, this chapter incorporates a bottom-up approach toward conflict prevention. This approach would empower communities to achieve better standards of living and opportunities by ensuring agricultural production is carried out in an environmentally sustainable way in the long term.

This chapter studies how a failure to provide human security or failure to address human insecurities can lead to regional instability and conflicts. As a case study, it takes environmental insecurity as an entry point to explore how it affects an array of human insecurities of Ferghana Valley residents. In particular, it explores the impacts of environmental insecurity on economic and community security in the area.

There are several reasons why this study identifies environmental insecurity as an entry point to analyzing the multidimensional causes and implications of water use in Central Asia. It creates less resistance from national authorities and communities because the risks and consequences of environmental deterioration reach beyond state borders. Existing transboundary water resources are central not only to the Ferghana Valley's economic and social development, but also to its environment. Due to the interdependence among the economy, social development, and ecosystem, any changes in water use in one country may have serious repercussions for the others. In particular, changing the natural flow of rivers and building cascades of reservoirs to generate electricity illustrate how actions can trigger transboundary effects. Addressing environmental insecurity would increase attention to the problem in the Ferghana Valley and help to gradually diffuse its adverse effects on community and economic insecurities. Additionally, in the authoritarian political settings inherent in Central Asia, an environmental entry point may be seen as an apolitical way of analyzing the context of the water problem. That way, the chances of increased public awareness of mutual interests and dependency will be higher.

Fundamentally, current water supply and management practices cannot meet the growing demand for enhanced economic well-being. Agriculture is essential to the region's economy, particularly cotton production. Currently, Uzbekistan is the world's seventh-largest cotton producer and third-largest supplier for world markets (MacDonald, 2012, p. 1). Moreover, agriculture accounts for 21 percent of its Gross Domestic Product (GDP) and about 40 percent of hard currency earnings. In both Kyrgyzstan and Tajikistan, agriculture accounts for about 20 percent of GDP, while the agricultural sector employs about half of the population (Central Intelligence Agency, 2013). Improvement of the local economic situation is a crucial task. Thus, supporting agriculture is essential for the region's economic health.

However, heavy irrigation has negative ecological effects. Today, approximately 90 percent of agriculture in Uzbekistan is produced on irrigated land (Aleksandrov, 2009). During the seventy years of Soviet power, mismanagement of water caused environmental problems, including reduced soil fertility and the shrinking of the Aral (Trucost, 2010). The fundamental problem is the inability of the water supply to meet growing demand and to help residents improve economic well-being. The importance of this demand is amplified by the severe poverty and economic conditions that depend on irrigated agriculture.

The Ferghana Valley faces severe poverty, as World Bank data shows. In Uzbekistan, GDP per capita in Ferghana Province and adjoining Andijan and Namangan provinces is $572, $566, and $377, respectively (IWRM-Ferghana, n.d.). The average GDP per capita in Uzbekistan rose from $558 in 2000 to $1,878 in 2013. Similarly, in Kyrgyzstan, GDP per capita increased tremendously from $280 in 2000 to $1,263 in 2013, and in Tajikistan it rose from $139 to $1,037 for the same period, according to the World Bank. Despite significant economic improvements in the last ten years, however, these countries remain among the poorest in the world. It is important to note that Uzbekistan leads the other two countries after increasing its GDP per capita in the last decade. This can be explained by its significant increase, 160 percent, in agricultural production.

To enhance economic well-being in the Ferghana Valley, higher agricultural production is necessary. However, that would put further pressure on the region's water resources and create more competition over its allocation. As competition over water allocation intensifies, tensions among the communities grow. A number of periodic small-scale intercommunity conflicts are emerging over water-sharing and allocation. In 2012–2014, close to twenty security-related incidents involving several thousand people were reported along the Uzbek–Kyrgyz, Tajik–Kyrgyz, and Uzbek–Tajik borders involving serious injuries, hostage-taking, property damage, and shootings by border patrols (Myrzabekova, Sikorskaya and Khaldarov, 2013; International Crisis Group, 2014). These intercommunity conflicts have a direct negative impact on social and economic health. Thus water serves not only as a source of conflict, but also as a conflict multiplier with a potential military dimension. This is particularly significant for ethnic minority groups in the Ferghana Valley because national borders do not represent ethnic distribution. Specifically, Uzbeks residing in Kyrgyzstan and Tajikistan, Kyrgyz residing in Uzbekistan and Tajikistan, and Tajiks residing in Kyrgyzstan and Uzbekistan are the likely victims of community-scale conflicts. Since these groups live next to one another, any ethnic tension in one country could easily spill over to another, drawing the entire region into the conflict. Such multi-causal problems illustrate the volatility of the Ferghana Valley.

A "human security-friendly" solution to the water problem

Existing traditional approaches, accompanied by differing priorities for water management and complicated territorial disputes, have brought state-to-state negotiations to a dead end. In contrast, community water management, as implemented by the Aga Khan Foundation in Pakistan, has shown benefits in empowering communities and enhancing their capacity to address acute needs and expand mutual cooperation. Hence, the chapter proposes an alternative solution based on a grassroots approach to ensure human security.

This proposed "human security-friendly" solution addresses what is called the "horizontal inequalities" of communities by Frances Stewart. She argues that the concept of horizontal inequalities differs from regular (or vertical) definitions of inequalities and focuses on multidimensional economic, social, cultural, and political inequalities across communities regardless of ethnic, racial, or religious origins (Stewart, 2007). Using the lenses of horizontal inequalities to design an alternative grassroots-based approach targets this solution toward the context of the greater Ferghana Valley. Aimed at the region's ethnically mixed communities, this alternative differs from traditional development-led interventions. While traditional projects specialize in water sanitation and building infrastructure for better access to a drinking water for individuals in *one* country, this proposed solution attempts to bring different communities *across* countries together and does not differentiate among specific individuals, ethnic groups, and communities.

An alternative to state-to-state negotiations should focus on communities and treat them as water users. This avoids ethnic labeling and addresses the problem of water distribution for agricultural purposes while also tackling both water-sharing and monitoring mechanisms. It advocates participatory, transparent, and fair community-based water management. Such solutions initiated at the grassroots level would diverge from the traditional blueprint policies pursued by multilateral financial institutions such as the World Bank, Asian Development Bank, and other donor agencies. Resting on a broad analysis of local context, it is designed to take on concrete insecurities faced by local communities.

Scrutinizing water disputes through a human security lens can provide a comprehensive analysis of multi-dimensional causes and implications of environmental insecurity and its ramifications for economic and community insecurities. This way of thinking also offers concrete mechanisms to deal with the scarcity of water resources in the Ferghana Valley. While focusing on human security, a contextual analysis shows that failure to address better water management can potentially escalate conflicts to include a military dimension. Clearly, the alternative solution proposed by this study would encompass the "human elements" of the security, development, and rights of Ferghana Valley communities. In addressing structural and systemic problems related to water access and distribution, grassroots-level initiatives empower residents and build community resilience. Furthermore, such initiatives empower residents to not only act on their own behalf, but also to find ways to ensure human security for their communities.

Conclusion and discussion

When states perceive competing interests and adversarial approaches in water use, it is clear that there is no comprehensive regional strategy that would satisfy all stakeholders. Furthermore, existing bilateral approaches driven by a state's seasonal interests consider only a short-term outlook. It is evident that such ad hoc tactics fail to deal with existing challenges and assess only the surface of existing complications in regional water management. One might claim that each state should and can best represent its own interests by ensuring enough water for its agricultural outputs or electricity generation. However, the *realpolitik* way of thinking fails to ensure sustainable and peaceful coexistence of competing interests. It also cannot guarantee against further escalation of tensions and potential violence associated with rivalry for limited access to water during the next several decades.

Irreconcilable values and diverging interests among states affect communities across Kyrgyzstan, Uzbekistan, and Tajikistan. Competition for scarce water resources leads to community-level conflicts that can easily spiral and metamorphose into inter-ethnic or inter-state conflicts. Thus, while states face deadlock in negotiations, community-level conflicts should be prevented from further escalation. To do so, communities should be treated as central and integral to water management strategy with a long-term vision. Communities should be treated horizontally—equally across the board—with their vulnerabilities addressed, and they must be empowered to remain resilient about any changes.

This chapter illustrates how a human security perspective can best explain the root causes of water policy problems in the Ferghana Valley. Furthermore, it shows how human security can be used in a comprehensive manner to uncover causes and implications of conflict and to help fill gaps in the causal chain of how environmental insecurity can generate economic and community insecurity among households and communities.

It also makes a case for a domino effect in that a problem in one location can impact or fuel problems in other locations. Furthermore, it illustrates considerable links among different elements of human security and shows that a threat is likely to spread across these elements. Such a comprehensive strategy to diagnose problems of water management and their effects can help design a carefully balanced intervention aimed at the root causes of the problems. Thus this proposed human security-based approach can improve community resilience in the face of volatile external environments, and it can open further avenues for sustainable regional development.

Acknowledgement

An earlier version of this study appeared in the journal *Central Asia & the Caucasus*.

Notes

1 "Freedom from want, freedom from fear, and freedom from indignities" is a concept in human security studies that addresses protection and promotion of human survival (freedom from fear), daily life with access to services, food, education (freedom from want), and a life of dignity (freedom from indignity). First pronounced by United Nations Secretary-General Kofi Annan, the concept has become an integral part of human security.

2 The project called the Water and Sanitation Extension program undertaken by AKPBS in northern Pakistan to provide water supply infrastructure and to improve water sanitation is considered a success. For more details, refer to Aga Khan planning and building services, Activities in Pakistan, viewed 12 May 2013, http://www.akdn.org/akpbs_pakistan.asp.

References

Agreement between the Government of the Republic of Kazakhstan, the Kyrgyz Republic, and the Government of the Republic of Uzbekistan on cooperation in the field of environmental protection and conservation (1998) Bishkek.

Aleksandrov, A. (2009) Uzbekistan gets credit it may not need to modernise irrigation system, *Central Asia Online*. Available at http://centralasiaonline.com/en_GB/articles/caii/features/2009/08/29/feature-06.

Bichsel, C. (2011) Liquid challenges: contested water in Central Asia. *Sustainable Development Law & Policy*, 12(1): 24–30, 58–60.

Central Intelligence Agency (2013) *CIA World Fact Book*. Washington, D.C. Available at https://www.cia.gov/library/publications/the-world-factbook/.

Commission on Human Security (2003) *Human Security Now: Final Report*. New York: Commission on Human Security.

Cooley, A. and Larelle, M. (2013) The changing logic of Russian strategy in Central Asia: from privileged sphere to divide and rule? PONARS Eurasia, Policy Memo 261, George Washington University.

Goudie, D. (1996) An overview of the Ferghana Valley. *Perspectives on Central Asia*, 1(1), Eisenhower Institute's Center for Political and Strategic Studies.

Human Rights Watch (2013) Uzbekistan: forced labor widespread in cotton harvest. Available at http://www.hrw.org/news/2013/01/25/uzbekistan-forced-labor-widespread-cotton-harvest.

International Crisis Group (2005) *The curse of cotton: Central Asia's destructive monoculture*, Asia Report #93. Available at http://www.crisisgroup.org/en/regions/asia/central-asia/093-the-curse-of-cotton-central-asias-destructive-monoculture.aspx

International Crisis Group (2014) *Water pressures in Central Asia*. Europe and Central Asia Report #233.

IWRM-Ferghana (n.d.) *Social-economic significance of water management and irrigated agriculture of Ferghana Valley*. Available at http://iwrm.icwc-aral.uz/socio_economic_en.htm.

Kazakhstan Ministry of Agriculture, Water Resources Committee (2006) Analysis of existing agreements between countries of Central Asia in the area of water relations from the standpoint of Kazakhstan's interests, ADB Project on Improving Common Water Resources of Central Asia. Available at http://www.ers.usda.gov/media/935015/cws12h01.pdf.

MacDonald, S. (2012) *Economic policy and cotton in Uzbekistan*, Washington, DC: United States Department of Agriculture. Available at http://www.ers.usda.gov/media/935015/cws12h01.pdf.

McKinney, D. (2004) Cooperative management of transboundary water resources in Central Asia. In *In the Tracks of Tamerlane: Central Asia's Path to the 21st Century*, eds. D. Burghart and T. Sabonis-Helf. Center for Technology and National Security Policy, National Defense University, Washington, D.C.

Myrzabekova, A., Sikorskaya, I. and Khaldarov, A. (2013) Kyrgyzstan enclave in turmoil, Institute for War and Peace Reporting. RCA Issue 693. Available at http://iwpr.net/report-news/kyrgyzstan-enclave-turmoil.

Siegfried, T., Bernauer, T., Guiennet, R., Sellars, S., Robertson, A.W., Mankin, J., Bauer-Gottwein, P. and Yakovlev, A. (2011) Will climate change exacerbate or mitigate water stress in Central Asia? *Climatic Change*, 112(3–4): 881–899.

Stewart, F. (2007) *Major findings and conclusions on the relationship between horizontal inequalities and conflict*. Oxford: Centre for Research on Inequality, Human Security, and Ethnicity.

Tadjbakhsh, S. and Chennoy, A. M. (2007) *Human Security: Concepts and Implications* (New York: Routledge).

Trucost (2010) *The Economics of Ecosystem and Biodiversity – TEEB report for business, annex 2.1 case studies*. Available at http://www.trucost.com.

United Nations Commission on Human Security (2006) Outline of the report of the Commission on Human Security.

United Nations Development Programme (2005) Transforming risks into cooperation, Central Asia—Ferghana/Osh/Khudjand area, ENVSEC initiative.

United Nations Development Programme (2012) *Tajikistan: poverty in the context of climate change*, National Human Development Report.

United Nations Trust Fund for Human Security (2009) *Human security in theory and practice: Application of the human security concept and the United Nations Trust Fund for human security*. Geneva: Human Security Unit of the United Nations Office for the Coordination of Humanitarian Affairs. Available at http://www.tr.undp.org/content/dam/turkey/docs/news-from-new-horizons/issue-41/UNDP-TR-HSHandbook_2009.pdf

World Bank (2010) *Joint economic assessment: reconciliation, recovery, and reconstruction.* Washington, DC: World Bank

World Bank (2014) Electricity production from hydroelectric sources (% total). Available at http://data.worldbank.org/indicator/EG.ELC.HYRO.ZS.

Part III
Energy

4 Energy exploration and the Caspian Region

Sturgeon, seals, and sulfur

Tracey German

Introduction

The Caspian Sea became the site of the world's first commercial oil industry, when oil reserves in Azerbaijan (then part of the Russian Empire) were developed at the end of the nineteenth century. Early exploitation of the region's hydrocarbons took place onshore. Offshore drilling technology was developed during the Soviet era, and the first major offshore field, Neftyanye Kamni (Oily Rocks), came on-stream in the 1940s. Oil and gas production during the Soviet era led to high levels of pollution in the Caspian, largely because of a lack of awareness of the potential negative environmental implications. According to Hekimoğlu, "[W]herever the oil industry had coastal and offshore operations, concentrations of contaminants in the Caspian were found to be several times the Soviet-recognized maximum permissible level" (Hekimoğlu, 1999, p. 86). By the end of the Soviet era, the average concentration of oil in Baku harbour was ten times the maximum permissible concentration (Hekimoğlu, 1999, p. 86). According to Azerbaijan's Ecology and Natural Resources minister, pollution in the Caspian has decreased markedly during the past two decades in spite of a rise in oil and gas production, largely because of the use of modern technology, although Soviet-era wells are still causing significant damage to the sea bed. Furthermore, not all pollution is the result of industrial pollution. Natural seepage contributes to the pollution of the Caspian Sea as well.

Following the collapse of the Soviet Union in 1991, the Caspian region was heralded as the Middle East of the future because of its potential hydrocarbon reserves. However, the euphoria and optimism that accompanied the initial involvement of foreign investors in the region has been tempered by difficult operating conditions, both political and geological. Although the Caspian has been lauded as the new Middle East, current proven reserves indicate a greater similarity with the North Sea than with the Persian Gulf (see Table 4.1), and foreign companies have begun to adopt a more moderate attitude toward the development of the Caspian's hydrocarbon reserves. Despite this, there has been considerable investment in oil and gas development, raising concerns about the potential environmental impact that increasing production could have on the Caspian's unique biodiversity. Large-scale exploitation of the sea's hydrocarbon resources necessitates a considerable increase in activity, including the production, transit, and processing of hydrocarbons, which heightens the risk of damage to the Caspian's distinctive ecosystem. Offshore developments can be more risky in their environmental impact, as demonstrated by the 2010 Deepwater Horizon accident in the Gulf of Mexico, which threatened more than 400 species.

The Caspian is home to a variety of unique species, including the Caspian seal, the white-tailed sea eagle (the largest bird of prey in Europe), and five of the most valuable species of sturgeon. The sea also lies on a seasonal migration route for thousands of birds from across Central Asia and the Mediterranean, including flamingos. The littoral states recognize the uniqueness of the sea; Russia's current maritime doctrine, approved in 2001 and looking forward to 2020, identifies the Caspian as a unique region in terms of the volume and quantity of its mineral and bio-resources (*Morskaya doktrina*). However, another unique aspect of the Caspian, which increases its vulnerability to oil spills and pollution, is that it is a closed, non-tidal system, meaning that pollution remains localized and is not dispersed as it would be on an open sea. Furthermore, it is located in an earthquake zone.

Research questions

This chapter examines rising oil and gas production in the Caspian region and assesses the potential environmental impact, investigating whether sustainable development is being sacrificed for rapid economic growth. It will focus on the Kashagan development in the northern Caspian, as this sector of the sea is the breeding ground for sturgeon and the endangered Caspian seal. The development of one of the biggest and most technically challenging oil fields in the world potentially threatens these species. The offshore Kashagan field highlights the complexities of the issues involved. It is located in shallow waters that freeze in winter, damaging equipment and making maintenance difficult. The field, thought to be one of the largest outside of the Middle East, also produces toxic hydrogen sulfide. A gas leak in October 2013 led to a halt in production and raised concerns about potential environmental damage. What steps are companies taking to mitigate the risk of environmental damage? Are regulations stringent enough? This chapter uses the Kashagan development as an example of modern-day production values and the challenges of balancing oil and gas production against the need for environmental protection.

Findings

The Caspian is composed of three very different sections: the northern, middle, and southern. The northern Caspian is composed of shallow waters with an average depth of 20 feet and low salinity, a consequence of the inflow of fresh water from the Volga River. This means it is ice-bound during the winter, which presents a serious technical challenge for energy companies. Caspian seal pups are born on these ice fields. The northern sector is also the location of sturgeon

Table 4.1 Comparison of proved reserves in the Caspian and Middle East, 2013

	Proven oil reserves (billion barrels)	Share of global total %	Reserves-to-production (R/P) ratio	Proven gas reserves (trillion cubic meters)	Share of global total %	R/P ratio
Azerbaijan	7.0	0.4	21.9	0.9	0.5	54.3
Kazakhstan	30.0	1.8	46.0	1.5	0.8	82.5
Turkmenistan	0.6	–	7.1	17.5	9.4	–
Saudi Arabia	265.9	15.8	63.2	8.2	4.4	79.9

Source: Figures from *BP Statistical Review of World Energy*, June 2014, www.bp.com. Reserves-to-production (R/P) ratio – "if the reserves remaining at the end of any year are divided by the production in that year, the result is the length of time that those remaining reserves would last if production were to continue at that rate." *BP Statistical Review of World Energy*, p. 6.

breeding grounds. The middle section, which has an average depth of more than 600 feet, holds about 35 percent of the Sea's total water volume, whereas the South is much deeper, averaging more than 1,000 feet, and has higher salinity (Huseynov, 2012). The south is not thought to contain as much oil and is possibly more gas-prone than the north. Meanwhile, exploratory drilling in the South Caspian basin has significantly reduced estimates of future oil potential.

Turkmenistan possesses some of the world's largest reserves of natural gas, as well as significant reserves of oil, although its ability to profit from these extensive hydrocarbon reserves has been restricted. In 2013 it had proven gas reserves of 17.5 trillion cubic meters (tcm), more than 9 percent of total global reserves of natural gas, most of them located onshore, in the east of the country. There is little in the Caspian. The majority of Turkmenistan's proven oil reserves of 0.6 billion barrels are in the South Caspian Basin and onshore in the west of the country.[1] It also claims to have significant oil reserves in areas of the Caspian that are subject to a dispute over ownership with Azerbaijan, notably the Serdar field (called Kyapaz by Azerbaijan), which lies on the maritime border between the two countries and has estimated recoverable reserves of 370 to 700 million barrels. Despite Turkmenistan seeking international arbitration to settle the boundary dispute, this issue, alongside its claims to portions of the Azeri and Chirag fields (called Khazar and Osman by Turkmenistan) being developed by Azerbaijan, remain unresolved.

Kazakhstan, where oil was first discovered more than 100 years ago, has the largest recoverable reserves of oil in the Caspian Sea region. According to BP's Statistical Review of World Energy published in 2014, the country has proven oil reserves of 30 billion barrels and was producing 1.7 million barrels a day (bpd) in 2013, making it a major producer (*BP Statistical Review of World Energy*). Kazakhstan's proven natural gas reserves stood at 1.3 tcm in 2012, the majority located in the west of the country. Oil is located primarily in the west, both

Table 4.2 Comparison of oil and gas production in the Caspian and Middle East, 2013

	Oil production (bpd)	Year-on-year change %	Share of global total %	Gas production (billion cubic meters)	Year-on-year change %	Share of global total %
Azerbaijan	877,000	0.4	1.1	16.2	3.8	0.5
Kazakhstan	1,785,000	3.5	2.0	18.5	0.8	0.5
Turkmenistan	231,000	4.1	0.3	62.3	0.4	1.8
Saudi Arabia	11,525,000	−1.1	13.1	103.0	4.0	3.0

Source: Figures from BP *Statistical Review of World Energy*, June 2014, www.bp.com.

on- and offshore. Current production is dominated by two giant onshore fields, Tengiz and Karachaganak, which combined produced more than 40 percent of the country's total output in 2013.[2] Tengiz is Kazakhstan's largest field, with daily production of more than 500,000 bpd. It is operated by Tengizchevroil, a joint venture that includes major U.S. oil companies Chevron and ExxonMobil, together with KazMunaiGaz and LukArco.[3]

Azerbaijan's sector of the Caspian Sea contains significant hydrocarbon reserves. Its proven crude oil reserves were estimated at 7 billion barrels in 2013, although there are indications that it may be more gas-prone than oil-prone and recent exploration in the Azeri sector of the Caspian Sea has been disappointing. The country's largest hydrocarbon basins are offshore with the majority of its oil being produced from the BP-led Azeri-Chirag-Guneshli (ACG) superstructure, which is composed of three fields with total reserves estimated to be at least 5.4 billion barrels of recoverable oil.[4] The 8 billion USD deal, which established the BP-led Azerbaijan International Operating Corporation to develop the Azeri, Chirag, and Guneshli offshore fields, was concluded in 1994. Dubbed the "contract of the century," it was the Azeri government's first international oil agreement with a consortium of global oil companies and marked the country's entrance into the international energy market. The ACG fields also produce a significant quantity of natural gas. In 2013, Azerbaijan's natural gas reserves were estimated at 0.9 tcm and, like its oil, most of Azerbaijan's natural gas is produced from a few fields in the Caspian: the ACG and the Shah Deniz. Situated in the Caspian Sea around 60 miles southeast of Baku, BP, the field's operator, claims that Shah Deniz is one of the world's largest gas-condensate fields with more than 1 trillion cubic meters of gas. Stage One of the field's development began operations in 2006 with an annual production capacity of 9 billion cubic meters (bcm). Shah Deniz is significant as the only major field development in the Caspian focused primarily on natural gas, rather than oil, despite the fact that the region is likely to be more gas-prone than oil-prone.

Russian production of oil and gas in the Caspian is insignificant compared to production elsewhere in the country. Although it is thought that Russia may have estimated hydrocarbon reserves of up to 32 billion barrels of oil equivalent in its sector of the Caspian, exploration has been limited to date. In 2010 Russian oil major LUKoil began developing the Yury Korchagin offshore field, which holds an estimated 270 million barrels of oil and more than 63 bcm of natural gas (*RIA Novosti*, 28 April 2010). Potential hydrocarbon reserves in the Iranian sector of the Caspian also remain largely unexplored, and there is no significant Iranian production in the sea. According to the National Iranian Oil Company, the country's Sardar Jangal field contains significant reserves worth more than 50 billion USD (*Tehran Times*, 9 July 2012). Iran announced at the end of 2011 that it had discovered the field, which it claims holds at least 1.4 tcm of natural gas and as much as 100 million barrels of oil (*Russia Today*, 16 July 2012). Despite these optimistic announcements, Iranian exploration and production in the Caspian is very limited, largely because its national sector of the sea is in extremely deep water and therefore difficult to explore with the technologies currently available.

An estimated two-thirds of future oil production will be from the North Caspian basin, predominantly from the giant offshore Kashagan field being developed under the North Caspian Sea Production Sharing Agreement (NCSPSA) by the North Caspian Operating Company (NCOC) consortium, which is composed of KazMunaiGaz, Shell, ENI, ExxonMobil, Total, Inpex, and the China National Petroleum Corporation (CNPC). Kashagan is thought to be one of the largest known fields outside of the Middle East and has been described as the "world's largest oil discovery in five decades" (Nurshayeva, 2013). Located 14,000 feet below the seabed, the total Kashagan contract area covers more than 3,400 square miles of the Northern Caspian and contains five separate fields: Kashagan, Kalamkas A, Kashagan Southwest, Aktote, and Kairan. It is hoped that the Kashagan reservoir will provide a reliable indicator of the Caspian's potential oil supply. Exploratory drilling has indicated that the field holds up to 35 billion barrels of oil, of which approximately 25 percent (7 to 9 billion barrels) can be produced.

According to Total, Kashagan is "one of the most complex projects ever undertaken by the oil industry" and requires the "use of exceptional and unusual resources and the implementation of large-scale innovative solutions."[5] The shallow water and extreme climate of the northern sector of the Caspian render conventional drilling and production technologies useless, so the infrastructure is built on artificial islands—small unstaffed "drilling islands" and larger staffed "hub islands"—linked by pipelines.[6] Production has been delayed several times, largely because of the challenges posed by the extreme operating conditions of the field, which is located in shallow waters that freeze in winter, damaging equipment and making maintenance difficult. The field's crude oil is highly pressured and its associated gas contains a high "sour gas" content (19 percent hydrogen sulfide), making it more difficult to produce and raising concerns about any possible environmental impact. Hydrogen sulfide is heavier than air, flammable, corrosive, and extremely toxic, necessitating the use of sour service steel pipe to prevent "sulphide stress cracking" (North Caspian Operating Company, 2014). A gas leak in October 2013 led to an indefinite halt in production and raised concerns about potential environmental damage from the complex offshore installation. An investigation into the leak concluded that two 55-mile pipelines linking the artificial islands with onshore processing facilities had suffered sulphide stress cracking—corrosion caused by hydrogen sulfide—and needed to be replaced, further delaying the project (Chazan, 2014). These findings highlight the potential environmental impact: oil in the Northern Caspian contains high levels of hydrogen sulphide, and there is the potential for this type of corrosion to occur in the future if the correct materials are not used. The challenges of developing a well that is highly pressured and contains high levels of hydrogen sulfide were demonstrated in June 1985 when Well 37 at the Tengiz onshore field suffered a massive blowout that burned for more than a year before being capped. Although this blowout resonates with contemporary developments in Kazakhstan such as Kashagan, the technologies and know-how available to international oil and gas majors are far more advanced than those available to the Soviets in 1985.

Some of the gas from Kashagan will go to the onshore Bolashak processing plant where the high levels of hydrogen sulfide will be removed (sweetened) and the sweetened gas used for power generation. The sweetening process will result in more than 1 million tons of sulfur being produced for sale annually at Bolashak. There are environmental risks associated with the storage of sulfur. These risks are highlighted by the controversy about its storage at the Tengiz field, which led to operator Chevron facing a significant fine after the Kazakh government accused it of not doing enough to dispose of the sulfur.

NCOC clearly recognizes the importance of protecting the biodiversity of the Northern Caspian, and its website claims that the operating company is "working hard to prevent and minimize any impacts on the environment that our operations may have."[7] Examples cited include the use of local companies to conduct on- and offshore Environmental Impact Assessments of NCOC operations, the funding of biodiversity research projects in the Caspian region, the installation of 20 air quality monitoring stations in Atyrau *oblast*, and annual soil, bird, and seal surveys.[8]

In addition to state scrutiny of its environmental impact, NCOC also faces pressure from the government about the persistent production delays at Kashagan. Continual delays mean that first production is now expected in 2016, with production increasing from 180,000 bpd during the first phase to as much as 370,000 bpd in the second. The development of Kazakhstan's "superfields" is the key to the country's long-term economic growth, and Kashagan in particular is vital for the country to achieve its goal of increasing crude oil output by 60 percent by the end of the decade. The continuing delays to the project have angered the Kazakh government, as it has had to lower its expectations for the country's long-term production. Kashagan is the only offshore "superfield" and therefore the only one currently with direct relevance to the northern sector of the Caspian. The complex requirements of developing the field highlight the difficult balance facing governments in the region as they seek to maximize the economic benefits from their natural resources while simultaneously protecting the unique ecosystem of the Caspian.

Pipelines and tankers

It is expected that Kazakhstan's oil exports will double once Kashagan is fully productive, and this will necessitate a significant expansion of export infrastructure capacity, pipelines, and cross-Caspian tanker routes. Most Kazakh oil is exported via the Russian pipeline network, including its shipment across the Caspian to terminals at Makhachkala and Taman and then on to Novorossiisyk, the Russian Black Sea port. Kazakhstan has signed a memorandum with Azerbaijan on the development of a Kazakh Caspian Transportation System (KCTS), an integrated system consisting of a pipeline to transport crude from Eskene and Tengiz to an oil terminal in Kuryk on the Kazakh coast of the Caspian, tankers and vessels to transport crude across the sea, an oil discharge terminal on the Azerbaijani coast, and facilities connecting to the Baku-Tbilisi-Ceyhan pipeline.[9] The original agreement envisaged the project being operational by 2013 or 2014, initially transporting up to 23 million tons of crude per year, increasing to 36 million tons. However, delays on the Kashagan project mean that the project has been suspended while the Kazakh Energy Ministry considers all alternative routes to the Russian one (Jafarova, 2014). Nevertheless, Kazakhstan still ships crude oil across the Caspian and exports it via Azerbaijan: Azerbaijan's Energy Ministry expected around 4 million tons of Kazakh oil to be transported via Azeri territory in 2014 (Hafizoglu, 2013). All of these transit projects increase the risk of an accident, such as a ruptured pipeline or a holed tanker. Not just the Caspian is at risk: so are transit routes for Caspian hydrocarbons across Russia, Georgia, Turkey, the Black Sea, and even the Mediterranean.

There is also a proposal to construct a subsea Trans-Caspian Gas pipeline linking Azerbaijan and Turkmenistan, which is supported by the EU. In November 2013, the EU made it clear that it was intent on pushing ahead with the project despite Russian unease about going ahead before all five littoral states reached agreement about the legal status of the sea, an issue that has remained unresolved since the collapse of the USSR. Denis Daniilidis, head of the EU mission in Turkmenistan, said that conditions were "most favourable" for construction of the pipeline and that the EU and Turkmenistan were in the final stages of their negotiations (*Today.az*, 20 November 2013). The 186-mile pipeline will cross the Caspian from Turkmenistan to Azerbaijan, where it will feed into the South Caucasus country's existing gas export infrastructure. It will enable Turkmen gas to reach European consumers without transiting through the Russian pipeline network. Igor Bratchikov, the Russian president's special envoy for the delimitation and demarcation of borders with CIS states, warned of the potential "catastrophic" impact the pipeline could have on the Caspian's "extremely sensitive ecosystem," stating that, in the event of an incident, it would not be the Europeans or Americans, but the littoral states that would have to tackle the aftermath (Sadykov, 2013). While potential environmental damage is clearly a concern, particularly as the Caspian is in a seismically active area, Russia is using these issues instrumentally to mask its real concerns, namely the loss of influence and transit tariffs that will result from the construction of the pipeline.

Sturgeon and seals

In addition to its significant hydrocarbon reserves, the Caspian contains another high-value natural resource: it is home to five of the world's most valuable species of sturgeon, which produce caviar. According to the Caspian Sea Fish Scientific-Research Institute, the commercial value of the sea's biological wealth, if properly managed, amounts to 1.1 trillion roubles (37 billion USD), equivalent to the total market value of the sea's recoverable reserves of oil and gas (Ustinov, 2004). This makes them highly desirable, by legal and illegal means, and poaching of sturgeon is a serious problem for the littoral states. Poaching and uncontrolled fishing have had a dramatic negative impact on the Caspian's sturgeon population since the collapse of the Soviet Union. Stocks of beluga sturgeon in the sea have fallen by 30 to 40 percent during the past decade, and some species of the fish are on the verge of extinction (Nekhai, 2013; Orujova, 2013). According to the Iranian International Scientific Research Institute, wild sturgeon may be extinct by 2021 at the current rate of decline (Nekhai, 2013; Orujova, 2013). In addition to these pressures, there are concerns that the development of the sea's oil and gas will put the Caspian's sturgeon stocks under further threat. Sturgeon are bottom-feeders and can live for up to 100 years, meaning that toxins can build up in their systems (Neville, 2001, p. 112). According to past research, increasing pollution levels in the Caspian basin caused muscle atrophy in sturgeon from cumulative toxicosis. The research quoted Altufiev's findings that common oil products, including diesel fuel, cause "anomalies" in the muscles of juvenile sturgeon similar to those seen in sturgeon with muscle atrophy (Khodorevskaya et al., 1997, p. 215).

Another species unique to the Caspian is the Caspian seal. Although they migrate across the whole area of the sea, almost all breeding takes place on the ice that covers the shallow northern sector in the winter. There has been a dramatic decline in the seal population in recent years. During the 1930s, there were more than 1 million seals in the Caspian, but this number has dropped to around 100,000, and they are listed as an endangered species by the International Union for Conservation of Nature and Natural Resources. Hunting by both people and predators such as wolves and eagles, large-scale fishing, and disease account for a significant number of deaths each year (Härkönen, 2008). Several thousand seals were killed by outbreaks of canine distemper virus (CDV) in 1997 and 2000 through 2001. Principal threats to their numbers and reasons for the continuing population decline appear to be a loss of habitat, and reduced fish stock linked to overfishing and a dramatic rise in comb jellyfish. The jellyfish, which were apparently introduced to the Caspian in ship ballast water in the Volga–Don Canal more than a decade ago, rapidly consume zooplankton, leading to a reduction in fish stocks, the primary food source of the seals. The rise in comb jellyfish is not directly connected with increasing oil production, but there could be an indirect link. An increased number of ships and barges entering the Caspian via the canal raises the risk of invasive species such as the comb jellyfish being introduced.

There are also concerns that the Kashagan development will disturb the seals and their pups. The construction of offshore drilling islands and associated infrastructure has led to a considerable growth in offshore activity, close to the breeding seals on the ice. One study found that breeding seals used shipping channels as artificial leads into the ice and gave birth close to the edge of these channels (Härkönen, 2008). Nevertheless, the principal threats to the seal population are not linked to the energy industry. Overfishing and hunting are the primary perils.

Conclusions and discussion

There is no doubt that that the large-scale exploitation of the Caspian's hydrocarbon resources is leading to a considerable increase in activity. Subsea pipelines, development of technically challenging fields such as Kashagan, more shipping traffic, and industrial complexes in environmentally sensitive areas such as the northern sector of the sea all heighten the risk of damage to the environment. This is compounded by pressure from local governments that hold stakes in these projects to press ahead with developments so the state can maximize the economic benefits from its natural resources. Delays and cost overruns are unwelcome. Nevertheless, major projects such as Kashagan come under considerable international scrutiny from governments, shareholders, non-governmental organizations, and the media, encouraging them to remain environmentally responsible. Economic and environmental risks are a liability and cost companies both in terms of their financial health and their reputation, as oil majors are held publicly accountable for their actions—or lack of actions—even more so in the wake of the Deepwater Horizon accident.

Governments in the Caspian region have demonstrated their willingness to hold companies accountable for environmental transgressions. However, the cloudy legal status of the Caspian Sea remains a serious impediment to the establishment of a stable security environment. During the Soviet era, only two states bordered the sea: the USSR and Iran. The collapse of the USSR saw the appearance of four new states in its place—Azerbaijan, Kazakhstan, Russia, and Turkmenistan—all of which had access to the sea's valuable natural resources. The sea's legal status was thrown into doubt, and a dispute has been simmering since 1991. Ongoing negotiations among the Caspian Five have so far failed to establish whether it is legally considered to be a lake or an inland sea. This lack of agreement means that the area remains one of political dispute that has, at times, threatened to turn into military action. In addition to the lack of clarity about its legal status and whether it is a sea or a lake, there is also disagreement among the littoral states about how to demarcate it and what legal regime to use: for example, median line or condominium. This lack of consensus hinders development of a clear environmental protection framework for the entire Caspian Sea and could enable oil majors to evade responsibility in the event of an accident.

Disclaimer

The analysis, opinions, and conclusions expressed or implied in this article are those of the author and do not necessarily represent the views of the Joint Services Command and Staff College (JSCSC), the UK Ministry of Defence, or any other government agency.

Notes

1 For further details, see Turkmenistan country analysis brief, US Energy Information Administration, http://www.eia.gov/countries/country-data.cfm?fips=TX.
2 For further details, see Kazakhstan country analysis brief, US Energy Information Administration, http://www.eia.gov/countries/cab.cfm?fips=KZ.
3 See http://www.tengizchevroil.com/.
4 For further details, see BP Caspian, www.bp.com/lubricanthome.do?categoryId=6070&contentId=7013331.
5 See more at: http://www.total.com/en/energies-expertise/oil-gas/exploration-production/projects-achievements/other-projects/kashagan#sthash.AZq7yflf.dpuf.
6 For further details, see www.ncoc.kz.
7 http://www.ncoc.kz/en/kashagan/technical_challenges.aspx.
8 http://www.ncoc.kz/en/kashagan/s_and_e.aspx.
9 See http://www.kmg.kz.

References

BP Statistical Review of World Energy (June 2014) Available at http://www.bp.com/en/global/corporate/about-bp/energy-economics/statistical-review-of-world-energy.html.

Chazan, G. (2014) Kazakhstan to extend contract for $50bn Kashagan oil project. *Financial Times*, 13 June. Available at http://www.ft.com/cms/s/0/9cbc3c7e-f2e1-11e3-a3f8-00144feabdc0.html#ixzz3DMt5gZQ9.

Hafizoglu, R. (2013) Azerbaijani Energy Ministry announces transit volumes of Kazakh oil for 2014. *Trend News Agency*, 2 December. Available at http://en.trend.az/capital/energy/2217306.html.

Härkönen, T. (2008) *Pusa caspica*. The IUCN Red List of Threatened Species, (IUCN SSC Pinniped Specialist Group). Available at http://www.iucnredlist.org/details/41669/0.

Hekimoğlu, L. (1999) Caspian oil and the environment: curse or cure? In M. P. Croissant and A. Bülent (eds) *Oil and Geopolitics in the Caspian Sea Region* (London: Praeger), pp. 83–98.

Huseynov, S. (December 2011–January 2012) Fate of the Caspian Sea. *Natural History*. Available at http://www.naturalhistorymag.com/features/112161/fate-of-the-caspian-sea.

Jafarova, A. (2014) No progress expected in KCTS project. *Today.az*, 23 October, http://www.today.az/news/regions/137175.html.

Khodorevskaya, R. P., Dovgopol, G. F., Zhuravleva, O. L. and Vlasenko, A. D. (1997) Present status of commercial stocks of sturgeons in the Caspian Sea basin. *Environmental Biology of Fishes*, 48: 215.

Konyrova K. (2010) Kazakhstan Caspian Transport System project postponed. *New Europe Online*, 27 June. Available at http://www.neurope.eu/article/kazakhstan-caspian-transport-system-project-postponed.

Morskaya doktrina Rossiiskoi Federatsii na period do 2020 goda (2001) Approved by Vladimir Putin, President of the Russian Federation on 27 July 2001. Available at http://www.scrf.gov.ru/documents/34.html.

Nekhai, O. (2013) Caspian Sea stocks to be restored. *Voice of Russia*, 3 May. Available at http://voiceofrussia.com/2013_05_03/Caspian-Sea-sturgeon-stocks-to-be-restored.

Neville, R. E. (2001) Two black golds: petroleum extraction and environmental protection in the Caspian Sea. *Journal of Public and International Affairs*, 12: 109–123. Available at http://www.princeton.edu/jpia/past-issues-1/2001/6.pdf.

North Caspian Operating Company (2014), Status of Kashagan Pipeline Integrity Issue. 25 April. Available at http://www.ncoc.kz/en/mediacentre/2014/news-25-04-2014.aspx.

Nurshayeva, Raushan (2013) 'Kazakh head reshuffles oil officials after Kashagan delays', *Reuters* 3 July, Available at http://www.reuters.com/article/2013/07/03/oil-kazakhstan-minister-idUSL5N0F90RC20130703.

Orujova, N. (2013) First sturgeon farm to open in Azerbaijan. *Azernews*, 7 November. Available at http://www.azernews.az/azerbaijan/61392.html.

RIA Novosti (2010) Putin kicks off oil project on Caspian Sea. 28 April. Available at http://en.rian.ru/russia/20100428/158790351.html.

Russia Today (2012) Iran claims $50bln oil field found in Caspian Sea. 16 July. Available at http://rt.com/business/iran-claims-vast-oil-field-found-in-caspian-sea-302.

Sadykov, M. (2013) Russia concerned about Caspian ecosystem, when expedient. EurasiaNet.org, 26 November. Available at http://www.eurasianet.org/node/67800.

Tehran Times (2012) Iran's oil deposits in Caspian Sea worth over $50bn. 9 July. Available at http://tehrantimes.com/economy-and-business/99479-irans-oil-deposits-in-caspian-sea-worth-over-50b.

Today.az (2013) EU satisfied with auspicious conditions for Trans-Caspian Gas Pipeline conclusion. 20 November.Available at http://www.today.az/news/business/128353.html.

US Energy Information Administration (2012) Turkmenistan country analysis brief. Available at http://www.eia.gov/countries/cab.cfm?fips=TX.

US Energy Information Administration (2013) Kazakhstan country analysis brief. Available at http://www.eia.gov/countries/cab.cfm?fips=KZ.

Ustinov E. (2004) Bioterrorizm: mesto deystviya – Kaspiy. *Krasnaya Zvezda*, 25 June. Available at http://old.redstar.ru/2004/06/25_06/3_02.html.

Zonn, I. (2001) The Caspian Sea: threats to its biological resources and environmental security. In G. Chufrin (ed.) *The Security of the Caspian Sea Region* (Oxford: Oxford University Press), pp. 69–82.

5 The 'great future of the country'?

Dams and hydroelectricity discourses in Kyrgyzstan

Amanda E. Wooden, Jeanne Féaux de la Croix and David Gullette

Introduction

Conversation among passengers and driver of a shared taxi, overheard when passing the Orto–Tokoi reservoir on the Naryn–Bishkek highway on September 24, 2014:

Woman 1:   My, the water reservoir is low now.
Driver: Yes, even though this region has had more rain than others this year.
Woman 2:   I drove past the Toktogul water reservoir the other day – there is almost no water left!
Driver (grunts):   Yes, they sold the water over the summer.
Woman 1:   It's good that they are building new hydropower stations higher up in Naryn region.
Driver: Yeah, but now there is no money for building. It all depends on Putin's policy.

Kyrgyzstan's government faces a water and energy supply conundrum. The country relies on Soviet-built hydropower stations on the Naryn River – its largest river – for up to 90 percent of its energy production. The system, however, suffers from inadequate and mismanaged storage capacities, aging infrastructure, and a limited national grid. It is also vulnerable to periods of low rainfall, as in 2014–2015. Kyrgyzstan, therefore, confronts regular electricity shortages, while attempts to raise energy prices to invest in improving the system put immediate pressure on a population that struggles to cope with electricity rate hikes.[1] As the taxi passengers noted, presidential administrations over the past decade have pursued Soviet-era plans to expand hydroelectricity production with a series of dams along the upper Naryn River and sought international investment and financial support to do so. This project – often referred to as the Naryn Cascade – entails a series of six medium- to large-sized dams. It began with construction of Kambar-Ata-2 and continues with construction of Kambar-Ata-1 and four dams on the upper Naryn. Neighboring Tajikistan is engaged in a similar endeavor, with a focus on the Rogun Dam on the Vakhsh River, which will be the highest dam in the world when completed.

Water infrastructure projects in both Kyrgyzstan and Tajikistan have roots in ambitious Soviet engineering plans developed from the 1930s and partially realized by the late 1980s. Such projects face much resistance from downriver countries, Uzbekistan in particular. The dam projects have also generated differing international contacts in each country, such as Russian investments in Kyrgyzstan and Iranian in Tajikistan, as well as differing levels of conflict with Uzbekistan. As the cost investments of imported fuels – coal, natural gas, oil – rose in the last decade, neighboring source countries Kazakhstan and Uzbekistan have charged higher prices and, on occasion, even cut off supplies due to indebtedness (Pannier, 2014). Kyrgyzstan and Tajikistan have not developed alternative energy plans to respond to such economic and trade pressures, but rather have advanced large hydropower development.

These multi-dam projects are odd choices in light of increasingly critical international discourses opposed to this approach. Many countries have shifted away from developing large dams, as local contestations became regular occurrences. In 2000, the World Commission on Dams (WCD) produced an influential report that critically evaluated large dams and contributed significantly to a shift in approach and a decline in international investment for such projects (WCD, 2000). Criticism has focused international attention on dams' environmental damage, social disruption, high economic cost, and low rates of return. Current international recommendations for dam-building highlight the need for improved decision-making processes, with increased transparency and early public involvement, acceptance by potentially impacted communities, full accounting of costs, and complete environmental impact evaluations (Ansar et al., 2014).

Part of Kyrgyzstan's reliance on a hydropower strategy can be explained by the nature of the dams and the places where they would be constructed. The impacts on pastureland and population displacement are described as minimal.[2] This is in contrast to countries with large-scale opposition mobilized to contest large dam construction, such as against the Sardar Sarovar (Narmada) Dam in India, the HidroAysén's Patagonian dam project in Chile, and the Belo Monte dam in Brazil. As a result of those projects, many people would be displaced. But also, environmental and indigenous rights movements that oppose large dam development are well established in India, Chile, and Brazil. There is widespread contestation of many industrial activities, while national NGOs networked with global civil society actors are poised to support local communities contesting negative impacts.

In the case of the Vakhsh and Naryn dams, we traced a relatively weak base of social resistance to dam-building plans *as such*, despite potentially negative political and economic impacts on citizens. This may be unsurprising in light of the atmosphere of censorship fostered in Tajikistan, but much more surprising in Kyrgyzstan, where other large-scale foreign investments in industry – mining in particular – regularly provoke public outcry about environmental impact (Gullette, 2014; Wooden, 2013).

Dam development, discourses and consequences: an enquiry

So why is critical discourse about this dam construction virtually absent, even among environmental NGOs? After all, as we saw from the taxi passengers' conversation, citizens tend to be quite aware of the political dimension of hydropower policies. What is different about hydroelectric projects? Why don't they draw the same kind of critical public attention as other contested industrial facilities in Kyrgyzstan? Can we attribute this difference to the particular riverine context, the kinds of environmental activism present, and the political and economic interests at stake? In this chapter we seek to answer these questions by evaluating the historical context of hydroelectricity development in Kyrgyzstan, with some comparisons to Tajikistan for perspective, and by dissecting discourses about the Kambar-Ata projects and the Naryn Cascade.[3]

Hydropower in Kyrgyzstan

Kyrgyzstan's government maintains that the expansion and increased generation of its hydropower capacity is the future of the country's energy security and essential to its economic development. Kyrgyzstan suffers from unbalanced energy distribution. The United Energy System – a Soviet-era high-voltage transmission network connecting all Central Asian republics except Turkmenistan – allowed balancing electricity needs, especially during peak hours. However, it is rapidly becoming obsolete. Uzbekistan withdrew from transmitting in December 2009, but still draws electricity from the system. To ensure its own energy security, Kyrgyzstan is constructing the Kemin-Datka high-voltage line to provide an internal grid circuit that does not rely on neighboring countries, especially at peak usage times.

Kyrgyzstan hopes to strengthen its energy security and meet domestic demand by constructing medium- and large-scale hydropower stations that were first planned in the Soviet period. The government argues that with the additional electricity generation capacity, it could sell surplus electricity to Afghanistan and Pakistan through the Central Asia South Asia Electricity Transmission and Trade Project known as CASA-1000.

In Kyrgyzstan, electricity through large-scale hydroelectric generation first became available in the 1960s, with successive dams on the lower Naryn coming online. This was an important part of the Soviet plan to provide electricity to modern homes in the region, but also served to regulate water flow for cotton crops downstream in the Ferghana Valley. The arrangement created a barter system through which upstream Soviet republics Kyrgyzstan and Tajikistan provided water in the summer for irrigation in return for electricity in the winter from downstream Kazakhstan and Uzbekistan – thus allowing upstream Soviet republics to accumulate water for the following summer.

Since independence in 1991, there has been a slow reversal of this arrangement. Kyrgyzstan, in particular, has increased electricity generation in the winter. This move brought water-sharing among the countries into sharp focus. President

Islam Karimov of Uzbekistan has suggested that large-scale hydropower dams and the subsequent limitation of water to downstream countries could lead to war in the region (International Crisis Group, 2014; Lillis, 2013).[4]

Dams as national symbols

The Kambar-Ata-1 and 2 dams, projects initiated in the late 1980s and re-launched by the otherwise unpopular regime of then-President Kurmanbek Bakiev, are probably Bakiev's only political initiative that continued unchallenged after his overthrow in 2010. Although questions of funding and implementation periodically occupy the parliamentary floor, the basic question of building or not building these large dams is not at issue. Interim President Roza Otunbaeva had asked highly critical questions of the project during Bakiev's rule, but once in power, she supported the project, as did the successor government (Menga, 2013, pp. 137–138). One reason might be that in the political crisis of summer 2010, when ethnic violence caused several hundred deaths, and amid fears the country might break apart, the inauguration of Kambar-Ata-2 – the smaller facility – on Independence Day was the only positive, potentially unifying piece of news. In this sense, Kambar-Ata-1 and 2 have at moments been used as national symbols, just as the Rogun dam project in Tajikistan has been enlisted in this way. Rogun has, at least since the early 2000s, served the government of President Emomali Rahmon as a symbol of national unity and a promise of development, with a host of speeches, posters, and other public relations activities dedicated to it.[5]

Considering the degree of government instability in Kyrgyzstan since 2010, forced sales of dam shares (as in Tajikistan) are out of the question. Despite that, significant state assets – or taxes that might be spent on other citizen services – are being invested in the Naryn hydro projects. Should attention become less monopolized by foreign profits from the Kumtor gold mine – a large, regularly protested Canadian-run mine that produces 10–12 percent of the country's annual GDP – the opposition, media, and public might also ask about the consequences of growing dependency on Russia as an investor in dams and energy. The public also might wonder whether such dependencies – on a single country or an organization like the World Bank – are desirable. After all, it has not been long since Kyrgyzstan balked at the International Monetary Fund's Heavily Indebted Poor Countries Initiative in 2007, fearing too much foreign interference and a roll-back of state services as a consequence.

However, there are many non-state and non-national actors involved, as is typical for large-scale infrastructure investments. In a fairly open "exchange" of favors, Russia offered to fund the Kambar-Ata-1 and 2 in return for Kyrgyzstan's closing of the American airbase near Bishkek. This deal was not fully realized, though the airbase closed in July 2014 under President Almazbek Atambaev. New, but as yet unspecified, investment interest from Russia in Kambar-Ata-1 has been voiced since. On the other hand, a Kyrgyz–Russian deal in 2013 began fairly quickly to build "small" hydropower stations on the uppermost reach of the Naryn.

A Kyrgyz–Russian joint venture manages the site (ZAO *Verkhnie Narynskie Gidroelektrostantsii*), bringing together Kyrgyzstan's Power Stations (*Elektricheskie Stantsii*) and Russia's RusHydro through an investment directly from the Russian state. This means that until these investments are paid off, RusHydro will own approximately 75 percent of the electricity produced at these sites. It has not been possible to view the actual contracts, and both regional administrators and residents in Naryn are unclear about whether, for example, they will benefit in any way from the dams on their territory, or how decisions about energy sales and pricing will be made. RusHydro itself claims there will be no preferential pricing or supply for the region of production. It also does not offer any kind of social or training programs in the construction area. Rather, regional administrators emphasize that taxes from the dams will ease their regional budget problems and that the dam sites will provide work (authors' fieldwork data, June 2014).

Cultural relationships to energy: everyday experiences and popular resonance

Focusing more on the immediate experience of dam-building, we see a common legacy of social acceptance for such projects as a solution to energy provision, which may partially result from the generally positive assessment of Soviet policies by Kyrgyzstani citizens (McMann, 2005).[6] It may also be because the narrative that dominates and resonates publicly is of hydroelectricity as the only large-scale solution to effectively tackle the regional energy dependency problem. Hydroelectricity framed as "the great future" may work, especially at times of insecurity such as when Uzbekistan cuts off gas supplies or when water levels are low and the population nervously expects a hard winter.

However, in conversation with villagers in 2014, and from a question-and-answer session with dam management on local Naryn TV (30 June 2014), it is evident that there have been, at the least, quite a few misunderstandings about the issue. The main concern raised by local people was employment, claiming that the company had promised 3,000 jobs to locals. During the TV discussion, the company representative carefully emphasized that it was primarily looking for skilled workers such as experienced engineers. Such people are, of course, extremely scarce in nearby villages, that subsist mainly on livestock. Anger over these disappointments led to threats and theft of equipment at the dam site in 2014.

Absence of activist criticism of dam construction

So why does this particular nation-building framing resonate now in Kyrgyzstan, and why are critical environmental voices largely absent? After all, there are firm indications of general environmental concern by a large proportion of the population, as well as specific worries about water supply and pollution, as evidenced in a public opinion survey and dozens of interviews (Wooden, 2013). This hydrosphere focus of worry may explain public support for investment in water system infrastructure, exemplified by large-dam construction. As is typical in many places around the world, environmental worries are often localized in Kyrgyzstan (Wooden, 2013). Those most likely to mobilize are residents of communities negatively affected by dam construction or who perceive that they would be adversely affected in the future. For the Naryn dams, the number of potentially impacted and likely dissenting communities is small. That, combined with difficulties created by water-dependent energy shortages for the majority of Kyrgyzstanis, drives popular acceptance of the government framing that hydroelectricity promises a better future.

Contemporary hydroelectricity discourses

In China, dam contestations have sometimes succeeded and sometimes failed, often depending on the political and social power of the narratives used by opponents in contrast with the power of the state's frames of the issue (Mertha, 2008). In the Kyrgyzstan case, the power of official frames of hydropower development challenges and neutralizes criticism before it forms. Dam development is difficult for environmentalists to battle, given widespread water concerns and energy demands at the household level. All of Kyrgyzstan's main hydropower stations are on the Naryn River. Low-water cycles in both 2009 and 2014, coupled with mismanaged electricity generation, nearly depleted the main Toktogul Reservoir.

The country's energy sector has been in stasis since the electricity crisis of 2009 and subsequent revolution (Wooden, 2014). Keen to appease a frustrated population, the government has continued to subsidize electricity rates. In addition, the rates for heating, hot water, and natural gas – where available – were kept stable until recently. Despite introduction of the National Sustainable Development Strategy (2013–2017), which includes goals for the energy sector and other adopted reform policies, the lack of sector funding results in poor quality and reliability of services.

The work on Kambar-Ata-1 has been slow to start, and there are concerns that projected costs may differ from the final, actual costs. For example, these costs do not consider the need to upgrade the existing infrastructure now operating well beyond its expected lifespan (Tetra Tech, 2011; UNISON, 2013).

Experts note other substantial issues to address. For example, Nurzat Abdyrasulova, director of the NGO UNISON Civic Environmental Foundation, said poor management, the complex financial structure, and technical issues allow corruption to flourish.[7] In addition, evidence suggests that the Bakiev government illegally sold electricity to Kazakhstan in 2009 (International Crisis Group, 2010). Public lack of trust in government structures means these challenges and the failure to overcome them through numerous reforms have exacerbated tensions toward the government. Coupled with the slow pace of improvements in the sector, it has created a situation where people do not see why rate increases should be accepted for poor service.

Rate increases have been sensitive since the 2010 ousting of President Bakiev, which was in part due to unpopular – and sudden – rate increases of 200 to 300 percent for electricity, heating, and hot water. Nonetheless, the topic has been gathering momentum in government. To overcome the energy crisis in both 2009 and 2014, rolling blackouts throughout the country attempted to reduce consumption, and emergency plans were in place to import electricity from Kazakhstan and Tajikistan. In short, there were strong parallels to the issues that led to the 2009 energy crisis and resulting political crisis the following year. *Bishkekteploset*, the capital's provider of hot water and centralized heating, introduced rate increases in July 2014. These, however, were challenged by human rights defenders who succeeded in having Bishkek's Inter-District Court cancel the increases. They argued that the government had not consulted with city residents ,and thus had neglected its duties (AKIpress, 2014).

Despite the critical situation, there has been no major discussion about examining other forms of renewable and alternative energy sources to complement the current infrastructure. For example, even the country's Law "On Renewable Energy" does not force development of alternative technologies or provide sufficient technical guidance on a number of topics, including feed-in tariffs for renewable energy generation sources. It is not just a matter of insufficient frameworks: "Nothing has been done regarding public awareness," said Abdyrasulova.[8] People have little awareness as to why the state should examine other forms of renewable and alternative energy sources when they have cheap electricity now.

In addition, mainstream environmental civil society groups face structural limitations and focus primarily on using sustainable development ideas with global and national goals rather than reflecting localized concerns outside of the capital (Wooden, Aitieva and Epkenhans, 2009). Henry's work underscores the political space limitations for the functioning of a healthy critical environmental civil society in authoritarian post-communist countries (Henry, 2009, 2010). The sustainability focus of most environmental NGOs – perhaps resulting from reliance on international donor grants – may preclude overly critical evaluations of industrial development that fits international conceptualizations of "green economics."

Most interestingly, the government's environmental and energy security talk is mismatched with what the United Nations Environment Programme identifies as unsustainable industrial development; that is, large dams. However, hydropower development divides the international community over the pursuit of greenhouse gas reductions, and this leads to little support for civil society criticism. For example, the 2000 WCD report critical of large dams pressured the International Bank for Reconstruction and Development (IBRD), a World Bank institution, into re-evaluating its hydroenergy funding policies, particularly regarding displacement (World Bank, 2000; World Bank, 2009). It withdrew funding from several projects, such as the Sardar Sarovar and Three Gorges dams. Yet the IBRD has since been criticized for a recent uptick in support for large dams as a result of climate change worries and pressure to reduce reliance on fossil fuels such as coal (Bosshard, 2013). The Kyoto Protocol Clean Development Mechanism – for which UNDP conducted workshops in Bishkek for environmental NGOs and power sector government agencies – has been criticized for giving credits to large hydropower dam construction and afforestation programs, meeting global emissions reduction goals but not local sustainability needs (Sutter and Parreño, 2007). The hydropower-support side of this international discourse aligns more with nationalistic framing of energy independence needs in Kyrgyzstan.

The arena in which Bishkek environmentalists are well versed and active is in environmental impact analysis (EIA) and ecological expertise, and thus this is where minimal criticism has occurred. The relevant international agreement that Kyrgyzstan signed is the United Nations Economic Commission for Europe Aarhus Convention on Access to Information, Public Participation in Decision-Making, and Access to Justice in Environmental Matters. Some anti-mining activists in Kyrgyzstan refer to the Aarhus Convention frame to demand access to independent monitoring and scientific information, public input in decision-making, and greater transparency. For the Kambar-Ata-1 and 2 dams, there were no functioning or publicly available environmental assessments as of early 2013. However, an EIA was started for Kambar-Ata-1 in August 2013. On 17 January 2014 the Ministry of Energy invited environmental groups with only one day's notice to attend a discussion about a 600-page EIA document and requested input and their organizations' position within five days (Abdyrasulova, 2014).

The unprofessional and incomplete nature of that document was criticized as a barrier to substantive public input. That critique was set out in a letter by the leader of the NGO UNISON and shared in the online forum Ekois. net (Abdyrasulova, 2014). According to key informants, the environmental assessment of Naryn dams conducted in 2012 is "locked in a drawer." The governments of Uzbekistan and Kazakhstan have insisted that EIAs must be conducted for hydroelectric dams in Kyrgyzstan and Tajikistan. Kyrgyzstani press coverage of the EIAs has been minimal and mostly presents politicians' responses to neighboring countries' demands (CARnet, 2010), including suggesting EIAs for downstream reservoirs or threatening enforcement of water-sharing quotas. This media coverage reinforces the regional independence and nation-building frames rationalizing dam construction and brushes over environmental impact concerns (Kenesh.kg, 2013).

Piecemeal international engagement: alternatives to hydropower?

A number of international organizations provide energy sector support, but as costs for creating new energy infrastructure is expensive, most provide assistance to revamp rather than replace that infrastructure. The Asian Development Bank and the World Bank are the main donor agencies in the sector and also support alternative and renewable energy technologies on a smaller scale. Organizations like the European Bank for Reconstruction and Development, German Development Bank, Japanese International Cooperation Agency (JICA), Swiss Agency for Development and Cooperation, the United Nations Development Programme (UNDP), and USAID provide support to parts of the energy network. JICA and UNDP, in particular, have promoted alternative and renewable energy technologies, such as biogas and solar panels. Many initiatives were pilot projects and have not been scaled up to a national level.

The lack of ability to maintain these technologies limits their wider implementation. There have thus been few debates about moving away from thermal power plants because there are no plans, and little willingness, on the part of the government to explore different technologies. Thus, the best option for many seems to be building on Soviet-era plans where profits can be made and can fit into the existing business structure without creating a new approach to energy production. The steady critical international discourse and increased information about the social and economic costliness of large dams recently led donor countries and organizations, such as the United States and the European Parliament, to withdraw contributions to international financial institution-supported dam construction projects (U.S. Congress, 2014; European Parliament, 2011). These shifts make funding a challenge for Central Asian countries. Kyrgyzstan has charged forward with big dam construction projects without acting on most of the suggested measures to evaluate and reduce their negative social and environmental impacts.

Conclusion

Kyrgyzstan's energy conundrum is also a water use conundrum. Central Asia has moved far from the Soviet system that, for a time, filled the energy needs of citizens and industry rather well, albeit at a high environmental cost – as it did elsewhere in the world during the same period. That legacy of the mid-20th Soviet century has, however, raised issues of regional and seasonal distribution of river flow in the post-Soviet period. Coping strategies in both Tajikistan and Kyrgyzstan have consistently envisaged new, large or medium-sized hydropower projects, all dependent on two transnational rivers: the Vakhsh and the Naryn.

This chapter has traced the histories and current political constellations around the Naryn projects. Due to heightened international – particularly Uzbekistani – attention to the Rogun project, the World Bank's recent environmental impact assessment looks much more rigorous than the stuffed-in-drawers nature of supposedly completed EIAs for the Kambar-Ata and upper Naryn cascade. And yet, even environmental NGOs in Kyrgyzstan tend to be silent about these hydropower projects.

There are a number of reasons why this might be so: the positive perception and experience of Soviet energy policies based on Naryn power stations – which both celebrated Soviet-era dams as national, heroic achievements, and did, indeed, fulfill Central Asian energy needs through sharing systems. Such rhetoric has continued, intermittently and with different degrees of intensity, in Tajikistan and Kyrgyzstan. This positive assessment is combined with a lack of information about potential alternatives, including energy-saving measures. Indeed, the sense that Kyrgyzstan simply has no viable alternatives to provide for its energy needs is a common trope: dams simply look like the most obvious option. In both countries, water is widely considered one of the few riches to be proud of, so why not tap it to make the country a stronger and better place? And indeed, it is easy to see that there are certainly *worse* choices in terms of potential environmental and social impacts, such as nuclear or coal plants. And although up to 40,000 residents will have to leave their homes for the sake of the Rogun dam project, it seems that only a handful of households in Kyrgyzstan are affected. These numbers compare favorably to the massive displacements seen in China, Brazil, and Turkey.

Nevertheless, popular endorsement of large dam projects *per se* is not to be confused with popular endorsement of actual government policy: just as the taxi driver quoted at the start of this chapter illustrated, there is widespread suspicion and expectation of corrupt practices both in energy sales and in the construction process. Apparently, however, this does not detract from the idea of dams, in principle, as useful and glorious things, promising a better future for the public. After all, while Kyrgyzstanis never immediately see the benefits of gold mining materialize in their own households, they can hold out the hope that in a decade or so they might no longer have to cope with long and painful power cuts in the cold, dark winters.

Notes

1 These price hikes hit urban residents hardest. But the fact that the rural population generally has access to alternative energy sources, such as wood and dried dung, has a long-term negative impact on their immediate environment and livelihoods.
2 According to company and ministry officials interviewed in 2014. Exact figures have proven extremely difficult to come by through the hydropower company, Ministry of Energy and Industry, or parliamentary channels. Some information on construction size can be found at www.narynhydro.kg.
3 For a fuller comparison of dam-building processes and discourses in Tajikistan and Kyrgyzstan, see Féaux de la Croix and Suyarkulova, Cahiers d'Asie Centrale (forthcoming 2015).
4 This statement should be seen as a rhetorical rather than an actual threat of war. Nevertheless, the high level of tension around regional water-sharing feeds into tense bilateral relations generally and the escalation or non-resolution of violent incidents, such as those along disputed borders in the Ferghana Valley.
5 For a more detailed comparison of dam-building in Kyrgyzstan and Tajikistan, see Féaux de la Croix and Suyarkulova (forthcoming 2015).
6 The Toktogul dam built on the Naryn River in the late Soviet period caused 35,000 residents to move from their homes, but discontent was and is not significantly reflected on a national scale.
7 Personal communication on 22 August 2014, Bishkek, Kyrgyzstan.
8 Personal communication on 22 August 2014, Bishkek, Kyrgyzstan.

References

Abdyrasulova, N. (2014) Obsuzhdenie OVOS v ramkakh razrabotki TEO stroitel'stva Kambaratinskoi GES-1 [Discussion of the EIA in the development of a feasibility study for Kambarata HES-1], letter published in *Ekois* (Ecological Information Service) 17 January 2014. Available at http://ekois.net/13702/.

AKIpress (2014) Nadeius', chto pravitel'stvo ne obzhaluet reshenie suda. Esli ono eto sdelaet, to prodemonstriruet prezrenie k sudu i naseleniiu – pravozashchitnik N.Toktakunov [I hope the government does not appeal against the court and people – human rights defender N. Toktakunov], 30 July 2014. Available at http://www.tazabek. kg/news:379407.

Ansar, A., Flyvbjerg, B., Budzier, A. and Lunn, D. (2014) Should we build more large dams? The actual costs of hydropower megaproject development. *Energy Policy*, 69(6): 43–56.

Bosshard, P. (2013) World Bank returns to big dams. *World Rivers Review* 28(3)., Available at http://www.internationalrivers.org/resources/world-bank-returns-to-big-dams-8077.

CARnet (Environment and Sustainable Development in Central Asia and Russia) (2010) Nazarbaev i Karimov trebuiut provedeniia ekspertizy proektov stroitel'stva GES v Kyrgyzstane i Tadzhikistane [Nazarbayev and Karimov require examination of the hydropower station construction projects in Kyrgyzstan and Tajikistan], 18 March 2010. Available at http://www.caresd.net/site.html?en=0&id=23474.

European Parliament (2011) European Parliament resolution on the World Bank's energy strategy for developing countries. Available at http://www.europarl.europa.eu/sides/getDoc.do?type=MOTION&reference=B7-2011-0128&language=EN#.

Féaux de la Croix, J. and Suyarkulova, M. (forthcoming 2015) Building big dams in Kyrgyzstan and Tajikistan: constructing state-society relations through water infrastructure projects. *Cahiers d'Asie Centrale*.

Gullette, D. (2014) Conflict sensitivity in the mining sector of the Kyrgyz Republic, OSCE Academy. Available at http://www.osce-academy.net/upload/file/Mining_report_final.pdf.

Henry, A. (2009) Thinking globally, limited locally: the Russian environmental movement and sustainable development. In Agyeman, J. and Ogneva-Himmelberger, Y. (eds) *Environmental Justice and Sustainability in the Former Soviet Union*. Cambridge, MA: MIT Press.

Henry, A. (2010) *Red to Green: Environmental Activism in Post-Soviet Russia*. Ithaca, NY: Cornell University Press.

International Crisis Group (2010) Kyrgyzstan: A Hollow Regime Collapses. Asia Briefing N° 102.

International Crisis Group (2014) *Water Pressures in Central Asia*. Europe and Central Asia Report No. 233.

Kenesh.kg (Official site of Kyrgyz Republic Jogorku Kenesh) (2013) Monitoring SMI v sfere mezhdunarodnykh otnoshenii na 15 ianvaria 2013 goda [Media Monitoring in the field of international relations on January 15, 2013], 15 January 2013. Available at http://kenesh.kg/RU/Articles/14889-Monitoring_SMI_v_sfere_mezhdunarodnyx_otnoshenij_na_15_yanvarya_2013_goda.aspx.

Lillis, J. (2013) In Uzbekistan, Kazakhstan leader conciliatory over water. EurasiaNet.org, 14 June 2013. Available at http://www.eurasianet.org/node/67119.

Menga, P. (2013) Power and Dams in Central Asia. Unpublished PhD thesis, University of Cagliari.

Mertha, A. (2008). *China's Water Warriors: Citizen Action and Policy Change*. Ithaca, NY: Cornell University Press.

McMann, K. (2005) Central Asians and the state: nostalgia for the Soviet era. NCEER report. Available at. http://www.ucis.pitt.edu/nceeer/2005_818_09_McMann.pdf.

Pannier, B. (2014) Kyrgyz ask, "Where's the gas? Won't you have some dung?" Available at http://www.rferl.org/content/qishlog-ovozi-kyrgyzstan-gas/25417176.html.

Sutter, C. and Parreño, J. C. (2007) Does the current Clean Development Mechanism (CDM) deliver its sustainable development claim? An analysis of officially registered CDM projects in Climate Change. *Climatic Change* September 2007, 84(1): 75–90.

Tetra Tech (2011) Management Diagnostic of the National Electricity System of Kyrgyzstan (JSC "NESK") Report on Phase 1: Preliminary Findings and Recommendations.

UNISON (2013) Sistema raspredeleniya i potrebleniya elektroenergii Kyrgyzstana: Analiz i otsenka upravleniya [Distribution System and Consumption of Electricity in Kyrgyzstan: Management Analysis and Assessment]. UNISON, Bishkek.

U.S. Congress (2014) Public Law No: 113-76. Available at https://beta.congress.gov/bill/113th-congress/house-bill/3547/text.

Wooden, A. E. (2013) Another way of saying enough: environmental concern and popular mobilization in Kyrgyzstan. *Post-Soviet Affairs*, 29(4): 314–353.

Wooden, A. E. (2014) Kyrgyzstan's Dark Ages: Framing and the 2010 hydroelectric revolution. *Central Asian Survey*, 33(4): 463–481.

Wooden, A. E., Aitieva, M. and Epkenhans, T. (2009) Revealing order in the chaos: field experiences and methodologies of political and social research on Central Eurasia. In Wooden, A. E and Stefes, C .H. (eds) *The Politics of Transition in Central Asia and the Caucasus: Enduring Legacies and Emerging Challenges.* London: Routledge.

World Bank (2000) Position on the report of the World Commission on Dams. Available at http://siteresources.worldbank.org/INTWRD/903857-1112344791813/20424179/TheWBPositionontheReportoftheWCD.pdf.

World Bank Group (2009) Directions in hydropower. Available at http://www-wds.worldbank.org/external/default/WDSContentServer/WDSP/IB/2010/05/27/0003349 55_20100527072807/Rendered/PDF/547270WP0Direc10Box349424B01PUBLIC1.pdf.

World Commission on Dams (2000) Dams and development: a new framework for decision-making. Available at http://www.unep.org/dams/WCD/report.asp.

Part IV
Public policy and mass media

6 Let there be science

Separating environmental misperceptions from reality in the Aral Sea Basin

Christopher Martius and John P.A. Lamers

Introduction

In 1992, the United Nations declared the Aral Sea Basin as a world "ecological disaster area," which Glantz (1999) defined as a typical example of a "creeping environmental problem" – that is a slow-starting, low-grade, long-term, and cumulative environmental change that evolves so slowly that perceiving it and starting counterbalancing measures is difficult. The term "Aral Sea Syndrome" was introduced as "environmental damage caused by large-scale projects aimed at restructuring natural landscape" linked to a "tendency towards top-down project planning and purely technological solutions" (WBGU, 1998).

Many authors recognized that the complexities involved in the syndrome, such as the need for water, food, energy, flood control, and navigation, were the main drivers of severe, often-unintended impacts on environment and society. Later the Aral Sea Syndrome was simplified to mean "bad" management of "centrally planned large-scale water schemes" as the only underlying driver. Decades of secrecy in the Soviet era further shrouded the syndrome in mystery. But often-questionable information about the Aral Sea Basin made its way into the media that influenced predominant thinking about the situation, adding confusion and hampering sound, knowledge-based decision-making. News of negative environmental developments took on a life of their own, creating what have almost become urban myths. Some misbeliefs are so engrained in the public mind that it is difficult to change them. And yet, doing so is imperative.

Before becoming part of the Soviet Union in 1924, the Central Asian region – now shared by Kyrgyzstan, Kazakhstan, Uzbekistan, Tajikistan, and Turkmenistan – had a history of irrigated agriculture, although at a much smaller scale than today. Sixty-seven years (1924–1991) of Soviet reign brought about drastic changes (Wehrheim et al., 2008). The Central Asia republics were transformed into suppliers of specific, strategically important agricultural commodities. Due to their warm and sunny climate and abundant river water, Uzbekistan and Turkmenistan were considered suitable springboards for achieving independence from cotton imports, while Kazakhstan was consigned to wheat production (Suleimenov, 2000). Agricultural production escalated massively, accomplished by an impressive expansion of the irrigated areas from 2 million hectares (4.9

million acres) to 7.2 million hectares (17.79 million acres) in six decades (1925–1985) and by diverting the flow from the Amu Darya and Syr Darya rivers, the main contributors to the Aral Sea. Concurrently, crop yields rapidly increased owing to extensive use of chemicals (mineral fertilizers and pesticides) and of heavy machinery in new, subsidized, centralized production units (Djanibekov, 2008). Maximizing production, not harmonizing it with the environment, was the goal (Granit el al., 2010).

Statement of the issue

Although often considered impressive, these achievements were realized at a cost: unprecedented environmental degradation in a fragile, human-environmental dryland system. The demise of the Aral Sea is just one, albeit perhaps the best-known, illustration (WBGU, 1998; Breckle et al., 2000). Until the 1960s, the Aral was the world's fourth-largest freshwater inland lake. It has shrunk from 66,900 to 6,700 square kilometers (25,800 to 2,600 square miles), while salinity increased tenfold, eradicating unique flora and fauna (UNEP, 2014). In contrast, the desiccated sea floor, now the Aralkum desert, spread over nearly 60,000 square kilometers (23,000 square miles), exposing previously deposited salts, pesticides, and toxic substances that were picked up by continental winds. Hence the area was regarded as a source of toxin-laden dust storms with harmful consequences for human health, such as respiratory diseases (UNEP, 2014).

As irrigated agricultural expansion at all costs was a major goal, it is no wonder that many present environmental challenges stem from unsustainable irrigated agricultural production practices with ill-designed irrigation and drainage networks (Tischbein et al., 2012), huge rates of water use, and low efficiency in irrigation (Awan et al., 2012). Today, it is widely accepted that the Aral cannot be "saved" (Micklin, 2008; Varis, 2014), although in public perception, this outcome may still be desirable (UNEP, 2014). Put simply: stopping irrigated agriculture, rolling back the irrigated areas, and concurrently allowing more water to flow into the remnants of the Aral would remove the basis of livelihoods for about 75 percent of the 40 million people in the Aral Sea Basin.

Recent evidence illustrates how science can play a role in developing sound options for more feasible, productive, and sustainable land use in the region (Martius et al., 2012; Lamers et al., 2014). We underscore this through analyzing three environmental problems considered the most daunting: the perceived water scarcity, rampant soil degradation due to salinization, and pesticide use. We scrutinize these problems in light of newly available scientific findings to debunk the associated myths and offer alternative explanations. We believe that doing so paves the way towards solutions based on a better understanding of cause–effect relationships. That will enable the design of more adequate, adaptive, and efficient solutions. It means bringing scientific evidence into a debate that is too often charged with emotionally laden but inaccurate or plainly wrong concepts.

Findings

Myth and reality on water scarcity

The perceived water problem is often presented as a physical water scarcity (Granit et al., 2010). Furthermore, physical water scarcity is seen as being caused by a combination of natural and anthropogenic factors. Indeed, most of the region is extremely dry, with annual rainfall not exceeding 400 millimeters (15.7 inches) over nearly 90 percent of Central Asia (de Pauw, 2008). Given that most precipitation falls outside the growing season and given the high level of aridity (de Pauw, 2008), crop water demands can be met almost only through irrigation, which in turn uses 85–95 percent of all surface water resources annually (Dukhovny and de Schutter, 2011). Hence, natural forces such as droughts severely exacerbate all other irrigation water problems. For example, during the drought years 2000 and 2001, the Tuyamuyun reservoir of the Amu Darya received 50 and 60 percent less water than in normal years, while downstream provinces such as Khorezm and Karakalpakstan in Uzbekistan and Dashovuz in Turkmenistan suffered severe water scarcity (Wegerich, 2002).

Central Asia does face a severe water problem, but we agree with Varis (2014) that the core issue is not an absolute water scarcity – and definitely not when considering "human" management factors – since the evidence for overly excessive water use is extensive. Four of the five countries (Kyrgyzstan, Tajikistan, Turkmenistan, Uzbekistan) rank among the top five per-capita water consumers worldwide and among the largest water consumers per unit of GDP (Granit et al., 2010; Varis 2014). According to United Nations classifications,[1] these countries are not water-stressed, except Tajikistan. In Uzbekistan, water use per hectare or acre is estimated at double the amount used in other regions on similar crops (Bekchanov et al., 2010). The water footprints of the two crops that dominate the irrigated agricultural landscape in Uzbekistan, cotton and winter wheat, are close to or beyond the global average (Chapagain et al., 2006; Rudenko et al., 2009). Of the 4 million irrigated hectares (9.9 million acres) in Uzbekistan, 0.7 million hectares (1.7 million acres) have soils too sandy for conventional irrigation. Ending irrigation in these areas would save a great amount of water. In addition, farmers in Uzbekistan may face water surplus and scarcity in the same growing season (Forkutsa et al., 2009a). Hence drought problems are exacerbated at the tail end of the river and irrigation systems. Also, remote sensing-based studies show that irrigation water supply is inequitably distributed among tail and head-end locations in the irrigation networks (Conrad et al., 2007).

In addition to using huge amounts of water, water productivity and overall water irrigation inefficiency are low; and so is Irrigation Water Use Efficiency, or IWUE. For instance, average overall system irrigation efficiency is about 30 percent in northwestern Uzbekistan (Awan et al., 2012), while Food and Agriculture Organization studies show a global mean of 38 percent (Bruinsma, 2003), and a maximum of about 70 percent (Bos et al., 2005) in ninety-three developing countries. IWUE for local cotton and conventional cropped wheat

(Ibragimov et al., 2011) is lower than that for wheat grown in similar conditions elsewhere (Alizadeh and Keshavarz, 2005). Furthermore, water-use efficiencies at the field and farm levels decreased during water-abundant years (Bekchanov et al., 2010), highlighting that water users know when, where, and how to save water – but that water saving is not always their priority (Saravanan et al., 2014). In Uzbekistan, the state uses its influence on irrigation water management to ensure that annually planned production goals for cotton and wheat are met, while day-to-day water management is arranged differently between farmers and local management (Veldwisch et al., 2012).

All this points to management problems, especially at the interface between farm and irrigation networks, and to farmers' perceptions rather than the realities of the water supply. We believe that the economic transition of most Central Asian economies will continue to rely on irrigated agriculture for a good many more years. Unless the real, underlying problems are identified, the search for solutions will yield ill-fated results. Previous oversimplification of the problem as absolute water scarcity has led to over-dominance of proposed solutions of a purely technical nature and interventions such as promotion of drip and sprinkler irrigation systems (Gadaev and Yasakov, 2012). But these are often too costly to be implemented in the short term (Bekchanov et al., 2010). Finally, the water challenge has a temporal dimension: water is often unavailable at the right moment. Hence, addressing the supply problem by raising technical irrigation efficiency alone is insufficient. Or seen from farmers' perspectives, investments in water-saving interventions make sense only when timely water availability is ensured. That requires, for example, strengthening water institutions or creating water storage facilities.

We argue that the actual water challenge is best understood as institutional and/or economic water scarcity. Therefore, a completely different set of solutions emerges (Lamers et al., 2014). These still comprise a set of technical solutions, but aim first to increase current low water-use efficiencies in the entire agricultural sector (Tischbein et al., 2014; Rudenko et al., 2012), as well as reducing field water application rates (Awan et al., 2012; Forkutsa, 2009a; Tischbein et al., 2014) and improving drainage systems (Tischbein et al., 2014). A second set of options also involves a change in cropping portfolios toward greater diversification (Bobojonov et al., 2013) and planting of tree crops to better use marginal, unproductive land (Khamzina et al., 2012; Djumaeva et al., 2013). However, technical options will become feasible only when accompanied by financial and institutional measures (Bekchanov et al., 2010).

Myth and reality on soil salinization

Central Asia is known for huge soil degradation challenges caused by soil salinization that adversely affects crop productivity (Ahrorov et al., 2012). Around 60 percent of Uzbekistan's irrigated croplands and more than 30 percent of Tajikistan's are salt-affected; the figures are 40 percent in Kyrgyzstan and about 90 percent in Turkmenistan (Ahrorov et al., 2012).

What is the actual – and dangerous – cause of this soil salinization? In an interesting twist that makes the victim into the murderer, some researchers blame the Aralkum. For example, Dukhovny and de Schutter (2011) are cited as a source for the statement in Varis (2014) that "half of Uzbekistan's soil has become salty owing to dust blown from the dry bed of the Aral Sea." In 2001, Vlek et al. (2001, p. 10) summarized some of the "disaster literature" related to salinity problems linked to the Aral. They cited assertions that the Aralkum had turned into a desert extending across 3 million hectares (7.4 million acres), frequent huge strong winds and dust storms move 100 to 140 million tons of sand and salt particles around the Aral Sea Basin annually, and widespread respiratory and dermatological ailments result.

But Vlek at al. (2001) cautioned that soil salinity should be assessed against a high background level of water-borne salinity. Available data on dust and salt deposition in the region show low levels of dust deposition in northwestern Uzbekistan (0.3–1.0 kg ha^{-1} year^{-1}; Opp et al., 2009) that are three orders of magnitude lower than two of the most rigorous standards of dust deposition – the West Australia Nuisance Standard and the Malaysia Air Quality Standard. At such low levels, the Aralkum can hardly be a significantly contributor to the salt load in agricultural soils.

In fact, the dominant reasons for ongoing soil salinization are a combination of factors linked narrowly to the huge rate of using surface water for irrigation, as well as insufficient drainage facilities (Akramkhanov et al., 2010). Under these conditions, groundwater reservoirs replenish quickly. For example, analysis of groundwater monitoring datasets from 1990, 1994, and 2000 in the Khorezm region showed that during the growing season, about two-thirds of the land had groundwater tables above the threshold that enables further soil salinization (Ibrakhimov et al., 2007). This rise of groundwater to levels at which salinization occurs is typical of irrigated agriculture in Central Asia (Ibrakhimov et al., 2011).

The salt content of river water used for irrigation is the first cause of soil salinization. The average mid-and-downstream salinity concentration in the Amu Darya is 0.7–0.9 g/l, or grams per liter. Even at the tail end of the river, average salinity varied around 1.1–1.2 g/l between 1991 and 2010 (Gaybullaev and Chen, 2013), which World Health Organization standards consider drinking-water quality. Only in the dry season (October to April) and during dry years can river water salinity rise higher (Gaybullaev and Chen, 2013). Even at such low salinity concentrations, large quantities of salt are deposited in the fields, given the huge amounts of irrigation water applied annually. Assuming a salt concentration of 1 g/l, merely supplying water to accommodate a 700 mm net irrigation demand for cotton means that 7,000 kg ha^{-1} of salts are deposited. As typical water application rates are about three times higher (Bekchanov et al., 2012; Awan et al., 2012), an average annual salt input of 20,000 kg ha^{-1} is no rarity.

A second cause of salinization is from high and rising groundwater tables (Ibrakhimov et al., 2011; Ahrorov et al., 2012). If groundwater levels lie below a critical soil depth, salts leach downward into the groundwater and are flushed out of the system along with drainage water. In addition, deeper groundwater tables lead to lower salt accumulation driven by capillary rise. In contrast, groundwater levels above a critical threshold – as often happens because many irrigated areas are flat and lack good drainage – lead to upward transport of water-soluble salts in the soil profile driven by evaporation, transpiration, and capillary effects. When water evaporates, those salts remain on the surface.

Options to reduce the levels of dust carried away from the Aralkum include afforestation, which would be a costly and herculean challenge given the size of the area (Breckle et al., 2000), although not the entire area would need to be planted with trees for the best impact (Rücker et al., 2004). While there are good reasons for afforesting the Aralkum, arresting soil salinization in irrigated croplands does not seem to be among them.

Possible mitigation options include: desalinizing irrigation water, which is expensive and resource-demanding; reducing water application rates; using salt-tolerant plants and halophytes to extract salts, a practice only moderately effective (Breckle et al., 2000), and regular leaching with scarce freshwater before the growing season, which is ineffective where groundwater levels are high and drainage systems inefficient (Forkutsa et al., 2009b). Other possibilities include planting salt-extracting crops such as sorghum, but extraction rates usually are modest (Begdullayeva et al., 2007), or introducing salt-tolerant perennials such as salt cedar and Russian olive (Khamzina et al., 2012; Djumeava et al., 2013). However, these do not lower soil salinity concentrations. Irrespective of effectiveness, such options would primarily mitigate symptoms of soil salinization rather than addressing underlying causes. Misidentifying the Aralkum as the dominant cause of soil salinization will not lead to successful reduction of soil salinity.

Thus it is essential that the discourse shifts to the actual problems. In the first place, mitigation must address drainage and outlet problems, reduce the amount of water input, and improve water use efficiencies (Akramkhanov et al., 2010). Next would be better adaptation of leaching amounts to site-specific needs based on advanced irrigation monitoring, a process that requires better infrastructure and equipment. At field level, use of laser-guided land leveling would be a win–win intervention. That is because the higher uniformity of irrigation/leaching water application achieved that way would increase efficiency due to more uniform leaching. It also would reduce patchiness of salt accumulation on elevations and waterlogging in depressions (Martius et al., 2012).

Myth and reality on pesticide abundance in the environment

During the Soviet era, farmers routinely sprayed cotton with pesticides, including defoliants to facilitate harvesting. Chemical substances such as DDT were widely employed to control insects (Bogdasarov et al., 2001; Galiulin and Bashkin, 1996). Although the U.S.S.R. officially banned DDT for agriculture in 1970, its use continued (Pryde, 1991). Pesticide use in Uzbekistan plummeted after independence, mostly due to economic difficulties (Crootof et al., 2015; Nishonov et al., 2009). But DDT, toxic to humans and wildlife, is persistent; as much as 50 percent can remain in the soil ten to fifteen years after application. Animals do not metabolize DDT, but deposit it in their fatty tissues.

Many scientists regard excessive use of agrochemicals as a source of surface and groundwater contamination (Bogdasarov et al., 2001; Galiulin and Bashkin, 1996). Furthermore, the movement of pesticides into groundwater is affected by plant uptake, evaporation, chemical/microbial breakdown, soil adsorption, and transport by water. Hence, the flow of huge amounts of water is considered the main driving force for the movement of pesticides.

The Research Center for Water Management Ecology in Uzbekistan demonstrated the presence of persistently high DDT concentrations in the Amu Darya Basin. In the Khorezm district, maximum concentrations of 1.33 parts per million (soil), 0.16 parts per million (groundwater), and 1.76 parts per million (drainage water) were found (Crootof, 2011). Although the study site was a former agricultural airfield and, thus, may have had higher than average DDT levels, that finding was alarming. Widespread occurrence of pesticides in groundwater has adverse health effects, particularly for people chronically exposed to contaminated drinking water from groundwater. For many rural inhabitants, such as those in Khorezm, groundwater is the main source of drinking water (Herbst, 2006), while many lakes in the region are used for aquaculture and fishing (Crootof et al., 2015). Therefore, determining the fate of these pesticides is imperative to assess risk and quality of life.

Water quality is of great significance. Studies of Khorezm lakes showed pesticide concentrations within ranges tolerable for aquaculture, while a chemical analysis of fish tissues underscored that overall DDT concentrations had not been accumulating in fish and, thus, did not threaten human health (Crootof et al., 2015). In addition, since only low concentrations of organochlorine pesticides were detected in lake sediments and in the Amu Darya (Nishonov, 2009), the lakes appear suitable for recreation and agriculture. Situations should be assessed locally because pesticide residues are heterogeneously distributed. Hot spots exist at former crop-duster airfields and pesticide storage depots and dumps, as well as sites where pesticide-laden agricultural runoff and wastewater from production accumulate (Crootof, 2011). One must therefore be cautious about the discourse of wide-scale contamination of persistent pesticides.

Summary and conclusions

Central Asia, and particularly the Aral Sea Basin, have long been associated with environmental disaster. While this view is correct in many aspects, it has led to serious but unsubstantiated assertions. In addition to the three myths detailed in this chapter, researchers should examine other deleterious fallacies and false beliefs related to management of natural resources in the region. Myths rather than facts often dominate the discourse, hampering proper problem definitions and impairing realistic debate about remedies.

A sound, science-based approach is needed to improve management of these natural resources –an approach that reveals the true causes behind what seems obvious but what is often misguided or plainly untrue. This requires scientists to engage more deeply with partners and stakeholders. We need to foster an understanding of the interactions of local actors with the environment that are often based on long traditions and experiences, and, thus, rational and premeditated – even if not always open to adaptation in a rapidly changing world. For the sake of Central Asia's people and environment, taking partners' knowledge and insights seriously will lead to understanding their motivations and getting a better grip on underlying causes of unfolding disasters.

Note

1 According to the UN: Annual water use per capita < 500 m^3 = extreme scarcity; 500–1,000 m^3 = water shortage/scarcity; 1,000 – 1,700 m^3 = water stress/moderate shortage; > 1,700 m^3 = sufficient.

References

Ahrorov, F., Murtazaev, O. and Abduallev, B. (2012) Pollution and salinization: compounding the Aral Sea disaster. In Edelstein M.R., Cerny A. and Gadaev, A. (eds) *Disaster by Design: The Aral Sea and its Lessons for Sustainability. Research in Social Problems and Public Policy*, 20, Bingley: Emerald Group Publishing Limited, pp. 29–36.

Akramkhanov, A., Ibrakhimov, M. and Lamers, J.P.A. (2010) Managing soil salinity in the lower reaches of the Amudarya delta: how to break the vicious circle? Case study #8–7. In Per Pinstrup-Andersen, P. and Cheng, F. (eds) *Food Policy for Developing Countries: Case Studies*: Cornell University, Ithaca, New York. Available at http://cip.cornell.edu/dns.gfs/1284648728.

Alizadeh, A. and Keshavarz, A. (2005) Status of agricultural water use in Iran. *Water Conservation, Reuse, and Recycling*. Proceedings of Iranian–American Workshop, Tunis, Tunisia. December 2002. National Academic Press, Washington, DC, pp. 94–105.

Awan, U.K.,Tischbein, B., Kamalov, P., Martius, C. and Hafeez, M. (2012) Modeling irrigation scheduling under shallow groundwater conditions as a tool for an integrated management of surface and groundwater resources. In Martius, C., Rudenko, I., Lamers, J.P.A. and Vlek, P.L.G. (eds) *Cotton, Water, Salts and Soums – Economic and Ecological Restructuring in Khorezm, Uzbekistan*. Springer, Dordrecht, pp. 309–327.

Begdullayeva, T., Kienzler, K.M., Kan, E., Ibragimov, N. and Lamers, J.P.A. (2007) Response of Sorghum bicolor varieties to soil salinity for feed and food production in Karakalpakstan, Uzbekistan. *Irrigation and Drainage Systems*, 21(3–4): 237–250.

Bekchanov, M., Karimov, A. and Lamers, J.P.A. (2010). Impact of water availability on land and water productivity: A temporal and spatial analysis of the case study region Khorezm. *Water* 2(3): 668–684.

Bobojonov, I., Lamers, J.P.A., Bekchanov, M., Djanibekov, N., Franz-Vasdeki, J., Ruzimov, J. and Martius, C. (2013) Options and constraints for crop diversification: a case study in sustainable agriculture in Uzbekistan. *Agroecology and Sustainable Food Systems*, 37(7): 788–811.

Bogdasarov, V., Sergeeva, I., Bolshakovaa, L. and Zubkov, D. (2001). Mapping of the degree of pollution by pesticides of agricultural irrigated areas in the Aral Sea regions. *Ecological Research and Monitoring of the Aral Sea Deltas. A Basis for Restoration*. Book 2. UNESCO Aral Sea Project. Final Scientific Report, pp. 225–230.

Bos, M.G., Burton, M.A. and Molden, D.J. (2005) *Irrigation and Drainage Performance Assessment: Practical Guidelines*. CABI, Trowbridge.

Breckle, S.W., Wuecherer, W., Agachanjanz, O. and Geldyev, B. (2000) The Aral Sea crises region. In Breckle S.W., Vesle M., Wuecherer W. (eds) *Sustainable Land Use in Deserts*. Springer, Heidelberg, pp. 27–37.

Bruinsma, J. (ed.) (2003) *World Agriculture: Towards 2015/30*, an FAO Perspective. London: Earthscan and Rome: FAO.

Chapagain, A.K., Hoekstra, A.Y. and Savenije, H.H.G. (2006) Water saving through international trade of agricultural products. *Hydrological Earth System Science*, 10: 455–468.

Conrad, C., Dech, S.W., Hafeez, M., Lamers, J.P.A., Martius, C. and Strunz, G. (2007) Mapping and assessing water use in a Central Asian irrigation system by utilizing MODIS remote sensing products. *Irrigation and Drainage Systems*, 21(3–4): 197–218.

Crootof, A. (2011) *Assessing Water Resources in Khorezm, Uzbekistan for the Development of Aquaculture*. MSc thesis, University of Nevada, Reno.

Crootof, A., Mullabaev, N., Saito, L., Atwell, L., Rosen, M.R., Bekchonova, M., Ginatullina, E., Scott, J., Chandra, S., Nishonov, B., Lamers, J.P.A. and Fayzieva, D. (2015) Hydroecological condition and potential for aquaculture in lakes of the arid region of Khorezm, Uzbekistan. *Journal of Arid Environments*, 117: 37–46.

De Pauw, E. (2008). ICARDA Regional GIS Datasets for Central Asia: Explanatory Notes. *GIS Unit Technical Bulletin*. International Center for Agricultural Research in the Dry Areas (ICARDA).

Djanibekov, N. (2008) *A Micro-economic Analysis of Farm Restructuring in the Khorezm Region, Uzbekistan*. PhD thesis, Bonn: University of Bonn, Germany.

Djumaeva, D., Lamers, J.P.A., Khamzina, A. and Vlek, P.L.G. (2013) The benefits of phosphorus fertilization of trees grown on salinized croplands in the lower reaches of Amu Darya, Uzbekistan. *Agroforestry Systems*, 87(3): 555–569.

Dukhovny, V.A. and de Schutter, J. (2011) *Water in Central Asia – Past, Present and Future*. CRC Press, Netherlands.

Forkutsa, I., Sommer, R., Shirokova, Y.I., Lamers, J.P.A., Kienzler, K., Tischbein, B., Martius, C. and Vlek. P.L.G. (2009a). Modelling irrigated cotton with shallow groundwater in the Aral Sea Basin of Uzbekistan: I. Water dynamics. *Irrigation Science*, 27(4): 331–346.

Forkutsa, I., Sommer, R., Shirokova, Y.I., Lamers, J.P.A., Kienzler, K., Tischbein, B., Martius, C. and Vlek. P.L.G. (2009b). Modeling irrigated cotton with shallow groundwater in the Aral Sea Basin of Uzbekistan: II. Soil salinity dynamics. *Irrigation Science*, 27(4): 319–330.

Gadaev, A. and Yasakov, Z. (2012) An overview of the Aral Sea disaster. In Edelstein, M.R., Cerny, A., and Gadaev, A. (eds) *Disaster by Design: The Aral Sea and its Lessons for Sustainability. Research in Social Problems and Public Policy*, 20. Emerald Group Publishing Limited, pp. 5–15.

Galiulin, R.V. and Bashkin, V.N. (1996) Organochlorinated compounds (PCBs and insecticides) in irrigated agrolandscapes of Russia and Uzbekistan. *Water, Air, Soil Pollution*, 89(3–4): 247–266.

Gaybullaev, B. and Chen, S.-C. (2013) Water salinity changes of the gauging stations along the Amu Darya River. *Journal of Agriculture and Forestry*, 62(1): 1–14.

Glantz, M.H. (1999) *Creeping Environmental Problems and Sustainable Development in the Aral Sea Basin*. Cambridge University Press, Cambridge, UK.

Granit, J., Jägerskog, A., Löfgren, R., Bullock, A., de Gooijer, G., Pettigrew, S. and Lindström, A. (2010) *Regional Water Intelligence Report Central Asia: Baseline Report*. Regional Water Intelligence Reports Paper 15. Stockholm: SIWI and UNDP.

Herbst, S. (2006) *Water, Sanitation, Hygiene and Diarrheal Diseases in the Aral Sea Area* (Khorezm, Uzbekistan), PhD thesis, Bonn: University of Bonn, Germany.

Ibragimov, N., Evett, S., Essenbekov, Y., Khasanova, F., Karabaev, I., Mirzaev, L. and Lamers, J.P.A. (2011) Permanent beds versus conventional tillage in irrigated Central Asia. *Agronomy Journal*, 103(4): 1002–1011.

Ibrakhimov, M., Martius, C., Lamers, J.P.A. and Tischbein, B. (2011) The dynamics of groundwater table and salinity over 17 years in Khorezm. *Agricultural Water Management*, 101(1): 52–61.

Ibrakhimov, M., Khamzina, A., Forkutsa, I., Paluasheva, G., Lamers, J.P.A., Tischbein, B., Vlek, P.L.G. and Martius, C. (2007) Groundwater table and salinity: spatial and temporal distribution and influence on soil salinization in Khorezm region (Uzbekistan, Aral Sea Basin). *Irrigation and Drainage Systems*, 21(3–4): 219–236.

Khamzina, A., Lamers, J.P.A. and Vlek, P.L.G. (2012) Conversion of degraded cropland to tree plantations for ecosystem and livelihood benefits. In Martius, C., Rudenko, I., Lamers, J.P.A., Vlek, P.L.G. (eds) *Cotton, Water, Salts and Soums – Economic and Ecological Restructuring in Khorezm, Uzbekistan*. Springer: Dordrecht, pp. 235–248.

Lamers, J.P.A., Khamzina, A., Rudenko, I. and Vlek, P.L.G. (eds) (2014) *Restructuring Land Allocation, Water Use and Agricultural Value Chains: Technologies, Policies and Practices for the Lower Amudarya Region*. Bonn University Press at V&R unipress.

Martius, C., Rudenko, I., Lamers, J.P.A. and Vlek, P.L.G. (eds) (2012) *Cotton, Water, Salts and Soums – Economic and Ecological Restructuring in Khorezm, Uzbekistan*. Springer: Dordrecht.

Micklin, P. (2008). Using satellite remote sensing to study and monitor the Aral Sea and adjacent zone. In Qi, J. and Evered, K.T. (eds), *Environmental problems of Central Asia and their Economic, Social, and Security Impacts*. NATO Science for Peace and Security Series – C: Environmental Stability. Dordrecht, the Netherlands: Springer.

Nishonov, B., Rosen, M.R., Fayzieva, D., Saito, L. and Lamers, J.P.A. (2009) Organochlorine pesticides residue in lakes of Khorezm, Uzbekistan. In *10th International HCH and Pesticides Forum How Many Obsolete Pesticides Have Been Disposed of 8 Years After Signature of Stockholm Convention*, 6–10 September 2009. RECETOX, Masaryk University, Brno, Czech Republic, pp. 157–161.

Opp, C., Lamers, J.P.A., Abdullaev, A., Groll, M. and Khamzina, A. (2009) Dust deposition in Khorezm under different site conditions. In Opp, C. and Groll, M. (eds) *Dust & Sand Storms and Desertification*. Philips University of Marburg, Germany, pp. 56–61.

Pryde, P.R. (1991) *Environmental Management in the Soviet Union*. Cambridge University Press, Cambridge UK.

Rücker, G.R., Conrad, C., Colditz, R.R., Strunz, G. and Dech, S. (2004) Remote sensing based mapping and characterization of soil and vegetation quality of potential plantation areas in the desiccated Aral Sea area. *ZEF Work Papers for Sustainable Development in Central Asia*, 7. Bonn, ZEF.

Rudenko, I. and Lamers, J.P.A. (2010). The Aral Sea: an ecological disaster. Case study #8–6. In Per Pinstrup-Andersen, P. and Cheng, F. (eds) *Food Policy for Developing Countries: Case Studies*. Cornell University, Ithaca, New York. Available at http://cip.cornell.edu/dns.gfs/1279121772.

Rudenko, I., Djanibekov, U. and Lamers, J.P.A. (2009) Water footprint of cotton products. Is more efficient water use possible in Khorezm? *Vestnik*, 3: 44–48 (in Russian).

Rudenko, I., Nurmetov, K. and Lamers, J.P.A. (2012) State order and policy strategies in the cotton and wheat value chains. In Martius, C., Rudenko, I., Lamers, J.P.A and Vlek, P.L.G. (eds) *Cotton, Water, Salts and Soums – Economic and Ecological Restructuring in Khorezm, Uzbekistan*. Springer, Dordrecht, pp. 371–387.

Saravanan, V.S., Ul-Hassan, M. and Schraven, B. (2014) Irrigation water management in Uzbekistan: analyzing the capacity of households to improve water use profitability. In Lamers, J.P.A., Khamzina, A., Rudenko, I. and Vlek, P.L.G (eds) *Restructuring Land Allocation, Water Use and Agricultural Value Chains. Technologies, Policies and Practices for the Lower Amudarya region*. V & R unipress. Bonn University Press. Göttingen, pp. 253–274.

Suleimenov, M. (2000) Trends in feed and livestock production during the transition period in three Central Asian countries. In Babu, S. and Tashmatov, A. (eds) *Food Policy Reforms in Central Asia: Setting the Research Priorities*. IFPRI, Washington DC, pp. 91–104.

Tischbein, B., Awan, U.K., Akhta, F., Kamalov, P. and Manschadi, A.M. (2014) Improving irrigation efficiency in the lower reaches of the Amu Darya River. In Lamers, J.P.A., Khamzina, A., Rudenko, I. and Vlek, P.L.G (eds) *Restructuring Land Allocation, Water Use and agricultural Value Chains. Technologies, Policies and Practices for the Lower Amudarya Region*. Bonn University Press, Göttingen, pp. 91–108.

Tischbein, B., Awan, U.K., Abdullaev, I., Bobojonov, I., Conrad, C., Forkutsa, I., Ibrakhimov, M. and Poluasheva, G. (2012) Water management in Khorezm: current situation and options for improvement (hydrological perspective). In Martius, C., Rudenko, I., Lamers, J.P.A. and Vlek, P.L.G. (eds) *Cotton, Water, Salts and Soums – Economic and   Ecological Restructuring in Khorezm, Uzbekistan*. Springer, Dordrecht, pp. 69–92.

United Nations Environmental Programme (2014) *The Future of the Aral Sea Lies in Transboundary Co-operation*. UNEP global environmental alert service, thematic focus: Environmental governance, Ecosystem management, Climate change. Available at http://www.unep.org/pdf/UNEP_GEAS_JAN_2014.pdf.

Varis, O. (2014) Curb vast water use in central Asia. *Nature*, 514(7520): 27–29.

Veldwisch, G.J., Mollinga, P., Zavgorodnyaya, D. and Yalcin, R. (2012) Politics of agricultural water management in Khorezm, Uzbekistan. In Martius, C., Rudenko, I., Lamers, J.P.A. and Vlek, P.L.G. (eds) *Cotton, Water, Salts and Soums – Economic and Ecological Restructuring in Khorezm, Uzbekistan*. Springer, Dordrecht, pp. 127–140.

Vlek, P., Martius, C., Wehrheim, P., Schoeller-Schletter, A. and Lamers, J.P.A. (2001) *Economic Restructuring of Land and Water Use in the Region Khorezm (Uzbekistan)*, No. 1. Centre for Development Research, University of Bonn. Available at http://www.zef.de/wps_khorezm.0.html.

WBGU (1998) *Worlds in Transition. Ways Towards Sustainable Management of Fresh Water Resources*. Springer-Verlag, Berlin.

Wegerich, K. (2002) Natural drought or human made water scarcity in Uzbekistan. *Central Asia and the Caucasus*, 2(14): 154–162.

Wehrheim, P., Schoeller-Schletter, A. and Martius, C. (eds) (2008) *Continuity and Change: Land and Water Use Reforms in Rural Uzbekistan Socio-Economic and Legal Analyses from the Region Khorezm*. Halle/Saale, Germany: Leibniz-Institut für Agrarentwicklung in Mittel-und Osteuropa (IAMO).

7 Tajikistan

An environmental scan

Shakhodat Saibnazarova

Introduction

Tajikistan is a country of high mountains and deep contradictions—economically poor and geopolitically wealthy. Its terrain offers many strategic advantages. It is a gatekeeper to the West for its development-hungry neighbor, China, and may be essential to any hegemonic power that seeks to control the Eurasian land mass. It possesses a vital natural resource: large and highly elevated glaciers that feed runoff into a network of rivers flowing downstream to neighboring states. This vast blanket of ice represents kinetic energy that, if harnessed, could generate electricity essential to Central Asia's development. Its location makes this relatively small nation the switchyard for gas pipelines, transmission lines, roads, and, for China, a much-desired proposed rail and telecommunications route dubbed the "New Silk Road" or, more formally, the Silk Road Economic Belt. Because Tajikistan is in the midst of multinational plans for high dams, hydropower plants, and communication corridors, it provides a case study in how policymakers can ignore climate change, although its effects are already being felt and could alter the balance of power throughout Eurasia.

Tajikistan experienced five years of civil conflict in the 1990s that debilitated the country socially, economically, and environmentally. Since 1997, political violence has ended, and there have been efforts to improve the condition of its natural resources, which suffered extensive damage during the long conflict.

Mountains cover 93 percent of its landmass, and about half of the territory lies at an altitude of more than 3,000 meters (9,800 feet) above sea level. The highest elevation is the peak of Ismoil Somoni (7,495 meters, or 24,590 feet) in the Pamir Mountains. Tajikistan glaciers, covering 6 percent of the country's landmass, regulate river flow and are the main glacial knot of Central Asia. The largest is the Fedchenko, which is more than 70 kilometers (43.5 miles) long. Manifestations of climate warming have already appeared as large and small glaciers have retreated dramatically and, according to some estimates, have lost 20 percent of their volume during the past 50–60 years (Kayumov, 2010).

Mountain and foothill areas host rivers that were the main source of replenishment of the Aral Sea straddling Kazakhstan and Uzbekistan. Both of those nations count on Tajik river flows to provide water for irrigation and

Figure 7.1 Pamirs, Tajikistan (photo: Alijon Boynazarov)

downstream power generation. Upstream–downstream competition for glacial runoff has led to conflict, including neighboring states' periodic cutoff of power, natural gas, and road access to Tajikistan over perceived threats to their water supplies. Oil and gas reserves are insignificant, and exploration of coalfields is not organized on an industrial scale because of their remote, mountainous locations. While the nation lacks carbon resources, its fast-running rivers and large height terrain differentials make Tajikistan a potentially leading supplier of hydropower. Yet for downstream neighbors, energy projects upstream translate into less water for crops and domestic use and less flow for their own dams and hydropower plants.

For growth if not for its own precarious survival, Tajikistan badly needs more hydropower for domestic use and for sale regionally to bring in essential revenue. Reduced winter flow on the Vakhsh River means a large drop in capacity at its one existing high dam, the Nurek, that can cause a serious shortage of electricity (Makhmedov, Madmusoev and Tavarov, 2012). Obstacles to the import and transmission of electricity from other countries make the problem more acute and strongly impair the country's socioeconomic security. Energy instabilities result in widespread blackouts, leaving large segments of the population to scramble for alternative fuel sources—wood, propane, cow chips, and teresken[1]—for heat and cooking.

Statement of the issue

Tajikistan's general economic contraction and loss of social services after the collapse of the Soviet Union in 1991 were exacerbated by the 1992 civil war that caused a drastic deterioration in living conditions. Poor land management practices and the adverse environmental legacy of Soviet central planning—

combined with a multitude of accumulating problems such as crumbling infrastructure and inadequate investment, heavy external debt, rising poverty among rural women, and limited institutional capacity—threaten the viability of the country's economic, social, and human development (United Nations Committee on Economic, Social, and Cultural Rights, 2015).

The impacts of climate change are expected to add to these continuing problems and pose additional risks to achieving national development priorities. From the available evidence on climate change effects that already have hit Tajikistan, it is clear that development aid as usual will not sufficiently address what is required (Aga Khan Development Network, 2010). Meanwhile, China stands ready to help—at a cost still unknown.

Recent droughts and weather extremes illuminate inadequacies in the nation's climate resilience, such as the inability of hydropower facilities to cope with increasingly extreme winter conditions. The nation's temperature spread runs from about +50° to −50° Celsius (122° to −58° Fahrenheit). Both droughts and torrential storms occur frequently.

Fragile economy and chaotic agriculture

Understanding the nation's vulnerability to extreme events provides a clue to the future. The limited climate projections now available suggest a future of higher temperatures, reduced rainfall, and higher evapotranspiration, with an increased frequency of weather events such as floods, droughts, and storms (Immerzeel, Lutz and Droogers, 2012).[2] Scientists predict these changes will lead to adverse impacts such as fluctuations in the hydrological cycle—especially flash floods from retreating glaciers—with downstream consequences for vulnerable communities, ecosystems, and water supplies needed for livelihoods, hydropower, potable water, irrigation, and food security. These potential changes directly threaten agricultural production and, with other economic and social factors, already have degraded Tajikistan's arable land, forests, pastures, and rangeland.

In a way not seen as directly in more developed countries, socioeconomic difficulties affecting Tajikistan are clearly entwined with the health of its ecosystems. While poverty has decreased considerably in the past fifteen years, more than 40 percent of the population still is deemed to live in poverty (Stein, 2011). The growth of new jobs lags the rate of population increase; the estimated real unemployment rate may be as high as 25 percent, although official figures are much lower. The government has failed to introduce minimum wage policies consistent with international standards, and frequent wage arrears remain a problem. Employment in the informal economy is common, resulting in a lack of social protection for the workforce (Stein, 2011).

The country's continued close association with Russia compounds its difficulties, including its ability to afford to tackle ecological problems. Due to the lack of job opportunities in Tajikistan, labor migration has been extensive in recent years, with devastating results. The Agency on Statistics under the President of the Republic of Tajikistan estimated that 877,335 citizens out of a national population of about 8 million worked abroad, almost all in Russia, in 2012 (Kurbanov, 2013). In 2014, workers sent home US$3.9 billion in remittances, or 42.2 percent of the national GDP—one of the world's highest remittance rates (World Bank, 2014b). In addition, devaluation of the Russian ruble against the U.S. dollar has created severe economic problems (Asia–Plus, 2015).

Economic growth is also slowing while vulnerability to unanticipated shocks is increasing as the nation faces a range of both external and domestic risks, according to the World Bank (2014b): "Weaker world economic growth and lower prices for cotton and aluminum adversely affected the major export-oriented industries, pushing total industrial growth below 3 percent from nearly 7 percent a year earlier." The World Bank reported that growth in agricultural output "also moderated due to heavy rains and low temperatures," but that inflation began to pick up as food prices rose and tariffs for utilities were adjusted, reaching 4.7 percent for the first half of 2014 compared to 1.6 percent a year earlier. "A Russian slowdown affects Tajikistan largely through the remittances channel" (World Bank, 2014b).

Increased stress from effects of climate change make Tajikistan a prime example of a country without the economic and social resilience to deal with environmental problems that are not of its causing. Perhaps nowhere is this more pronounced than in the agricultural sector, already weakened by the loss of younger males working in Russia. But other systemic problems are multiplying, representing a threat not only to the nation's food security but also to land management programs to address soil degradation and water pollution.

Connectivity and transportation—the New Silk Road

As Russia goes through an economic crisis, the Central Asia republics are turning increasingly toward China for investment and trade. In 2013, Tajikistan was one of the first countries in the region to support China's initiative to build out the Silk Road Economic Belt. This project would especially benefit Tajikistan (Fedorenko, 2013) since it is Central Asia's least-connected nation, with only limited regional and international transportation links. Limited—and difficult—road transport is often the only option, given the alpine topography and minimal rail network. Most of its transportation system was built during the Soviet era and has deteriorated badly since then because of insufficient investment and maintenance. However, Tajikistan has begun major development in its transportation sector, including its aviation industry.

More east–west connectivity is badly needed. China's use of the legacy Silk Road title, observers point out, was a calculated attempt to connect the project with memories of what was once the world's most important trading route, linking East and West, Asia with Europe. The original trade routes created a conduit to exchange prized silks, spices, and jewels, as well as philosophies, cultures, and religions. Its very name is iconic and synonymous with exoticism, adventure, and mystery (Hedin, 1898a, 1898b; Kuzmina, 2007; Beckwith, 2009; Liu, 2010; Hansen, 2012).

But observers and analysts of the proposal see something far less romantic about its enormous scale and purposes. Beijing expects to gain by boosting the economies of its post-Soviet trading partners along the route. It already has collected them into an economic and military pact called the Shanghai Cooperation Organization, which includes Russia, Kyrgyzstan, Uzbekistan, Kazakhstan, and Tajikistan. Although Russia belongs to it, the Shanghai Six widely is seen as competing with President Vladimir Putin's ambitions for a "Eurasian Union" and with the organization he supports, the Interstate Council of the Eurasian Economic Community, which brings together Russia, Belarus, Kazakhstan, Kyrgyzstan, Uzbekistan, and Tajikistan. China's interest in the region's energy resources, raw materials, and markets is only part of the geopolitical equation. "The New Silk Road is undeniably related to security issues in China's Western Frontier, beset with what Beijing calls the 'three evils' of terrorism, separatism, and fundamentalism," Ooi and Trinkle wrote for *The Diplomat* (2015).

According to this analysis, Tajikistan is China's essential double firewall between radical Muslim groups to Tajikistan's west and the restive Uygur Muslim population to the east, on China's side of the Pamirs. As a result, China is making direct investments in the republic. Of the US$6 billion China pledged in September 2014 to invest in Tajikistan, US$3.2 billion was designated to construct the Tajik branch of a 1,830-kilometer (1,137-mile) pipeline network connecting the gas fields of Central Asia with China (Farchy, 2014).

U.S. and European diplomats and aid organizations also have sought to exert influence over the region's natural resources. The World Bank decided in February 2015 to invest in Tajikistan's regional transport connectivity and allocated US$45 million to finance the second phase of the bank's transformative Central Asia Road Links Program to be implemented between 2015 and 2020. The program aims to increase transport connectivity among neighboring countries while supporting improved road operations and maintenance practices (World Bank, 2015). While road construction projects are planned mostly to use existing rights of way, the vast scale of the Silk Road project is expected to impact the environment.

Water resources

Central Asia is plagued by an uneven distribution of water resources. More than 80 percent of water contributed to the Aral Sea comes from upstream Tajikistan and Kyrgyzstan. Both upstream and downstream nations depend on the seasonal glacier melt water. Tajikistan has more than 14,500 glaciers covering about 12,000–14,000 square kilometers (4,600–5,400 square miles) (Kotlyakov, Osipova and Tsvetkov, 2008), and there are 947 rivers more than 10 kilometers (6 miles) long (Luterbacher, Kuzmichenok, Shalpykova and Wiegandt, 2008).

The region's water supply is essential. If there is plenty of water, people prosper; if there is little, they starve (Huntington, 1912). Irrigated crops account for up to 90 percent of agricultural production, and that, in turn, constitutes up to 20 percent of the nation's GDP.

The Russian Empire was the first occupying power to orient the local economy toward producing goods for distant markets, first domestic and eventually international. From the late 1920s to the early 1980s, the Soviet Union built dams, drained swamps, uprooted orchards and vineyards, plowed under pastureland, and dug canals from two major Tajik rivers, the Amu Darya and Syr Darya (McNeill and Mauldin, 2012). By 1985, cotton—a notably thirsty crop—grew on more than 85 percent of the cultivated land in the basins of the Amu Darya and Syr Darya. Uzbekistan alone produced more cotton than the U.S., while the Soviet Union had become the world's second-leading cotton producer behind China.

Consequently, by the mid-1980s, the two rivers delivered a mere trickle of water to the Aral. As the sea contracted, the adjacent region suffered violent dust storms that originated on the exposed, windswept ex-seabed. In addition, more than half of the irrigated land had become highly salinized, and more than a million hectares (2.5 million acres) were lost to production. At the same time, some lakes, swamps, and lush meadows in the lower parts of the river basins dried up altogether. The desiccation of subsoils, in turn, reduced vegetation by 20 to 40 percent throughout the lower stretches of the river valleys, pushing many mammal and bird species to local extinction (McNeill and Mauldin, 2012).

By contrast, Tajikistan is water-rich with about 1,300 lakes, 80 percent of them above 3,000 meters (9,800 feet) with an area of less than 1 square kilometer (0.39 square miles). The largest saltwater lake is Karakul in Eastern Pamir. Believed to have formed when a meteor struck Earth millions of years ago, its aquamarine waters appear oasis-like amid the barren, stony landscape of the mountains. Despite its beauty, the ancient lake is home to few forms of marine life, and area residents claim the water is so dense with salt that anyone who tries to sail a boat across the surface would capsize from top-heaviness.

Groundwater resources regenerated by rivers and lakes play an important role for conservation of ecosystems, especially wetlands and protected areas—the most important of which is the Tigrovaya Balka Nature Reserve close to the Afghan border. The reserve hosts a rich diversity of fauna and flora, including rare Bactrian deer and valuable bird species, earning its designation as a UNESCO World Heritage Centre. The Tajik National Park in the center of the Pamir range shelters rare and threatened birds and mammals, including Marco Polo argali sheep, snow leopards, and Siberian ibexes. It is a forbidding place, subject to frequent strong earthquakes and isolated from agriculture and permanent settlements. It hosts the longest valley glacier outside Antarctica.

But the wealth of Tajik water may not last. Beginning in the second half of the 20th century, its glacial resources have declined at an average rate of 0.6–0.8 percent per year in ice area and about 0.1 percent in ice volume annually (Hagg, 2013). Its largest glacier, the Fedchenko, has shrunk by 11 square kilometers (4.2 square miles) and has lost about 2 cubic kilometers (0.48 cubic miles) of ice during the previous century (Iwata, 2009). The Garmo glacier has retreated more than 7 kilometers (4.3 miles) since 1932, the most significant retreat in Central Asia. This trend appears to be continuing steadily at an as-yet unknown rate. Forecast scenarios indicate river runoff is expected to drop 5–10 percent in the short term and 10–40 percent over the long term (Kayumov, 2010). As runoff declines, water and energy shortages already are felt acutely. Abnormal weather conditions such as prolonged winter frosts are occurring. Ecological changes exacerbate the region's hydropower capacity shortage and lack of reliable water resources management.

The Rogun Dam: real or fantasy?

Dam-building on transnational rivers is a geopolitical concern throughout Asia, where the world's fastest economic growth is accompanied by the world's fastest increase in military spending and fiercest competition for natural resources, especially water and energy (Chellaney, 2012; Hannam, 2013). As a result, dams, reservoirs, irrigation networks, and other infrastructure have sparked cross-border conflicts, sometimes verging on war.

No better example exists than the interrupted construction of the Rogun hydropower plant in southern Tajikistan, which has become a major dispute among resource experts, policymakers, and heads of state. All want cheap electricity, but at the same time they avoid confronting the many fiscal, engineering, and environmental problems this project presents. Planning and construction of the country's second high dam began in 2006 and has become the defining feature of strained relations between Tajikistan and Uzbekistan over much of the last ten years (Makhmedov, Madmusoev and Tavarov, 2012). The most contentious feature is its height. Soviet engineers began construction of the 335-meter (1,100-foot) giant in 1976, but construction was suspended multiple times. If completed, it would overtake Tajikistan's other high dam, Nurek (300 meters, 984 feet)— also on the Vakhsh River—as the world's highest dam. Its size and location create engineering challenges that pushed its cost to more than US$3 billion. In August 2012, construction was suspended again pending a World Bank assessment. Since then, alternative and less grandiose designs have been proposed. Its unfinished status and the World Bank's review represent continued hope for energy security in Tajikistan and Afghanistan. Planners assert it also would alleviate the problem of interconnected economies and resource conflicts in post-Soviet Central Asia.

Tajikistan's hydropower potential is estimated at 527 billion kilowatt-hours of electricity per year, which would more than triple existing electricity production in Central Asia (Stern, 2008). In terms of potential hydropower resources, Tajikistan ranks eighth after China, Russia, the United States, Brazil, Zaire, India, and Canada (Makhmedov, Madmusoev and Tavarov, 2012). The existing use of hydropower resources in Tajikistan generates about 17 billion kWh of electricity per year, or about 3 percent of the potential hydropower capacity (Rahimov, 2014).

Until late 2009, Central Asia had a unified energy system—an energy "ring" that coordinated output from eighty-three power stations in the region. But when Uzbekistan announced it was taking its system offline, the unified scheme collapsed. Tajikistan was left with no sources of imported electricity, and its existing Nurek Dam couldn't meet demand. Completing the Rogun Dam would enable Tajikistan to generate about 13 billion more kilowatt-hours of electricity annually (Stern, 2008). This not only would help meet all its domestic needs, but would let Tajikistan expand its aluminum industry and become a net exporter of electricity.

Other countries remain less enthusiastic about the prospect of a completed Rogun Dam. In particular, Uzbekistan argues that the dam would decimate its cotton production and add to desertification. Uzbekistan also fears the large volume of water stored behind the dam would trigger higher-scale earthquakes in an already seismically active area. At a more fundamental level, Uzbekistan worries that controlling the flow of the Vakhsh will give Tajikistan crucial geopolitical leverage.

The World Bank commissioned an independent assessment of the potential social and environmental impacts of the Rogun Dam. The resulting "Assessment Studies for the Proposed Rogun Hydropower Project in Tajikistan" was finalized after riparian consultants completed work, and comments from government and civil society stakeholders were carefully considered. The study resulted from four years of independent, transparent, and consultative analysis to assess the feasibility of the project from the technical, economic, environmental, and social perspectives. Anna Bjerde, the World Bank director for strategy and operations in Europe and Central Asia, said that throughout the process, the report's authors were "committed to ensuring that the studies meet the highest standards for technical quality, transparency, and consultation" (World Bank, 2014a).

A consulting report to an independent World Bank panel of experts advised that it would be feasible to build and operate a dam at the site within modern international norms, but contingent on incorporating the experts' recommendations on modifying the original design, implementing mitigation measures, and establishing monitoring systems. After the World Bank gave assurances of a redesigned dam's benefits, on February 27, 2015, Tajikistan announced a tender offer to help finance construction, but it drew little investor interest. The financial aspect of the project was still problematic since the plant's price tag was estimated to have escalated from as much as US$3 billion to US$5 billion, which Tajikistan did not have (Asia-Plus, 2015).

Experts say a new US$1 billion electricity transmission system to connect Kyrgyzstan, Tajikistan, Afghanistan, and Pakistan would make the most efficient use of clean hydropower resources by enabling them to transfer and sell surplus electricity during the summer to energy-deficient countries in South Asia, such as Pakistan and Bangladesh. The Inter-Governmental Council, which consists of Afghanistan, Kyrgyzstan, Pakistan, and Tajikistan, put a key framework in place for making CASA (Central Asia-South Asia)-1000 a reality. In addition to their own commitment, CASA-1000 has support from the World Bank Group, Islamic Development Bank, U.S. Agency for International Development, U.S. Department of State, United Kingdom Department for International Development, Australian Agency for International Development, and other donors.

Domestic criticism emerged regarding Tajikistan's participation in CASA-1000 because of the electricity deficits. However, the project focuses on transporting the available summer electricity surplus from Tajikistan; thus it would not negatively impact winter electricity deficits. To the contrary, revenue from summer surpluses could alleviate problems with winter energy deficits. Another advantage of the project would be direct transmission links between Tajikistan and Kyrgyzstan, thus strengthening the electrical interchange network in Central Asia (Fedorenko, 2013).

Conclusions

For Tajikistan, peace, stability, and development depend heavily on availability of water resources, the energy they could produce, and international cooperation on economic growth. Given the tight interrelationship between water and energy—and the problem of energy insecurity down to the household level—it is critical that the government strongly support investment in and expansion of renewable energy sources and off-grid household energy systems. Examples include microhydro, solar, and wind power. If the Rogun Dam can be finished with a new design and if the World Bank's cautions are heeded, it would represent social value with minimum environmental cost and an opportunity to create jobs and improve living conditions for hundreds of thousands of people.

Although glaciers across the Pamirs may not be disappearing at as rapid a rate as had been previously thought, uncertainties about their future remain high. Even without extensive data, the need remains for mitigation of and adaptation to glacial retreat.

One key point of regional tension remains accurately predicting water flows, glacial decline, and permafrost changes. Support for scientific research, particularly in glaciology and hydrology, should be a high priority. In Tajikistan, the need is particularly acute for instrumentation to monitor glaciers, producing information that would benefit all Aral Sea Basin states. It is difficult to see how assessments of climate impacts can be taken into account in regional planning without more data and better documentation of baselines for Tajikistan's many glaciers.

In sum, scientists and policymakers are urging these steps, many of which they contend would directly or indirectly improve Tajikistan's environment:

- Improve regional and international collaboration on glacier monitoring;
- Engage local residents and authorities in monitoring activities to aid research efforts, allow for better early warning systems for climate-related disasters, and provide jobs;
- Create knowledge hubs throughout Central Asia so scientists and policymakers can learn from each other and offer rational options to aid sustainable development;
- Coordinate ecosystem protection among mountain peoples;
- Provide financial support for fact-based planning and needed investments in infrastructure that will provide jobs;
- Ensure that regional planning takes into account real-world, science-based environmental risks.

Notes

1 Teresken is a small, woody shrub that is one of the few plants that survive in the semi-arid plateau of the Eastern Pamirs, where temperatures can reach –50° Celsius (–58 ° Fahrenheit).

2 Eight severe droughts hit the country during the last sixty years, the latest in 2000, 2001, and 2007. The last was so strong and prolonged that it caused widespread drying of subsoils. Little is known about the impact of droughts on permafrost at Tajikistan's higher altitudes.

References

Aga Khan Development Network (2010). *Rural Development in Tajikistan*. Available at http://www.akdn.org/rural_development/tajikistan.asp.

Armstrong, R.L. (2010). Melting glaciers: current status and future concerns. National Resources Management & Development Portal. Available at http://rmportal.net/news/news-usaid-rmp-featured-stories/melting-glaciers-current-status-and-future-concerns.

Asia-Plus (2015). Tajik labor migrants may work in Russia this year under paten[t]s received last year. Available at http://news.tj/en/news/tajik-labor-migrants-may-work-russia-year-under-patens-received-last-year.

Bakanova, M. and Sobirzoda, R. (2014). Tajikistan: moderated growth, heightened risks. *Tajikistan Economic Report*, 6. Available at http://documents.worldbank.org/curated/en/2014/01/20302396/tajikistan-moderated-growth-heightened-risks.

Beckwith, C.I. (2009). *Empires of the Silk Road: A History of Central Eurasia from the Bronze Age to the Present* (Princeton, NJ: Princeton University Press).

Chellaney, B. (2012). From arms racing to "dam racing" in Asia: how to contain the geopolitical risks of the dam-building competition. Transatlantic Academy Paper Series. Available at http://www.transatlanticacademy.org/publications/arms-racing-dam-racing-asia-how-contain-geopolitical-risks-dam-building-competition.

Farchy, J. (2014). Tajikistan looks to China as Russian remittances dry up. *Financial Times*. Available at http://www.ft.com/intl/cms/s/0/2c87ee20-58f9-11e4-9546-00144feab7de.html#slide0.

Fedorenko, V. (2013). The New Silk Road initiatives in Central Asia. Rethink Institute. Available at http://www.rethinkinstitute.org/the-new-silk-road-initiatives-in-central-asia.

Hagg, W. (2013). *Glaciers: Frozen Treasures of the Pamirs*. Eurasia travel. Available at http://eurasia.travel/tajikistan/tajikistan_facts/geology/glaciers_frozen_treasures_of_the_pamirs/.

Hannam, I. (2013). Transboundary resource management strategies in the Pamir mountain region of Tajikistan. In *Land and Post-Conflict Peacebuilding*, eds Unruh, J. and R. Williams (London: Earthscan).

Hansen, V. (2012). *The Silk Road: A New History* (New York: Oxford University Press).

Hedin, S. (1938). *The Silk Road*, trans. F. H. Lyon (New York: E.P. Dutton and Company).

Hedin, S. (1898a). *Through Asia Volume I* (London: Methuen & Company).

Hedin, S. (1898b). *Through Asia Volume II* (London: Methuen & Company).

Huntington, E. (1912). *Asia: A Geography Reader* (Chicago, IL: Rand McNally & Company).

Immerzeel, W.W., Lutz, A.F. and Droogers, P. (2012). Climate change impacts on the upstream water resources of the Amu and Syr Darya river basins. FutureWater Report,

107. Available at http://www.futurewater.nl/wp-content/uploads/2012/03/Upstream_Report_FW_web.pdf.

International Partnership for Human Rights (2015). Tajikistan: UN review of economic, social and cultural rights. Available at http://www.iphronline.org/tajikistan-un-review-of-economic-social-and-cultural-rights-20150224.html.

Iwata, S. (2009). Mapping features of Fedchenko Glacier, the Pamirs, Central Asia from space. *Geographical Studies*, 84(1): 33–43.

Kayumov, A. (2010). Glaciers resources of Tajikistan in condition of the climate change. State Agency for Hydrometeorology of Committee for Environmental Protection under the Government of the Republic of Tajikistan. Available at https://www.wmo.int/pages/prog/www/OSY/Meetings/GCW-IM1/glaciers.pdf.

Kotlyakov, V.M., Osipova, G.V. and Tsvetkov, D.G. (2008). Monitoring surging glaciers of the Pamirs, Central Asia, from space. *Annals of Glaciology*, 48(1): 125–134.

Kurbanov, S. (2013). Gender shape of labor migration in the Republic of Tajikistan. Available at http://www.stat.tj/img/en/Gender%20aspects%20in%20migration(1).pdf.

Kuzmina, E.E. and Mair, V.H. (2007). *The Prehistory of the Silk Road* (Philadelphia, PA: University of Pennsylvania Press).

Liu, X. (2010). *The Silk Road in World History* (New York: Oxford University Press).

Luterbacher, U., Kuzmichenok, V., Shalpykova, G. and Wiegandt, E. (2008). Glaciers and efficient water use in Central Asia. In *Darkening Peaks: Glacier Retreat, Science, and Society*, eds Orlove, B.E., Wiegandt, E. and Luckman, B.H. (Berkeley, CA: University of California Press).

Makhmedov, Y., Madmusoev, M. and Tavarov, S. (2012). Water and energy disputes between Tajikistan and Uzbekistan, and their negative influence on regional co-operation. Norwegian Institute of International Affairs.

McNeill, J.R. and Mauldin, E.S. (eds) (2012). *A Companion To Global Environmental History* (Chichester, West Sussex: Wiley-Blackwell).

Ooi, S-M. and Trinkle, K. (2015). China's New Silk Road and its impact in Xinjiang. *The Diplomat*. Available at http://thediplomat.com/2015/03/chinas-new-silk-road-and-its-impact-on-xinjiang.

Pilot Programme for Climate Resilience (2011). Tajikistan: strategic programme for climate resilience. Available at https://www.climateinvestmentfunds.org/cif/sites/climateinvestmentfunds.org/files/SPCR_Tajikistan_revised_012511.pdf.

Rahimov, S. (2014), Tajikistan: turn water into cooperation. *EP Today*. Available at http://eptoday.com/tajikistan-turn-water-cooperation/.

Statistical Agency under the President of the Republic of Tajikistan (2010). Tajikistan in figures. Available at http://stat.tj/ru/img/9f5268b192177e16d1066c1e16aea04a_1287832044.pdf.

Stein, M. (2011). Conflict over water related resources in Uzbekistan and Tajikistan and its impact on local security. Foreign Military Studies Office. Available at http://fmso.leavenworth.army.mil/documents/Conflict-Over-Resources.pdf.

Stern, D.L. (2008). Tajikistan hopes water will power its ambitions. *New York Times*. Available at http://www.nytimes.com/2008/09/01/world/asia/01tajikistan.html?_r=0.

United Nations Committee on Economic, Social, and Cultural Rights (2015). Tajikistan: UN review of economic, social and cultural rights. Session in Geneva on 24–25 February 2015. Available at http://www.iphronline.org/tajikistan-un-review-of-economic-social-and-cultural-rights-20150224.html.

United Nations Development Programme (2011). The glaciers of Central Asia: a disappearing resource. Available at http://www.envsec.org/publications/brochure_the_glaciers_of_central_asia_dec_2011.pdf.

World Bank (2014a). Fifth and final riparian meetings on Rogun Assessment Studies. Available at http://www.worldbank.org/en/news/press-release/2014/07/18/fifth-and-final-riparian-meetings-on-rogun-assessment-studies.

World Bank (2014b). Comprehensive structural reforms needed to bolster growth, create jobs, and reduce poverty, says World Bank. Available at http://www.worldbank.org/en/news/press-release/2014/10/27/comprehensive-structural-reforms-needed-to-bolster-growth-create-jobs-and-reduce-poverty.

World Bank (2015). World Bank invests in Tajikistan's regional transport connectivity. Available at http://www.worldbank.org/en/news/press-release/2015/02/25/world-bank-invests-in-tajikistans-regional-transport-connectivity.

8 Newspaper coverage of water and other ecological issues in Kazakhstan during *Perestroika* and today

Ardak Yesdauletova and
Aitmukhanbet Yesdauletov

Introduction

The Soviet period had distinctive features in various spheres beyond ideology and politics. Soviet styles of administration were reflected in many aspects of society, including the environment and the press.

The rise of coverage of environmental problems in newspapers during *glasnost* reflected more openness and democratization in the Kazakh Soviet Socialist Republic. Coverage of ecological problems was the impulse for starting more than one social movement organization when people got the opportunity to talk more openly with each other and to discuss issues that had been closed for decades.

The first part of this chapter recounts the catastrophe at the Chernobyl nuclear plant in Ukraine on 26 April 1986, and how Soviet mass media did not cover it until three weeks had elapsed. The leadership of the USSR tried to hide this tragic event from the public. Even with that three-week delay, however, press coverage played a role in assisting some residents around the nuclear plant with enough time to help those living in the radioactive zone.

The second part of this chapter explores a proposal to divert Siberian rivers to Central Asia. It was a grandiose project, planned in the Kremlin. After successful construction of the Karakum Canal in the 1950s, the Soviet administration decided to build a canal to connect Siberian rivers and Uzbekistan to irrigate the dry soil to cultivate cotton. The canal called the Siberia–Central Asia was intended to be the first stage of this ambitious plan that would include construction of a canal from the Ob River to Uzbekistan through the Kazakh steppe. The second stage was to be the "anti-Irtysh" canal that would reverse the flow of Siberia's Irtysh River. Instead of flowing north, which is its natural course, it would go south to Central Asia and Russia. The project was not completed because of lack of financing and technical difficulties.

The third part of this chapter examines press coverage of the Aral Sea disaster. The troubles of the Aral began on August 6, 1956, when the Central Committee of the Communist Party of the Soviet Union (CCPU) and the USSR Council of Ministers adopted a resolution titled "On irrigation and development of virgin lands the Hungry Steppe in the Uzbek and Kazakh (Soviet Socialist Republics) to increase cotton production." The problems of the disappearing sea, the reasons, and the consequences were covered constantly in newspapers and magazines, including *Pravda* (Truth), *Literaturnaya Gazeta* (Literary Newspaper), *Izvestia* (News), and *Sotsialistik Kazakhstan* (Socialist Kazakhstan).

The print media served as a tool for raising ecological issues and as a discussion forum. As a result of newspaper coverage, the first nongovernmental eco-organizations were formed. Among them were "Initiative," "Ecology and Public Opinion," and "Semey Nevada."

Research questions

The research questions for this study are as follows:

1   What was the impact of the interaction of mass media and ecological problems in the Kazakh Soviet Socialist Republic on the process of *Perestroika* (restructuring) in the 1980s?
2   What differences are evident by comparing mass media coverage of water resources in the 1980s and currently?

Methodology

The authors of this chapter used commonly accepted methodologies in social and political science, including secondary analysis[1] and comparison of policies during the Soviet era and under the Kazakhstan government today. This study evaluated cases in Central Asia, particularly in Kazakhstan, and focused on newspaper coverage of water policy and their explanation of urgent issues.

Findings

Ecological propaganda in the media began with the first days of Soviet power in the 1920s. Many books and newspaper articles were devoted to environmental protection. However, they were limited to coverage of such non-controversial topics as protection of specific natural features, the rational use of natural resources, and the so-called "environmental upbringing" of the public. Full and objective coverage of ecology in accordance with existing Western-style journalistic practices did not occur; instead, the main problems were concealed.

For the people, transparency came slowly in the first years of *Perestroika*. Coverage was limited at the beginning as newspapers started publishing stories about previously off-limits environmental topics. From national newspapers, readers learned that "voluntarism"[2] had led to many mistakes.

The growth of industrial activity caused negative impacts on the environment that affected present and future generations. In 1984, a joint decree of the Central Committee of CPSU and the Council of Ministers, "On a long-term program of land reclamation, more efficient use of land reclamation for sustainable building food stocks of the country," was released. It caused excitement in the press, and all publications covering agricultural issues referred to the decree.

As journalist L. Sizova wrote at the time:

> If you look at the newspaper at least ten years ago, we can see that the bio-economic publications were not so widespread. But it was not just because of quantity, it was not the severity of the problem; guidance on the specific perpetrators of pollution, digital, and statistical material was superficial because of the "secrecy" of environmental indicators. And the tone of these publications was more educational and instructive than offensive and combative. Without denying the importance of these areas, it should be noted that in the "stagnant" years, they have contributed little to the practical solution of pressing environmental problems.
>
> (Sizova, 1989, p. 132)

Another decree of the Central Committee of the CPSU and Council of Ministers, "On the fundamental restructuring of the nature conservation in the country," appeared in *Pravda* in January 1988. This second decree proposed allowing new enterprises and businesses to start work only if they fully met environmental requirements. Attention was paid to the replacement of outdated command-administrative methods of natural environment management with economic methods. What changed in the intermediate four years, and what was the reason for the second decree?

The book *Journalism and Perestroika* noted that environmental education of the public was the leading environmental objective of the press (Sizova, 1989, p. 131). The political and legal arenas had largely discredited themselves, and social and class analysis of environmental problems was often limited to promotion of the thesis that "they" are naturally all bad, and "we" have only some drawbacks. Detachment from reality led to the opposite effects of propaganda. Real environmental information seeped into society, and voices were raised asking whether it is more important to analyze environmental experiences and to use them rather than to glorify non-existent achievements. Meanwhile, Mikhael Gorbachev's reforms led to a weakening of state control, and the transformation of Soviet society intensified the environmental movement.

Perestroika changed public attitudes toward environmental problems. A huge flow of information about everything that had previously been secret began and many new environmental organizations appeared. A series of mass demonstrations in defense of the environment, many of which ended in victory, occurred throughout the country. This was the green movement of *Perestroika* as characterized by a wide variety of forms of social activity and a wide range of political and ideological activities. For some time, the movement was even fashionable (*Ekologicheskoye dvizheniye v SSSR i v sovremennoy Rossii*, Environmental movement in the Soviet Union and in modern Russia, 2014).

Press coverage of the Chernobyl disaster

The Chernobyl disaster on 26 April 1986 was unprecedented in its scope and played a significant role in promoting the "green movement." It was not reported in the Soviet press until after the May Day holidays. But broadcasts from Western radio stations and from a few Soviet media outlets in late April disclosed that "something" happened at the nuclear power plant near Kiev.

The Chernobyl event focused new attention on the development of nuclear energy and other potential human-made hazards. It was only after the disaster that such information began to penetrate into the free press through various channels (Dyachenko, 2004). Media coverage of the consequences of the disaster destroyed the myth of the absolute safety of nuclear energy as many of its accumulated problems became publicly known. Discussion regarding the safety of nuclear energy became socially significant. Differing and sometimes opposite opinions were expressed – for its further development or for elimination of all existing nuclear power plants. For example, Viktor Snitkovsky, a firefighter who worked at Chernobyl after the explosion, expressed a sharply negative view toward nuclear plants in post-Soviet territory (Snitkovsky, 1998).

Thus the disaster sparked coverage of a wide range of environmental themes on newspaper pages. The first and most important achievement was publicity about the disaster.

Press coverage of potential diversion of Siberian rivers to Central Asia

Addiction to gigantic projects was inherent in the Soviet economy. Many buildings were declared constructions of the century, and most newspapers gave space to these undertakings. However, Stalin stopped many of them, and others were dropped after his death. Ambitious plans for greening the Hungry Steppe, building tunnels, and adding railway branches in the countryside were announced every five years.

One such project prior to the Siberian rivers scheme was the Main Turkmen Canal, built between 1950 and 1955. Intensely covered by the newspapers at the beginning of the 1950s, it was called "Stalin's construction of the century" and "the epitome of Stalin's plan to transform nature." The purpose of the large-scale irrigation and land reclamation project was cotton cultivation, development of new land in Karakalpakstan and in the Karakum Desert, and facilitating shipping from the Volga River to the Amu Darya (Zholdasov, 2003). In 1953, after the death of Stalin, construction of the canal was suspended and then terminated.

Diverting Siberian rivers – one of the USSR's largest and most ambitious projects – aimed to redistribute the flow of the Irtysh, Ob, and other rivers into desert regions. The project was intended to bring fresh water to Kazakhstan, Uzbekistan, and Turkmenistan for irrigation, to refill the Aral Sea, and to accommodate navigation on the canals (Verkhoturov, 2014). The Siberia-Central Asia canal was the first stage of the project and consisted of construction of a water channel from the Ob River through Kazakhstan to the south to Uzbekistan. "Anti-Irtysh" was the second phase of the project. Water would be sent upstream on the Irtysh, then through the Turgai deflection to Kazakhstan and to the Amu Darya and Syr Darya rivers. The government was supposed to build a series of dams and ten pumping stations. Later, in 1983, examination of the project by the USSR State Planning Committee concluded that the central planners' flow projections were at least two times too low. Water was needed not only to drive against the flow of the Ob, Irtysh, and Tobol rivers, but also to drive it uphill to a height of 360 feet. The estimated need for electricity for the pumps in the first stage was 10.2 billion KW/h and for the second stage 35–40 KW/h (Verkhoturov, 2014).

In 1986, the Central Committee of CPSU decided to discontinue work on water transfer from the Siberian rivers. The resolution adopted by the Central Committee and the Council of Ministers included more focus on effective conservation and efficient use of available water resources to intensify agricultural production (Zalygin, 1986). The editor of the literary journal *Novyi Mir* (*New World*) noted, "Thus the longstanding dispute between supporters and opponents of the transfer projects ended. This decision was one of the most important and convincing evidences of the overall process of restructuring, which lives today [in the] country" (Zalygin, 1986: 14). He meant that the resolution symbolized a changing country where even old, grandiose projects might be revised and stopped. It was, in effect, a challenge to Communist Party decisions.

Numerous articles in the press in that period opposed the project and played a great role in affecting the outcome. "The situation with the rotation of the flow of northern rivers could not stir up the public if publicists have failed to show the social consequences of the wrong decision" (Fomicheva, 1989).

Press coverage of the Aral Sea

Gradually, due to newspaper coverage, it became clear that the Soviet government was one of the most environmentally unfriendly in the world. The environmental theme was on the agenda, and one of the first issues raised by the press was the tragedy of the Aral Sea.

Literaturnaya Gazeta was among the first major newspapers to sound the alarm on the Aral Sea when it published an article by S. Azimov in November 1986. Then in the March 1987 *Bulletin of Society Knowledge*, Institute of Water Resources director G. Voropayev drew attention to the issue. Discussing the causes of the environmental disaster, he suggested that "only 40–60 percent of the irrigated land needed to be allocated for cotton," with the rest used for other crops, and "In the last twenty to thirty years cotton took all the developed lands" (Yesdauletov, 2013).

Gradually other national newspapers joined the discussion. In June 1987, *Pravda* published an article by an expert who studied deserts in Central Asia (Petrov, 1987). He noted that almost two million acres of land in Uzbekistan had become salty. In addition, scientist M. Muhamedzhanov wrote in *Pravda* that the drying of the Aral had led to 3.2 million acres becoming takyrs. A takyr is usually formed in a shallow depressed area with a heavy clay soil, which is submerged by water after seasonal rains. In 1987, *Izvestia* published an article, "The Aral from Space," stating that the sea would disappear by 2010, according to scientists.

The press in Kazakhstan first timidly, then boldly, sounded alarm bells: The sea was dying. One of the first articles in the Kazakh language about the tragedy was published in *Sotsialistik Kazakhstan*[3] on 19 June 1987. The author wrote that in some places the water had receded 75 miles from the coast, despite the fact that the region had struggled with flooding until 1967. In some springs, the water poured in from the Syr Darya River 50 to 75 miles from the coast, but 115 square miles had become a lifeless desert. The tragedy of the sea turned into a tragedy of humans. In one year, 12,000 people migrated from the village of Bugunsk and 48,000 from the district to more hospitable places. What used to be 1,300 small lakes were now dried up.

The climate changed journalistically, politically, geographically, and scientifically. An editorial in a Kazakh newspaper referred to stories in the Moscow press. The editorial was a review of national press coverage, and prohibitions by party organs were not followed. As the saying goes, "The gateway was opened," and *Sotsialistik Kazakhstan* published a series of articles about the problems of the Aral Sea on 5, 10, 17, and 21 July 1987. The value of these articles is that the readers could understand the tragedy, and an objective picture was created. In addition to *Sotsialistik Kazakhstan* (in Kazakh) and *Kazakhstanskaya Pravda* (in Russian), correspondent Bahytzhan Bektepov raised the problem in a newly created newspaper column, "Save the people and the Aral Sea!"

The press determined the culprit to be localism, sectarian ministries, and government departments. The ministries and departments did not care about local inhabitants and the environment. "They behave in their own country as colonizers. Where they dig, what and where to build, they never ask the inhabitants about their own land" (Baklanov, 1988).

Such publications were perceived as particularly critical because they opened the perpetrators of environmental tragedy to the public. The main issue was the "narrow departmental approach," which had brought nothing but harm. "It was unfortunate, but a widespread feature of stagnant decades: the ministries and departments were much easier and more likely to understand each other, rather than those whose interests they had to defend. Perverted professional consciousness has enormous troubles for society" (Shkondina, 1989, p. 142).

In the second half of the 1980s, environmental themes in the press became popular and understandable. Readers faced a flood of environmental information. An ecological map of Kazakhstan blossomed with hot spots of disasters. The world gradually learned about the problems of the Aral, the Semipalatinsk Nuclear Test Site, Lake Balkhash, and more. Media began to shape and reflect public opinion about the most important environmental problems in the country and to work out practical solutions.

By shaping public opinion on the country's critical environmental issues, the media provided a powerful impetus for the revitalization of social and political movements, which accelerated the process of politicization of social consciousness in Kazakhstan. Non-governmental organizations called *neformal* (*informals*), proliferated. Initially, their activities were fragmented and dispersed. Then *neformal* groups began to make political demands, and often the word *neformal* had a negative connotation.

The press and informal social associations

In those years, politicization of the mass consciousness and the rise of social and political organizations occurred throughout the country. Everywhere there were informal community groups, unions, associations, and environmental movements. But they did not appear immediately after *Perestroika* began.

Democratization of society, openness, and pluralism of opinions as declared by the XIX Congress of the Communist Party of the Soviet Union became the impetus for the emergence of associations in Almaty and other regional centers. Such movements served as the basis for political practices that were new in the history of modern Kazakhstan.

The Central Committee of the CPSU adopted the decree "On the negative tendencies in the activities of some informal social associations" on 18 June 1987. Soon after, the Bureau of the Communist Party of Kazakhstan took immediate steps to implement the decree, noting that the "negative tendencies" mentioned in the decree existed in Kazakhstan (Yertysbaev, 2001, p. 196).

Activities of environmental groups had not gone beyond action teams, and their organizations were fragmented. In the book *Nazarbayev and Kazakhstan: the Logic of Change*, Ermuhanbet Yertysbaev – who was an advisor to President Nursultan Nazarbayev at the time – noted "in July 1987 in Pavlodar, the Ecological Organization (Environmental and Public Opinion) was created under the directive of the XX Congress of the Young Communist League delegate P. Lihacheva. The organization set a goal to prevent the construction of the protein-vitamin concentrates plant in the town. This decision on construction had been made in Moscow on the government level, and several times coordinated with local authorities" (Yertysbaev, 2001, p. 197).

But this time, the powers-that-be in Moscow and Pavlodar met strong resistance from informal youth organizations that protested construction of the plant in newspapers, radio, and television. "What happened was unprecedented: a handful of informals won power, the decision to build the plant was canceled. The organization Environmental and Public Opinion drew attention to other problems in the town and had stimulated the creation of other associations in other regions of Kazakhstan" (Yertysbaev, 2001, p. 197).

Another example cited by Yertysbaev was formation of the Socio-Ecological Association Initiative in August 1987. Even its name signaled that the organization was not going to deal only with environmental issues. One goal of the movement was to promote public activities based on the anti-war, environmental, humanitarian, and peacekeeping ideals of transparency, democratization, social equity, and justice. Initiative acquired a significant role in the capital by its noisy campaign about Zhamankum Lake (from the Kazakh, *Zhaman* – bad, *kum* – sand) wastewater storage facility thirty miles from Almaty. Mud overflow from the lake blew away highway and railway bridges, the Aul restaurant, and part of a village, causing great damage.

Motivated by Initiative's work, new associations were formed, including Green Salvation and Green Front. Many activists went further, creating the Social Democratic Party of Kazakhstan. One of their leaders, Sergey Duvanov, wrote that the Social Democrats have "green" roots, saying that "we all came from the socially political association Initiative" (Yertysbaev, 2001, p. 199).

It was a time when environmental organizations proliferated in the form of associations, groups, foundations, and clubs. Among them were Green Movement and an association of ecological small enterprises and cooperatives in Jambul [now Taraz]; in Taldy-Kurgan [now Taldykorgan], it was the environmental association Zhety-su; in Temirtau it was Nour; in Shymkent, the Committee for Rescue of the Koshkar-Ata River; Aktobe Ecologist, a public committee for protection of the northern outskirts of the town of Aktyube, and many others. In one East Kazakhstan region, more than ten environmental associations sought to create a unified environmental organization called Rudnyi Altay (Ore Altay is the name of Kazakhstan's part of the Altay Mountains). At a November 1988 meeting, the Bureau of the Central Committee of the Kazakhstan Communist Party emphasized that "in several towns of the country we observed the real attempts to create groups and associations which were clearly extremist. Their initiators, judging by their own programs [and] agreed-upon slogans, calling for the elimination of the leading role of the Communist Party, elimination of any centralized authority, disobedience to the Soviet laws, and even direct resistance to public order" (Yertysbaev, 2001, p. 203).

In 1989, for an initiative of the ecological club Biosphere, residents of the town of Leninogorsk opposed construction of a lead factory and sent the Supreme Soviet of the USSR an appeal demanding an independent investigation. It held several meetings, and the issue received constant press coverage.

Also that year, the Supreme Soviet adopted a resolution, "On urgent measures on ecological rehabilitation of the country," that noted the country's alarming, and sometimes critical, environmental situation. It proposed a long-term national program through 2005 to protect the environment. One cause of the environmental problems was lack of funding. In the context of a ban on political activity, statements from environmental associations often became the only voices of opposition. Members of these movements exhibited ecological awareness at the beginning, and then gradually moved to political demands. Media coverage of environmental issues was a powerful impetus for the revitalization of social and political movements, accelerating the politicization of social consciousness in Kazakhstan.

What has changed after thirty years?

Ecological themes are still present in newspapers and scientific journals. However, press coverage of water now carries more of an economic dimension. "Water is intrinsically linked to the most immediate challenges we face today, including food security, health, climate change, economic growth, and poverty alleviation" (Asia Society, 2009).

The ex-Soviet states of Central Asia are engaged in an increasingly bitter standoff over water resources, adding another element of instability to the volatile region that neighbors Afghanistan. For example, plans for two of the world's biggest hydroelectric power stations in mountainous but energy-poor Tajikistan and Kyrgyzstan have enraged their powerful downstream neighbor Uzbekistan, which fears losing water that is valuable for agriculture (Borisov, 2012).

One of the main problems in modern water policy involves the transboundary rivers among Central Asian countries and between Kazakhstan and China, raising national security and economic and environmental concerns at the highest levels of government. For example, Kazakhstan President Nursultan Nazarbayev and Uzbekistan President Islam Karimov discussed the water situation in September 2012. Uzbekistan ranks fourth and Kazakhstan ranks eleventh among the world's nations in per capita water consumption (Varis, 2014, p. 28). According to one account of that presidential meeting, "Leaders of the two countries are pleased with the results of the visit and have once again reiterated their positions on the hydro-technical facilities being constructed upstream of the Syr Darya River that require independent international inspection and consideration of interests of all the involved parties" (KTK.kz, 2012).

Another problem directly related to Kazakhstan involves rivers that originate in China. Although Kazakh-Chinese talks on water issues began in the late 1990s, no positive effect for Kazakhstan has been achieved so far. Kazakhstan cannot meet Chinese plans to increase water intake from the Irtysh and Ili rivers. Meanwhile China plans to improve the economic and social situation in the desert area in the northwestern part of the country, the Xinjiang Uygur Autonomous Region, by using more water resources and increasing oil production there.

In addition to Uzbekistan and China, Kyrgyzstan has competing water interests with Kazakhstan. In an August 2014 visit to the Kirov reservoir in the Talas region, Kyrgyzstan Prime Minister Djoomart Otorbaev said, "We will not put conditions for Kazakhstan on water allocation. Kazakhstan is a friendly country, and unilaterally, we will not review the intergovernmental agreement on water sharing. Kyrgyzstan will not unilaterally revise the intergovernmental agreement on water sharing with Kazakhstan" (Kyrgyz Telegraph Agency, 2014).

A key problem is the approach that treats water resources as a good that carries its own cost. Kyrgyzstan and Tajikistan contend that downstream countries must pay for water because water resources have an economic cost, and thus consumers must pay that cost. It is their way of surviving in a difficult economic situation. At the same time, Uzbekistan refuses to pay for water use. Uzbekistan's leadership argues that water is a renewable resource that people do not work to produce. Kazakhstan, in general, agrees with Uzbekistan that water – the rivers – belongs to all transboundary countries. But now Kazakhstan's government is helping to maintain the old water infrastructure in Kyrgyzstan.

Conclusion

Water issues impact the economy and public policy among neighboring countries in Central Asia and newspapers in Kazakhstan regularly cover these aspects. In the 1980s, they devoted space to wrongheaded Soviet ecological policies and raised public awareness about problems of the Aral Sea. These publications led to the green and ecological movements, which became the first informal organizations opposing the Soviet government's ignoring of environmental catastrophes.

Now, a quarter-century after gaining independence, Kazakhstan is shaping its own policy in this field. However, water is perceived as a main resource not only for the environment, but also for economic development and interstate relations. Tensions related to transboundary rivers cause instability and dissatisfaction among neighboring countries. Lack of water influences agriculture, especially in the spring and summer. It also leads to problems in the energy sector. That is true, for example, in the Toktogul cascade between Kyrgyzstan and Kazakhstan and in construction of a controversial new hydropower plant in Tajikistan, a project that created a strong negative reaction from Uzbekistan. That is why coverage by mass media must play a greater role in disseminating information and drawing attention to the environmental problems of the region.

Notes

1 Secondary analysis refers to re-analysis of previously collected data. The intent is to provide knowledge, conclusions, or interpretations that supplement or differ from that of the first report using the same data.
2 This term was widespread in the Soviet system. According to one definition, voluntarism is a "metaphysical or psychological system that assigns a more predominant role to the will (Latin, *voluntas*) than to the intellect." http://www. merriam-webster.com/dictionary/voluntarism.
3 The newspaper is now named *Egemen Kazakhstan*.

References

Asia Society (2009). *Asia's Next Challenge: Securing the Region's Water Future*, The Leadership Group on Water Security in Asia. Available at http://asiasociety.org/files/pdf/WaterSecurityReport.pdf.

Baklanov, G. (1988). Nothing better than democracy has not yet been invented. *Izvestia*, 2 November.

Borisov, A. (2012). Water tensions overflow in ex-Soviet Central Asia. Available at http://phys.org/news/2012-11-tensions-ex-soviet-central-asia.html.

Dyachenko, A. (2004). The experience of the Chernobyl disaster. Scientific and journalistic monograph to the 18th anniversary of the disaster. Available at http://lizard.jinr.ru/~tina/world/proza/chernbl/glav-1-1.htm.

Ekologicheskoyedvizheniye v SSSR i v sovremennoy Rossii (Environmental movement in the Soviet Union and in modern Russia) (2014). Available at http://aarhus.ngo-tm.org/appendix/Kniga/013.html.

Fomicheva, I.D. (1989). Tribune for public dialogue (Tribuna dlya obshchestvennogo dialoga), in Shkondina, M.V. (ed.), *Journalism and Restructuring (Zhurnalistika i perestroyka)*. Moscow: Moscow State University.

KTK.kz (2012). Karimov arrived in Astana in search of allies. Available at http://www.ktk.kz/ru/news/video/2012/09/08/18911.

Kyrgyzstan Telegraph Agency (2014). Agreement on water allocation will not be revised. Available at http://news.mail.ru/inworld/kazakhstan/economics/19146697/?frommail=1.

Literaturnaya Gazeta (1970). February 11.

Literaturnaya Gazeta (1987). April 22.

Petrov, M. (1987). *Pravda*. June 20.

Shkondina, M. (1989). *Journalism and Perestroika*. Moscow: Moscow State University.

Sizova, L. (1989) The main directions of environmental journalism (Osnovnyye napravleniya ekologicheskoy zhurnalistiki), in Shkondina, M.V. (ed.), *Journalism and Restructuring (Zhurnalistika i perestroyka)*. Moscow: Moscow State University.

Snitkovsky, V. (1998). Chernobyl divination. *Vestnik*. 14 April, p. 189.

Varis, O. (2014). Resources: curb vast water use in Central Asia. *Nature* 514(7520): 27–29.

Verkhoturov, D. (2014). Water myth. *Cawater-info.net*. Available at http://www.cawater-info.net/review/water_myth.htm.

Yertysbaev, E. (2001). *Kazakhstan and Nazarbayev: The Logic of Change*. Elorda: Astana.

Yesdauletov, A. (2013). Environmental issues in the periodical press in Kazakhstan in the years of perestroika (Ekologicheskaya tematika na stranitsakh periodicheskoy pechati kazakhstana v gody perestroyki). Available at enu.kz/repository/repository2014/Aytmuhanbet%20ESDAULETOV.doc.

Zalygin, S. (1986). Turn. Lessons from the same debate. *New World (Novy Mir)*. Available at http://evartist.narod.ru/text8/16.htm.

Zholdasov, A. (2003). Main Turkmenian Canal: lessons from the great building (Glavnyy Turkmenskii kanal: uroki velikoi stroiki). Available at http://cyberleninka.ru/article/n/glavnyy-turkmenskiy-kanal-uroki-velikoy-stroyki.

9 Western news coverage of environmental issues in post-Soviet Central Asia

Eric Freedman, Mark Neuzil, Bruno Takahashi and Christine Carmichael

Introduction

Most Central Asian countries have press systems controlled tightly by their governments and their proxies – political parties, members of the presidents' family and friends, and financial-industrial groups. Those press systems, even that of Kyrgyzstan – the most democratic of the countries on a comparative scale – are rated as "not free" by the nongovernmental organization Freedom House (2015). The Reporters sans Frontières (2014) press freedom survey ranks the region's two most repressitarian[1] governments among the near180 countries: Uzbekistan (166th) and Turkmenistan (178th). Domestic and international press and human rights advocacy organizations frequently criticize all five regimes for individual and systemic rights violations. Overall, as one study observed, "the pattern of press controls in Central Asia remains disturbing. At no time since independence has any of these countries seriously pursued comprehensive liberalization of constraints or *de facto* recognition of the importance of free expression. Although several countries – most notably Kyrgyzstan – have undergone periods of liberalization, there has been no sustained improvement" (Freedman and Shafer, 2014).

As for environmental coverage, Justin Burke, editor of EurasiaNet, an international news organization that intensively reports on policy issues in Central Asia, described the environment as "one of the more underreported topics, and we feel a commitment to cover it wherever we can and whenever we can, whatever the country. There are certain areas where there are glaring needs: water pollution and water usage is a vital issue. Mining and energy production and the consequences thereof is obviously something we follow." He added, "There are some stories that local news can't cover so much, especially when it comes to corruption" (Burke, 2014).

Not all news organizations share that same level of commitment to environmental stories. The Institute for War and Peace Reporting (IWPR), another Western news organization that reports on Central Asia, has reduced its environmental coverage in recent years because that issue hasn't been a priority for its funders, its Central Asia editor, Saule Mukhametrakhimova, said in a 2015 interview with one of the authors.

Any dearth of media coverage of the environment carries severe ramifications. It limits the agenda-setting role of the press, impedes potentially powerful advocates of government and corporate transparency, minimizes awareness of threats to the environment and public health, and reduces the ability of international funders and multinational agencies to remediate ecological threats.

Meanwhile, the region's ministries are generally opaque in their operations, and regimes are reluctant to undertake measures to encourage citizen engagement on environmental issues. One limited exception is a small network of Aarhus Centres,[2] which exist to promote public environmental knowledge and participation in Kazakhstan, Tajikistan, and Kyrgyzstan. In late 2014, the Organization for Security and Cooperation in Europe (OSCE) and Kyrgyzstan's State Agency on Environmental Protection and Forestry announced plans to open an Aarhus Centre in the capital of Bishkek. That initiative was intended to "promote access to environmental information, enhance the capacity of the state to ensure greater public participation in decision-making, and ... help to create an atmosphere of trust amongst all relevant stakeholders, most importantly civil society," according to an OSCE official. The country's second-largest city, Osh, already had an Aarhus Centre focused on such topics as "sustainable mining; biodiversity conservation; participatory environmental assessments and action planning; compliance with environmental legislation; and the monitoring of uranium tailing sites." The Osh and Bishkek centers would work closely together "to build a national dialogue on environmental issues," according to the announcement (*Times of Central Asia*, 2014).

Statutory and regulatory barriers also make it difficult to establish grassroots eco-NGOs (ENGOs). In a survey-based study of ENGOs in Kazakhstan, Soltys examined the effectiveness and influence of both "authentic" ENGOs and those that are fronts for government.

> Are ENGOs the harbingers of the democratisation of the country that many observers hope to see? Given increases in the nation's budgets for the environment and easing of NGO/ENGO legislation, the institutionalising project would seem to have some prospects for success. Concomitantly, the participation of civic groups in the policy arena has contributed to better governance through experiments in new forms of state-society partnership. However, these partnerships have under-performed. Local governments face conflicting demands, while the insufficient administrative and technical capacity of state agencies highlights the need for capacity building. On the political level, authentic ENGOs must compete for policy inclusion with co-opted "front" organisations selectively favoured by the national government, at the same time that the government's ambiguity towards ENGOs retards the latter's institutionalisation. The immediate future of environmental civic society is uncertain.
>
> (Soltys, 2013, p. 342)

This chapter is a content analysis of English-language news stories posted in 2012–2013 by United States-based EurasiaNet (www.eurasianet.org) and United Kingdom-based IWPR (www.iwpr.net). Both news outlets post their stories in English; EurasiaNet also posts its stories in Russian, and IWPR posts in national languages. We selected these two well-established media organizations because they regularly cover a broad range of public policy issues in Central Asia, use Western-style methods of newsgathering and news dissemination, and follow Western-style standards for fairness, balance, accuracy, and ethical reporting. While other Western news organizations such as the British Broadcasting Corporation, *Financial Times*, and Associated Press also report about the region, their coverage is either more sporadic or focused on a specific non-environmental theme (for example, Forum 18 News Service covers religious freedom issues). To illustrate: While the Kumtor gold mining controversy in Kyrgyzstan received extensive coverage by EurasiaNet, *The New York Times* published only one article on the topic in 2012–2013 (Roth, 2013). Also during the two-year study period, the Aral Sea received only passing references in the *Times*.

IWPR in London describes itself as "an international not-for-profit organisation governed by senior journalists, experts in peace-building, development and human-rights, regional specialists and business professionals ... IWPR employs skilled staff and expert consultants in a variety of fields to support its capacity-building activities and to assist in providing journalists, civil society, and civic activists with the basic and advanced skills and knowledge that support sustainable and positive change..." (IWPR, 2015). It has about ten staff members in offices in Kazakhstan, Kyrgyzstan, and Tajikistan, as well as a couple of dozen contributing writers in the region.

EurasiaNet, headquartered in New York City, is part of the Open Society Foundations Eurasia Program. It describes itself as providing "information and analysis about political, economic, environmental, and social developments in the countries of Central Asia and the Caucasus, as well as in Russia, Ukraine, Moldova, Turkey, and Southwest Asia ... EurasiaNet.org advocates open and informed discussion of issues that concern countries in the region. The web site presents a variety of perspectives on contemporary developments, utilizing a network of correspondents based both in the West and in the region. The aim of EurasiaNet.org is to promote informed decision making among policy makers, as well as broadening interest in the region among the general public" (EurasiaNet. org, 2015).

EurasiaNet has a Moscow-based Central Asia editor, David Trilling, who oversees a network of about twenty journalists who contribute to the news outlet. He assigns stories, receives story pitches – ideas – from those contributors, and spends a week or two every six weeks in the region to do his own reporting.

Speaking about environmental coverage in the region, EurasiaNet editor Burke said in an interview, "There are certain areas where there are glaring needs. Water pollution and water usage is a vital issue. Mining and energy production and the consequences thereof is obviously something we follow. In Kyrgyzstan in particular, the Kumtor mine is something we always stay on top of because it's the most valuable asset in the Kyrgyzstan state." The Kumtor story involves questions of environmental damage, corruption, economics, and political control (Trilling, 2014).

In a 2015 interview, Trilling said many sources for environmental stories "are too difficult to get or are hung up in local political controversies." In a region with vast expanses of land and many remote communities, economics also limit coverage because of travel expenses and available time.

David Mould, a Western journalism educator and trainer with extensive Central Asia experience, discussed lessons he learned from conducting workshops about environmental coverage:

> Compared with politics, celebrity sex scandals, crime and other contact sports, the environment seems dull. It's a challenge to convince editors that the issues are worth covering, and to have journalists conduct research on complex topics involving statistics, scientific data, and sometimes conflicting evidence. They are overly reverent towards scientists and experts. I ask them: You don't trust politicians, right? The heads nod. Well, should you trust scientists and environmental experts any more than politicians? They agree, at least in principle, but faced with bulky reports and tables of data, it's easier to package rather than to probe.
>
> (Mould, 2016)

Research questions

The research questions examine the environmental issues covered by EurasiaNet and IWPR, the countries involved in those news events, the sources used, and the balance of views in those stories.

- RQ1: What environmental issues did these news organizations cover in 2012–2013?
- RQ2: With what frequency did news organizations cover environmental issues in each Central Asian country?
- RQ3: What types of sources did reporters use in these stories?
- RQ4: To what extent do news stories reflect balanced reporting?
- RQ5: To what extent were issue-experts used as sources in these environmental news stories?
- RQ6: To what extent did these environmental news stories use non-experts as sources?

Methodology

Few published studies have incorporated content analysis of Central Asia news coverage in general and environmental coverage in particular. Principal reasons include the limited lifespan of many media outlets and the lack of comprehensive, accessible archives. Many news media in the region are short-lived, sometimes created by a political party or an aspiring politician in the run-up to an election. Because of the scarcity of advertising and circulation revenue, news outlets supported by international NGOs may stop publishing or broadcasting when foreign subsidies end. Others are shut down directly by government action or court orders, including financially crippling libel judgments. Even longer-lived media often maintain poor electronic archives or do without archives that researchers could use for their studies. Additionally, under autocratic regimes, constraints on academic freedom deter local media scholars, especially when their inquiries might highlight weaknesses in coverage of public affairs such as environmental controversies.

An exception is a recent study (Sultanalieva and Freedman, 2015) of environmental coverage by two leading Russian-language news organizations in Kyrgyzstan, the newspaper *Vecherniy Bishkek* and the online news website 24.kg. Using content analysis, survey research, and interviews, that study found: ecological issues did not appear regularly in either news outlet during the study period; government agencies and officials were the dominant news sources for both news outlets; and ENGOs failed to effectively convey information, analysis, and opinion to journalists. In addition, the study found a stark disconnect between the environmental issues those news organizations covered and the issues that local ENGOs considered most pressing.

Rather than look at domestic coverage of environmental issues, some scholarship has content-analyzed foreign media's coverage of public affairs topics. One such study (Freedman, 2005) examined how three Western news organizations – IWPR, EurasiaNet, and the United Nations-affiliated IRIN News – covered environment and environmental health in the region. It found that about 25 percent of the articles cited unnamed sources and that the three most commonly covered topics were environmental health, water, and natural disasters. It observed that those Western news organizations do the type of reporting that domestic Central Asian media usually cannot do.

This study looks at foreign coverage of environmental issues, specifically fairness, balance, and sourcing in stories about environmental and environmental health issues and events in the five countries in 2012–2013. Its core assumption is that most environmental stories involve more than one "side" or perspective, that major contenders in these issues can be identified, and that assertions made about them can be isolated. It is then possible to examine how the news organizations treat the contending sides by measuring the space and prominence they get in news stories. These stories focus on environment-related policies, events, research findings, and controversies. To be included, a story must have at least three paragraphs about the environment or environmental health. Stories may involve legislative, judicial, or executive branches of government at local, district, national, or international levels. They also may involve businesses, NGOs, researchers, educational institutions, and/or multinational organizations.

The data set includes stories by staff, freelancers, and correspondents, as well as stories reposted from partner news organizations such as Radio Free Europe/ Radio Liberty. Editorials are excluded.

We define a news source as a person, organization, or document that gives information to reporters. A source is explicitly identified when reporters quote or paraphrase information from that source. In media studies, the means by which reporters publicly credit a source for a story is called "attribution." Attribution is signaled when a source's name is linked with verbs such as "said" or "claimed." Attribution may also be made by verbs denoting a source's state of mind, such as "thinks," "feels," or "wants." Broad categories of individuals to whom an assertion is attributed (for example, "residents say" or "experts state …") are not considered sources. Also, we assume that information not clearly attributed to a source originated from the reporter's direct observation of actions or events. Sources can be considered advocacy or non-advocacy as determined by their publicly declared position on an issue or event.

Our study divides sources into three categories:

- Advocacy sources: An *advocacy source* is one whose assertions suggest a specific course of political action or point of view on an issue. This category excludes assertions from expert sources intending to define or identify a problem.
- A *non-advocacy issue source* has not explicitly advocated a position on the topic in any relevant story. Rather, such sources illuminate or explain some aspect of the issues it raises. An issue-expert source is any person cited in stories because of his or her institutional or background credentials to evaluate or interpret the issues.
- Ordinary people: These are *non-expert, non-advocacy sources* who comment on an environmental or environmental health issue – for example, "a farmer in Osh." They or their family, business, or community are usually affected by the issue.

Sources in any of these categories may be anonymous. If so, their full names are omitted or changed in the story to protect their identities. This is common in a region where people may fear official or unofficial repercussions if they are identified in the press as critics of government or other powerful interests. For example, an IWPR article about electricity cut-offs in the capital of Uzbekistan quoted "a Tashkent-based economist who asked to remain anonymous" and "an energy-sector employee in Tashkent," while identifying only one source by name, "an Uzbek political analyst based in the United States" (IWPR, 2012a). Mukhametrakhimova (2015) explained, "As a reporter or as a journalist, you want to get as close to a source as possible, but we are sometimes happy to accept an anonymous source. Otherwise we don't get any. Anonymity also extends to some people, ordinary people on the street, if we interview them on topics that are very sensitive for political reasons or any other reason, mostly political reasons."

Intercoder reliability with two coders was calculated for all the variables reported using fourteen news articles. Reliability scores, based on Krippendorff's Alpha, ranged from 0.71 to 0.85 and were deemed acceptable for coding of the full sample and analysis. Two coders then split the sample in half and coded the rest of the articles.

A cautionary note: As Soltys (2013) explained, some ENGOs are "fronts" for government. That status is not transparent but is apt to influence the views expressed by their experts and leaders, whether classified as advocacy sources or non-advocacy expert sources.

Interviews with two EurasiaNet journalists and an IWPR editor supplement our content analysis.

Findings

RQ1 asked about the environmental issues that EurasiaNet and IWPR covered in 2012–2013.

The analysis (see Table 9.1) shows that coverage focused mostly on mining (32.1 percent of stories) and energy (29.4 percent). Most mining-related stories involved the Canadian-owned Kumtor gold mine in Kyrgyzstan, and most of those reported primarily on political and economic aspects rather than on environmental aspects of the controversy. For example: mine officials "have regularly complained about shakedowns and threats from locals purporting to represent villagers' environmental concerns" (Trilling, 2013). Similarly, energy-related articles often centered on regional political conflict – such as tensions between Tajikistan and Uzbekistan concerning the supply of natural gas and a proposed hydroelectric dam project – rather than environmental ramifications.

Other issues in stories overlap as well, such as water and agriculture. Although IWPR now provides less environmental coverage than in the past, the environment sometimes provides an important component in stories that fit the organization's current priorities. Mukhametrakhimova (2015) gave the example of how a story about the impact of oil production on the population along Kazakhstan's side of the Caspian Sea may include its effects on wildlife.

The two news organizations paid limited attention to major global issues such as climate change, a fact that may reflect the interests of the correspondents and their editors, the perceived interests of their audiences, or the relative ease or difficulty in covering more localized environmental controversies.

RQ2 asked about the frequency of coverage of each country. The analysis (see Table 9.2) found that most news stories were about Kyrgyzstan (35.8 percent) and Kazakhstan (21.1 percent), with limited coverage of the other countries. Only 5.5 percent of stories were about Tajikistan. There are at least two possible explanations for this result.

First, it is easier for Western journalists to get into and travel around Kyrgyzstan and Kazakhstan. Citizens of the United States, Canada, United Kingdom, and most European Union countries no longer need a visa for visits of up to three months in Kyrgyzstan. Meanwhile, Kazakhstan is experimenting with waiving the requirement for visas for stays of up to fifteen days for visitors from the U.S., U.K., France, Italy, Netherlands, and Germany. The other three countries require visas. The comparatively tighter constraints on the media in Tajikistan and especially

Table 9.1 Dominant environmental issue

	Frequency	Percent
Mining	35	32.1
Energy	32	29.4
Water	10	9.2
Animal issues	9	8.3
Agriculture	6	5.5
Pollution	4	3.7
Other	13	11.9
Total	109	100

Uzbekistan and Turkmenistan make it more difficult for Western journalists and for domestic freelancers for Western news organizations to operate.

Second, the region's most contentious and high-profile environmental controversies during the two-year study period occurred in Kyrgyzstan and Kazakhstan.

RQ3 asked about the number of advocacy sources cited in environmental news stories. The results of the analysis show that slightly more than half of the stories, 53.2 percent, included more than one advocacy source. Approximately 46 percent of the stories included one source or none.

The 4th research question asked about balance in environmental news stories. The results (see Table 9.3) show that only 11.9 percent of these stories presented a balanced use of assertions. More than 60 percent of stories favored one advocacy position over others.

RQ5 asked the extent to which issue experts appeared as sources in environmental news stories.

More than half the stories included at least one issue expert source (see Table 9.4). Among them, stories citing one (24.8 percent) or two (20.2 percent) experts were the most frequent. In addition we tallied the number of paragraphs attributed

Table 9.2 Country of coverage

	Frequency	Percent
Kyrgyzstan	39	35.8
Kazakhstan	23	21.1
Uzbekistan	13	11.9
Turkmenistan	12	11.0
Tajikistan	6	5.5
Central Asia as a region	11	10.1
Other	5	4.6
Total	109	100

Table 9.3 Balance

	Frequency	Percent
Favors A	66	60.6
Favors B	12	11.0
Balanced	13	11.9
None	18	16.5
Total	109	100

Table 9.4 Issue expert sources

	Frequency	Percent
None	47	43.1
1	27	24.8
2	22	20.2
3	4	3.7
4	7	6.4
5	2	1.8
Total	109	100

to issue experts in each story. In this respect, about half the stories included from one to five paragraphs attributed to issue experts (see Table 9.5). At one end of the spectrum, there were no expert sources cited in an article about how a brewery in Kazakhstan is donating part of the proceeds from souvenir cans of beer to protect golden eagles, "the endangered bird of prey that has iconic status" in the country (Bartlett, 2013). At the other end of the spectrum, a heavily expert-dependent story about an energy project cites experts from the Asian Development Bank and a Russian parliamentary think tank analyst, among others, although only one is named (EurasiaNet, 2013).

Table 9.5 Issue expert paragraphs

	Frequency	Percent
None	47	43.1
1	18	16.5
2	13	11.9
3	7	6.4
4	8	7.3
5	4	3.7
6 or more	12	11.0
Total	109	100

Table 9.6 Non-expert sources

	Frequency	*Percent*
None	91	83.5
1	9	8.3
2	4	3.7
3	1	0.9
4	3	2.8
5	1	0.9
Total	109	100

The 6th research question asked how often non-experts appeared as sources in environmental news stories. The analysis (see Table 9.6) found that non-expert sources were rarely used (16.5 percent). Among them, most included only one non-expert source (nine stories). Given the repressive nature of governments in the region and the fear many residents have of retaliation for public criticism, it is unsurprising that many ordinary people agree to be interviewed as non-expert sources only on condition of anonymity. To illustrate, an article about extensive industry-related and electric power-related pollution in the city of Angren, Uzbekistan, identifies a local resident only by his first name, Berdimurat, and age, 57, as he blames pollution for his worsening respiratory problems (IWPR, 2012b).

Journalists also must consider the credibility of prospective sources. Trilling points to such factors as lack of education, the prevalence of rumors, and the fact that "people are easily swayed when someone comes by and says something is damaging the land." In an interview (2015), he commented, "In Central Asia, a lot of people will scream but not have evidence." He gives the example of villagers in southern Kyrgyzstan who may claim that gold mining in a nearby valley is causing their beards to fall out and killing their livestock, "but without any evidence I can use or follow up on."

In addition, the number of paragraphs attributed to non-experts in each story was relatively low (see Table 9.7) compared to the number of paragraphs attributed to issue expert sources.

Discussion and conclusions

Research into foreign rather than domestic coverage of environmental issues offers advantages and limitations. Among the advantages from scholars' perspective are the availability of current and archived content to analyze and the wider ability to present and publish their results outside Central Asia in an atmosphere of academic freedom.

Unfortunately, there have been few qualitative studies published about environmental journalism in Central Asia (for example, Toralieva, 2011;

Table 9.7 Non-expert paragraphs

	Frequency	Percent
None	91	83.5
1	3	2.8
2	3	2.8
3	1	0.9
4	1	0.9
5	2	1.8
6	5	4.6
7 or more	3	2.7
Total	109	100

Freedman, 2014). Given the importance of environmental and environmental health news, we hope future content analysis by scholars in and outside of Central Asia will contribute to a better understanding of how local private, state, and independent media report on such issues.

Foreign news organizations and their journalists – even their local freelancers – often can operate more freely than their domestic counterparts because their economic survival does not depend on the good graces or corruption of government officials and regulatory agencies. Even so, they do run the risks of censorship, website blockages, and expulsion of non-citizen journalists. Foreign correspondents often lack proficiency in Russian and the region's national and ethnic languages, as well as an incomplete understanding of local culture and history, hampering their ability to communicate with sources and possibly coloring their reporting. As one study observed, "Western journalists who report from the region take an arguably valid gloom-and-doom perspective on such stories" (Freedman, 2005, p. 303).

In addition, coverage of environmental issues by foreign media can influence decision-making about projects and financial commitments from international funders and environmental advocacy groups such as the United Nations Environmental Programme, World Bank, Nature Conservancy, and United Nations Development Programme. Such coverage can also affect investment and project decisions by businesses already operating in the region or thinking about doing so.

Foreign coverage can impact the news agenda for local media outlets. That is because domestic news organizations sometimes reprint, rewrite, or follow up on foreign news stories that they missed, lacked the resources to cover, or were afraid to cover on their own. EurasiaNet's Burke (2014) noted that about one-quarter of his organization's Twitter followers are journalists, adding, "We are basically serving as a tripwire for story ideas." In effect, the fact that a foreign news outlet initially breaks an environmental story can provide cover for local follow-up, especially in the less repressitarian countries.

Yet it is crucial to remember that most audience members for these and other Western news organizations live outside Central Asia. For example, about 35 to 45 percent of EurasiaNet readers are in North America, 25 percent in Western Europe, and only 30 percent in Central Asia and the Caucasus, according to Burke. A significant share of its audience in the countries it covers read EurasiaNet in Russian, as does 22 percent of its overall audience globally. The interests of foreign audiences play a role in what issues are covered as well, according to Trilling (2015). For example, he said EurasiaNet readers have high interest in tailings from Soviet-era uranium mines, especially in the Ferghana Valley. Access to those sites is tough except in Kyrgyzstan, where "you can just drive up to these places." Yet readers are less interested in environmental problems with small mining enterprises. Even so, "we can write stories without worrying about the number of clicks," he said.

For IWPR, Russian speakers in the region are the major target audience. It is Russian-language local newspapers and local websites that are most interested in reprinting or posting its stories, especially if they include interviews with well-known sources, according to Mukhametrakhimova (2015). However, newspapers and websites in national languages sometimes use IWPR material as well.

Local residents who lack access to objective news reports are most at risk from eco-threats. Consider the area of the Kazakhstan steppes near the Semipalatinsk test zone known as the Polygon where the USSR carried out hundreds of nuclear tests. During and after Soviet times, deaths and severe medical problems caused by exposure to radiation have plagued area residents and their animals. Radiation enters the herders' food chain when their livestock graze on contaminated pastures, according to Mould. Yet people stay in the Polygon. He quotes this explanation from a Western medical anthropologist doing research in a small village there: "People believe they are sick from radiation ... but they accept it. Life is hard, anything can kill you – that's their attitude. They have accepted a very difficult life and they are survivors" (Mould, 2016). The local population doesn't receive full information from the government or health officials, nor is there a domestic media system to accurately fill that information gap.

Another limitation is the comparatively greater influence in the region of Russian-language media. For example, a survey in Kazakhstan by the Public Opinion Research Institute in Almaty found that more respondents in that country read newspapers and magazines in Russian (48.5 percent) than in Kazakh (36.9) or both languages (14.6 percent) (Rakisheva, 2014). The reasons include geographic proximity, the stationing of more Russian media journalists in the region, the large number of Central Asians who currently work in Russia, and the fact that more Central Asians are fluent in Russian than in English.

Burke (2014) noted, "There are some stories that local news can't cover so much, especially when it comes to corruption." At the same time, we reiterate the conclusion that Freedman (2005) reached that these Western news outlets do the type of reporting that domestic media cannot carry out because of official, cultural, economic, and self-imposed obstacles, as well as insufficient resources. "This is certainly not to say that many Central Asian journalists lack the professional skills or interest to report about and access such issues with a multiplicity of views and with factual accuracy" (pp. 313–314).

It is unrealistic to believe that a dramatic liberalization of the Central Asian media environment is on the horizon. Interlocking factors of authoritarian traditions, legal and extra-legal constraints on the media, public mistrust of the press, inadequate professional training and ethical standards, self-censorship, cultural and religious values, and weak media resources and economics combine to put such aspirational changes beyond reach – at least for the foreseeable future. One directly related impact is the likelihood that Western journalists will continue to rely heavily on unidentified sources, although that practice can conflict with Western standards of journalism ethics and professionalism. Even experts and government officials are apt to continue demanding anonymity.

That has practical implications for journalistic coverage of the environment, even for foreign news organizations. As EurasiaNet's editor explained, "It's frustrating to try to do anything in Turkmenistan and Uzbekistan. In Kazakhstan, an increasing barrier is the cost of travel, in addition to bureaucratic delays and obstacles. To get our people out of Almaty requires significant travel costs, and we operate on a relatively small – you might even say shoestring – budget, and therefore we have to pick our spots very well" (Burke, 2014).

Notes

1 Repressitarian means both repressive in human rights practices and authoritarian in governance (Freedman et al., 2010).
2 The centers are part of an effort to implement the 1998 United Nations Economic Commission for Europe's Convention on Access to Information, Public Participation in Decision-Making and Access to Justice in Environmental Matters. "By providing a venue where members of the public can meet to discuss environmental concerns, the Aarhus Centres strengthen environmental governance. They assist the public with participating in environmental decision-making and facilitate access to justice on environmental matters sensitizing the public and governments to their shared responsibility for their natural surroundings" (United Nations Economic Commission for Europe, 2015).

References

Bartlett, P. (2013). Kazakhstan: drink beer, save eagles. Available at http://www.eurasianet.org/node/66463.
Burke, Justin (2014, October 24). Interview with E. Freedman, New York City.
EurasiaNet (2013). Central Asia: South Asia energy project a pipe dream? Available at http://www.eurasianet.org/node/67151.
EurasiaNet (2014). About EurasiaNet. Available at http://www.eurasianet.org/node/14733.
Freedman, E. (2005). Coverage of environmental and environmental health news of Central Asia by independent news web sites. In Gervers, M., Bulag, U. E. and Long, G. (eds), *History and Society in Central and Inner Asia* (University of Toronto Asian Institute: Toronto), pp. 297–316.
Freedman, E. (2014). Barriers to coverage of transborder issues in the Ferghana Valley of Central Asia. *Applied Environmental Education & Communication*, 13(1): 48–55.

Freedman, E. and Shafer, R. (2014) Contrasting regional portraits of press rights on post-Soviet terrain: the Baltics vs. the Caucasus and Central Asia. Paper presented to the International Association for Media and Communication Research, Hyderabad, India.

Freedman, E., Shafer, R. and Antonova, S. (2010). Two decades of repression: the persistence of authoritarian controls on the mass media in Central Asia. *Central Asia and the Caucasus*, 11(4): 94–110.

Freedom House (2015). *Freedom of the Press.* Available at www.freedomhouse.org.

Institute for War and Peace Reporting (2015). About. Available at https://iwpr.net/about.

Institute for War and Peace Reporting (2012a). Uzbek capital hit by power cuts. Available at https://iwpr.net/global-voices/uzbek-capital-hit-power-cuts.

Institute for War and Peace Reporting (2012b). Industrial plans prompt health fears in Uzbek city. Available at https://iwpr.net/global-voices/industrial-plans-prompt-health-fears-uzbek-city.

Mould, D. (2016). *Postcards from Central Asia* (Ohio University Press: Athens, OH).

Mukhametrakhimova, S. (2015, 3 February). Skype interview with E. Freedman.

Rakisheva, B. (2014). Impact of media on public opinion. Public Opinion Research Institute. Presentation at Media, Security and Central Asia Seminar, Helsinki, 9 December.

Reporters sans Frontières (2014). *World Press Freedom Index 2014.* Available at http://rsf.org/index2014/en-index2014.php.

Roth, Andrew (2013). Kyrgyzstan declares state of emergency after clashes. *New York Times*, 31 May.

Soltys, D. (2013). Challenges to the institutionalization of environmental NGOs in Kazakhstan's corporatist policy arena. *Journal of Contemporary Asia*, 44(2): 342–362.

Sultanalieva, C. and Freedman, E. (2015). Press coverage of environmental news in Kyrgyzstan and the role of eco-nongovernmental organizations. *Central Asia and the Caucasus*, 16(2): 144–169.

Times of Central Asia (2014). Aarhus Centre to open in Bishkek in 2015. 25 December.

Toralieva, G. (2011). Environmental reporting in Kyrgyzstan. *Problems of Post-Communism*, 58, pp. 58–66.

Trilling, D. (2013). Kyrgyzstan: is purported extortion video a bid to boost foreign investor confidence? EurasiaNet.org. Available at http://www.eurasianet.org/node/67451.

Trilling, D. (2014). Kyrgyzstan's parliament accepts controversial gold mine deal. EurasiaNet.org. Available at http://www.eurasianet.org/node/68011.

Trilling, D. (2015, 29 January). Skype interview with E. Freedman.

United Nations Economic Commission for Europe (2015). Aarhus Centres. Available at http://www.unece.org/env/pp/acintro.html.

Part V
Environmental health

10 Radiation health risk studies associated with nuclear testing in Kazakhstan

Bernd Grosche, Steven L. Simon,
Kazbek N. Apsalikov and Ausrele Kesminiene

Introduction

Detrimental health effects from environmental radiation exposures in Kazakhstan derive from nuclear weapons testing and uranium mining. With respect to uranium mining, some efforts have been made to assess its impact on the environment (Kazymbet and Seisebaev, 2002; Stegnar et al., 2013) but with little attention paid to possible health consequences, either to miners or to the general population living close to the mines. However, possible health consequences of nuclear weapons testing have drawn greater attention from researchers.

The former Soviet Union's Semipalatinsk nuclear test site (SNTS) is located on the border of the Semipalatinsk (now East Kazakhstan), Pavlodar, and Karaganda oblasts (regions) of Kazakhstan. The test site is named after the city of Semipalatinsk (in Kazakh: Semey) 150 kilometers (90 miles) to its east. The site covers about 18,500 square kilometers (7,140 square miles), which is almost the size of Wales and is larger than Connecticut. In comparison, the United States' Nevada nuclear test site was about 3,500 square kilometers (1,360 square miles).

The SNTS was a major center for nuclear weapons testing by the USSR and where the country conducted its first nuclear bomb test on 29 August 1949. That test replicated the first U.S. nuclear device, Trinity, as a consequence of information leaked from the U.S. Manhattan Project. During the following forty years, 456 nuclear detonations took place, including 111 atmospheric tests (eighty-six in the atmosphere and twenty-five surface events) between 1949 and 1962 (Mikhailov, 1996; Nugent et al., 2000). A further 130 tests took place at the USSR's second nuclear test site, Novaya Zemlya, plus 129 outside those sites (Mikhailov, 1996).

After the Limited Test Ban Treaty, signed in 1963, detonations at SNTS were restricted to underground shafts and tunnels. With a few exceptions, little or no offsite environmental contamination resulted. The exceptions were four cratering events occurring between 1965 and 1968 within the framework of a program for peaceful uses of nuclear energy. That program was designed for earth-moving purposes such as construction of artificial lakes, canals, and harbors. The last event at the SNTS was on 19 October 1989. The total yield of atmospheric events at the site was reportedly the equivalent of 6.58 megatons of TNT, which corresponds to approximately two-thirds of the total estimated Soviet bomb yield (Dubasov et al., 1994).

The SNTS had three major testing areas: Ground Zero, where atmospheric bomb tests were carried out; the Degelen Mountains, where more than 200 underground nuclear explosions occurred; and the Balapan area, where 123 underground explosions were performed with one excavation leading to Lake Chagan (also known as Lake Balapan). The latter is sometimes called "Atomic Lake" because of the still-existing radioactive contamination there (Nugent et al., 2000). During the nuclear testing period, Soviet armed forces strictly controlled access, and no civilian use of the area was permitted.

Research question

Given this history and its continuing legacy for residents of the region and the environment, it is important to understand past studies of the health consequences, including dosimetry efforts, from nuclear testing at the SNTS.[1] Beyond an overview on past health risk studies, it is possible to discuss directions for further research that has implications for the public, as well as for medical costs, the expense of remediation, and future use of the land.

Findings

Exposure of the public

The 111 atmospheric tests at the SNTS were responsible for regional radioactive contamination of the environment and exposure of the public. The most damaging tests in terms of public exposure were conducted on 29 August 1949 (with a yield equivalent to 22 kilotons (kt) of TNT), 24 September 1951 (38 kt), 12 August 1953 (400 kt), and 24 August 1956 (27 kt). The other detonations led to exposure primarily within the confines of the testing ground and not beyond the site.

Settlements adversely affected by the 1949 test were primarily northeast of the site, e.g., Dolon and Cheremushka, although some scientists documented exposure of people living further away, as in the Altai Region of Russia (Shoikhet et al., 2002). The tests of 1951, 1953, and 1956 affected settlements south and southeast of the site, among them Kainar, Karaul, Kaskabulak, Sarzhal, and Znamenka.

Sources of radioactivity – both external and internal exposures – must be considered when estimating the individual doses that inhabitants received. Two types of events caused external exposure: immersion in a radioactive cloud as it passed locations where people resided, and exposure to radioactivity deposited on the ground. In general, exposure to fallout deposited on the ground was greater due, primarily, to the longer exposure time. In contrast, internal exposure resulted from intake of radioactivity into the body as a consequence of breathing, drinking, and eating. Ethnic groups living in the contaminated areas

– predominantly Kazakhs, Russians, and Germans – have different diets so their exposure from food products varied. Generally, intake of contaminated foods such as dairy products, vegetables, and meat resulted in exposure.

In addition, the location of the settlements was significant for the degree of contamination. Studies estimated both external and internal exposure of residents near the SNTS. One of the first such studies, Kurakina et al. (2000), provided dose estimates, although its combination of methods and inputted data were later judged to have overestimated actual exposures. Several international teams have made intensive efforts to assess the doses received and used measurement data from the village of Dolon as the basis to compare methods and findings (Gordeev et al., 2002, 2006; Simon et al., 2003). In particular, progress was made in such assessments during a meeting at the University of Hiroshima, Japan, in 2005 (Stepanenko et al., 2006).

The most evolved dosimetry system to date that estimates both external and internal doses is based on a joint U.S.–Russian dose reconstruction methodology developed from the experience of dose-reconstruction scientists in the two countries (Gordeev et al., 2006; Simon et al., 2006; Beck et al., 2006).

Researchers applied this methodology in a cross-sectional study of thyroid diseases that reconstructed individual thyroid doses from external and internal radiation sources for 2,994 subjects who had been exposed to the 1949, 1951, or 1953 tests. For control purposes, the study included a village thought to be relatively unaffected by the tests. Doses were reconstructed from fallout deposition patterns, residential histories, and data from individual interviews on their diet, in particular consumption of fresh milk and other dairy foods during childhood. Individual external and internal doses to the thyroid averaged 0.04 Gy (range 0–0.65) and 0.31 Gy (0–9.6), respectively (Land et al., 2008). Gray (Gy) is the unit for exposure to ionizing radiation.

Based on the same dosimetric approach used in Land et al. (2008), external whole-body doses were estimated for 7,699 individuals in six of the ten affected settlements included in an analysis of mortality from solid cancers, meaning a malignancy that forms a tumour mass within organ(s), in contrast to lymphoproliferative malignancies like leukemias and lymphomas (Bauer et al., 2005). Estimation was impossible for other settlements because of missing information. The external whole-body doses for these individuals were estimated to range between 0 and more than 0.630 Gy, with an average of about 0.092 Gy (Grosche et al., 2011).

The doses to the thyroid of the cohort considered in Land et al. (2008) were reassessed using additional information on behavioral patterns and more detailed dietary habits from the same cohort, but derived from focus group interviews (Schwerin et al., 2010). The additional data, combined with a Monte Carlo-based statistical sampling strategy to quantify dosimetric uncertainty of doses, was used to reassess the doses (Simon et al., 2015). From that analysis, researchers determined a mean dose from both external and internal exposures of 0.28 Gy (range 0–4.2 Gy) (Land et al., 2015).

Health effects

The first studies of possible negative health consequences from nuclear weapons testing at the SNTS were descriptive. One of the earliest reports examined the age-specific incidence rates of malignant tumors in the Semipalatinsk oblast compared to the general Soviet Union and Kazakhstan populations (Bulbul'ian et al., 1991). Based on survey data collected in five-year intervals from 1949 onward, increased cancer incidence rates were reported in highly exposed villages compared to villages of the Kokpektinskii district (control area) (Gusev et al., 1998). In a study comparing the incidence of childhood cancers in four administrative regions adjacent to the SNTS from 1981 to 1990, higher relative risks for all cancers, leukemia, and brain tumors were reported in children living less than 200 kilometers (125 miles) from the test epicenter compared to those residing more than 400 kilometers (250 miles) from the site (Zaridze et al., 1994). A comprehensive book included information on the incidence and mortality of selected diseases such as cancer, cardiovascular diseases, and mental retardation, as well as the prevalence of congenital malformations (Nugent et al., 2000). Overall, the unfavorable health situation of people living around the test site was clearly demonstrated. None of these studies quantitatively assessed the health outcomes in relation to radiation doses, however.

A cross-sectional study of the prevalence of thyroid diseases was conducted among 2,994 residents of eight villages. It involved ultrasound screening and determined malignancy by cytopathology. In terms of excess relative risk per unit dose, the findings for nodule prevalence were compatible with those from populations exposed to medical X-rays and with atomic bomb survivors (Land et al., 2008). A reanalysis of this data set, using a new approach for dealing with uncertainties (Simon et al., 2015), revealed risk estimates higher (Land et al., 2015) than those calculated in the earlier analysis (Land et al., 2008) based on simple point estimates of dose without uncertainty characterization. In contrast to the earlier findings, the new methods led to the conclusion that the biological effectiveness for internal and external doses was similar.

Regarding thyroid nodules, estimates of excess relative risk per unit dose (ERR/ Gy) from both external and internal exposure for males were markedly higher than for females. This result is based on 177 male and 571 female cases and might partly be due to much higher baseline rates in females. The study found only a small number of thyroid cancers (seven in males, twenty-eight in females). Nonetheless, the ERR/Gy for confirmed cases of papillary thyroid cancers (three in males, eighteen in females) was also comparable to risk estimates from other studies, but not significantly different from zero.

Based on data collected from 1960 to 1991 by the National Research Institute of Radiation Medicine and Ecology (NIIRME), a "historical cohort" was established. It comprised 19,453 individuals, 9,859 from exposed villages and 9,604 from a comparison area. The first analyses of this cohort used the dosimetry system developed by Kurakina et al. (2000) and focused on solid cancer mortality with a follow-up through 1999 (Bauer et al., 2005, 2006). A more recent analysis of mortality from cardiovascular diseases employed improvements of the U.S.–Russian dosimetry system described in Simon et al. (2006) that was developed primarily to study thyroid diseases and was based on application of the method to determine external doses (Grosche et al., 2011; Land et al.; 2008). Findings showed no effects at the given doses, which were 92 milliGray (mGy) on average, with a maximum of 630 mGy (1 milliGray is 1/1000 Gy).

Although higher risks, in particular for cardiovascular diseases, were observed in the population close to the test site compared to those in the comparison area, analysis did not show a dose dependency. It is apparent that the updated doses should be used to re-analyze mortality from both solid cancers and cardiovascular diseases.

Two studies looked into possible genetic radiation effects. The first investigated whether the exposures led to a significant change in the sex ratio – the ratio of males to females – of newborns. Based on 11,464 singleton births from 3,992 mothers exposed to radiation during 1949–1956, the overall sex ratio was 1.07, which was comparable to the current sex ratio in Kazakhstan (1.06) (Mudie et al., 2007). A further 141 deliveries to the 3,992 mothers were twins, and researchers investigated whether radiation exposure and other risk factors influenced the delivery of either same-sex twins or different-sex twins. Only different-sex twinning increased with maternal age. The increase occurred after radiation exposure [OR = 4.08 (95% CI: 1.11, 15.07)] when comparing five years to more than twenty years after exposure. However, this effect was similar in villages with both low and high radiation exposure (Mudie et al., 2010).

Another study, which focused on the frequency of mini-satellite mutation in the control and exposed offspring, found a negative correlation between mutation rate and the parental year of birth in the exposed offspring generation. The highest mutation rate occurred in the most exposed cohort of parents born before 1960 (Dubrova et al., 2002).

To our knowledge, no further studies have been conducted on mental retardation and on congenital malformations as discussed in Nugent et al. (2000).

Databases and registries

Several databases and registries of residents around the SNTS were developed over the past decades. One of these resources is the "historical cohort" that is described earlier in the chapter and comprises almost 20,000 individuals (Bauer et al., 2005). That cohort became a subset of a larger database, the registry of the population in areas of the former Semipalatinsk oblast living near the site. Going back to 1949, that registry is a valuable source of health data, including information on residential histories, vital statistics, and causes of death for more than 100,000 individuals (Katayama et al., 2006). NIIRME in Semey holds the database and updates it annually. More recently, a joint Japanese–Kazakh effort was made to set up a database of exposed residents and those from a comparison area different from that used for the "historical cohort" – including residential history and causes of death (REA, 2010). An ongoing evaluation of these databases within the European Union-funded SEMI-NUC project indicates that they include approximately 100,000 individuals and can be used to set up a cohort for future epidemiological studies (SEMI-NUC, 2015).

Biological material

Numerous studies have collected biological samples from residents of affected areas, of which, to our knowledge, not all have been stored (Gusev et al., 1997; Stephan et al., 2001; Dubrova et al., 2002; Salomaa et al., 2002; Lindholm et al., 2004; Tanaka et al., 2006; Sigurdson et al., 2009). In recent years, NIIRME started collecting blood samples and teeth from people still residing in villages close to the former SNTS and keeping the annotated material in a biological repository (NIIRME, 2013).

Conclusion and discussion

Although nuclear weapons testing is not the only environmental source of radioactive contamination in Kazakhstan, studies of health effects from radiation exposure in the country relate primarily to the area around the SNTS. Effects studied to date include all-cause mortality, cancer mortality, congenital malformations, birth outcome, including the sex ratio of newborns, mortality from cardiovascular diseases, and the occurence of thyroid cancer and nodules.

Overall, people residing close to the test site have a worse health status than residents of a comparison area. There is growing evidence that radiation exposure from the testing adversely impacted the health of the affected population. Because of the long latency times for many cancers, we assume a lingering effect remains among those exposed as children.

Available information from biological studies, with very few exceptions (Sigurdson et al., 2009), have not linked the studied endpoints to the individual exposure characteristics and are, therefore, difficult to evaluate. In the future, a deliberate evaluation of existing biomaterials would be beneficial. Such an evaluation should assess the methods and procedures used for processing and storing samples. Possibilities of applying modern technologies to biological samples collected long-time ago have been validated, and standard operating procedures are available (STORE, 2015).

In particular, it is necessary to properly integrate existing biomaterial into a future multidisciplinary study. Follow-up mechanisms must be developed to allow not only use of mortality data, but also incidence data from such sources as hospital records and the newly established nation-wide population-based cancer registry. Outcomes of interest are non-cancer diseases as well as cancer.

Significant improvements have been made in recent years in retrospective dose estimation. These methods include not only better dosimetry methods for fallout, but also take uncertainties into account. Using these improved methods, further steps should be taken to more accurately estimate the exposure of those affected.

There are additional interesting prospects for future research on the transgenerational effects of exposures from nuclear testing in Kazakhstan. For example, the large NIIRME dataset includes a subset of biological material collected from three generations.

However, one must bear in mind that epidemiological research related to the SNTS faces a number of difficulties: exposures are dominated by the radioactive plumes, but internal exposures also are relevant for some health endpoints. Meanwhile, exposure estimates must be carried out many years after the events, and dose uncertainties which may be substantial should therefore be taken into account (Simon et al., 2015). In the past, biological materials from affected people were not always stored, and it is difficult to link still-available biological material to individuals included in epidemiological studies. NIIRME conducts medical monitoring, but it is a major task to collect information available elsewhere in scattered places.

Studies of individuals affected by atomic bomb testing have the potential to contribute to a better understanding of the risks from radiation exposure. That is especially true because such populations are not selected, unlike nuclear workers, and their exposures are to low doses with low dose rates, in contrast to the population of atomic bomb survivors (Akleyev et al., 2002; Gilbert et al., 2002). Meanwhile, dosimetry remains a difficult task for internal exposure.

Acknowledgements

The participation of Steven L. Simon was made possible by the Intramural Research Program of the National Institutes of Health, National Cancer Institute, Division of Cancer Epidemiology and Genetics. The SEMI-NUC project is funded by the European Commission under Grant Agreement 323310 (FP7).

Note

1 Numerous biological studies have been conducted in the past that are outside the scope of this review.

References

Akleyev, A. V., Grosche, B., Gusev, B. I., Kiselev, V. I., Kisselev, M. F., Kolyado, I. B., Romanov, S., Shoikhet, Y. N. and Neta, R. (2002). Developing additional resources. *Radiation and Environmental Biophysics*, 41(1): 13–18.

Bauer, S., Gusev, B. I., Pivina, L. M., Apsalikov, K. N., and Grosche, B. (2005). Radiation exposure due to local fallout from Soviet atmospheric nuclear weapons testing in Kazakhstan: solid cancer mortality in the Semipalatinsk historical cohort, 1960–1999. *Radiation Research*, 164(4): 409–419.

Bauer, S., Gusev, B. I., Pivina, L. M., Apsalikov, K. N. and Grosche, B. (2006). Esophagus cancer and radiation exposure due to nuclear test fallout: an analysis based on the data of the Semipalatinsk historical cohort, 1960–1999. *Radiatsonnaya Biologiya Radioecologiya*, 46: 611–618.

Beck, H. L., Anspaugh, L. R., Bouville, A. and Simon, S. L. (2006). Review of methods of dose estimation for epidemiological studies of the radiological impact of Nevada test site and global fallout. *Radiation Research*, 166(1): 209–218.

Bulbul'ian, M. A. and Tokareva, G. D. (1991). Deskriptivnoe epidemiologicheskoe issledovanie zlokachestvennykh novoobrazovanii v Semipalatinskoi oblasti Kazakhskoi SSR [Descriptive epidemiological study of malignant neoplasms in the Semipalatinsk district of the Kazakh S. S. R.]. *Vestnik Akadademii Meditsinskikh Nauk SSSR*, 7: 59–63.

Dubasov, Y. V., Zelentsov, S. A., Matushchenko, A. M., Tsyrkov, T. A., Logachev, V. A. and Chernyshov, A. K. (1994). Chronology of nuclear testing at the Semipalatinsk Polygon and the radiation characteristics of nuclear tests. In *Radioactivity from Nuclear Test Explosions: The Human and Environmental Consequences*. Institute of Regional Medico-Ecological Problems, Barnaul.

Dubrova, Y. E., Bersimbaev, R. I., Djansugurova, L. B., Tankimanova, M. K., Mamyrbaeva, Z. Z., Mustonen, R., Lindholm, C., Hulten, M. and Salomaa, S. (2002). Nuclear weapons tests and human germline mutation rate. *Science*, 295(5557): 1037.

Gilbert, E. S., Land, C. E. and Simon, S. L. (2002). Health effects from fallout. *Health Physics*, 82: 726–735.

Gordeev, K., Shinkarev, S., Ilyin, L., Bouville, A., Hoshi, M., Luckyanov, N. and Simon, S. L. (2006). Retrospective dose assessment for the population living in areas of local fallout from the Semipalatinsk nuclear test site Part I: External exposure. *Journal of Radiation Research (Tokyo)*, 47 Supplement A: A129–136.

Gordeev, K., Vasilenko, I., Lebedev, A., Bouville, A., Luckyanov, N., Simon, S. L., Stepanov, Y., Shinkarev, S. and Anspaugh, L. (2002). Fallout from nuclear tests: dosimetry in Kazakhstan. *Radiation and Environmental Biophysics*, 41: 61–68.

Grosche, B., Lackland, D. T., Land, C. E., Simon, S. L., Apsalikov, K. N., Pivina, L. M., Bauer, S. and Gusev, B. I. (2011). Mortality from cardiovascular diseases in the Semipalatinsk historical cohort, 1960–1999, and its relationship to radiation exposure. *Radiation Research*, 176(5): 660–669.

Gusev, B. I., Abylkassimova, Z. N. and Apsalikov, K. N. (1997). The Semipalatinsk nuclear test site: a first assessment of the radiological situation and the test-related radiation doses in the surrounding territories. *Radiation and Environmental Biophysics*, 36(3): 201–204.

Gusev, B. I., Rosenson, R. I. and Abylkassimova, Z. N. (1998). The Semipalatinsk nuclear test site: a first analysis of solid cancer incidence (selected sites) due to test-related radiation. *Radiation and Environmental Biophysics*, 37(3): 209–214.

Izrael, Y. A. (2002). *Radioactive Fallout After Nuclear Explosions and Accidents* (Elsevier: Amsterdam).

Katayama, H., Apsalikov, K. N., Gusev, B. I., Galich, B., Madieva, M., Koshpessova, G., Abdikarimova, A. and Hoshi, M. (2006). An attempt to develop a database for epidemiological research in Semipalatinsk. *Journal of Radiation Research (Tokyo)*, 47 Supplement A: A189–197.

Kazymbet, P. K., and Seisebaev, A. T. (2002). Problems of the complex assessment of radiobioecological situation and public health in uranium-extraction regions of Kazakhstan. *Radiatsonnaya Biologiya Radioecologiya*, 42: 750–753.

Kurakina, N. N., Sekerbaev, A. K., Gusev, B. I., and Ospanov, E. K. (2000). *Otsenka pogloshchennikh i effektivnykh doz ioniziruiushchikh izluchenii u naseleniia, prozhivaiushchego na radioaktivnikh sledakh iadernikh vzryvov. Metodicheskie ukazaniia dlia spetsialistov po radiatsionnoi meditsine i radioekologii* [Assessment of absorbed and effective radiation doses in the population living on the radioactive traces of nuclear tests. Methodological guidelines for experts in radiation medicine and ecology]. Semipalatinsk/Almaty.

Land, C. E., Kwon, D., Hoffman, F. O., Moroz, B., Drozdovitch, V., Bouville, A., Beck, H., Luckyanov, N., Weinstock, R. M. and Simon, S. L. (2015). Accounting for shared and unshared dosimetric uncertainties in the dose response for ultrasound-detected thyroid nodules after exposure to radioactive fallout. *Radiation Research*, 183(2): 159–173.

Land, C. E., Zhumadilov, Z., Gusev, B. I., Hartshorne, M. H., Wiest, P. W., Woodward, P. W., Crooks, L. A., Luckyanov, N. K., Fillmore, C. M., Carr, Z., Abisheva, G., Beck, H. L., Bouville, A., Langer, J., Weinstock, R., Gordeev, K. I., Shinkarev, S. and Simon, S. L. (2008). Ultrasound-detected thyroid nodule prevalence and radiation dose from fallout. *Radiation Research*, 169(4): 373–383.

Lindholm, C., Murphy, B. P., Bigbee, W. L., Bersimbaev, R. I., Hulten, M. A., Dubrova, Y. E. and Salomaa, S. (2004). Glycophorin A somatic cell mutations in a population living in the proximity of the Semipalatinsk nuclear test site. *Radiation Research*, 162(2): 164–170.

Mikhailov, V. N. (1996). *Nuclear Weapons Tests and Peaceful Nuclear Explosions in the USSR 1949–1990*. (Ministry of the Russian Federation on Atomic Energy and Ministry of Defense of the Russian Federation: Moscow).

Mudie, N. Y., Gusev, B. I., Pivina, L. M., Schoemaker, M. J., Rijinkova, O. N, Apsalikov, K. N., and Swerdlow, A. J. (2007). Sex ratio in the offspring of parents with chronic radiation exposure from nuclear testing in Kazakhstan. *Radiation Research*, 168(5): 600–607.

Mudie, N. Y., Swerdlow, A. J., Gusev, B. I., Schoemaker, M. J., Pivina, L. M., Chsherbakova, S., Mansarina, A., Bauer, S., Jakovlev, Y. and Apsalikov, K. N. (2010). Twinning in the offspring of parents with chronic radiation exposure from nuclear testing in Kazakhstan. *Radiation Research*, 173(6): 829–836.

NIIRME (2013). The Research Institute for Radiation Medicine and Ecology. Available at http://de.slideshare.net/IRPslideshare/inst-radiology-med.

Nugent, R. W., Zhumadilov, Z. S., Gusev, B. I. and Hoshi, M. (2000). *Health Effects of Radiation Associated with Nuclear Weapons Testing at the Semipalatinsk Test Site* (Hiroshima: Nakamoto Sogo Printing Co.).

Radiation Effects Association (2010). *Study on Health Effects of Radiation on Residents Near the Former Semipalatinsk Nuclear Test Site. The Final Report of the 2001–2009 Study*. Radiation Effects Association, Tokyo.

Salomaa, S., Lindholm, C., Tankimanova, M. K., Mamyrbaeva, Z. Z., Koivistoinen, A., Hulten, M., Mustonen, R., Dubrova, Y. E. and Bersimbaev, R. I. (2002). Stable chromosome aberrations in the lymphocytes of a population living in the vicinity of the Semipalatinsk nuclear test site. *Radiation Research*, 158(5): 591–596.

Schwerin, M., Schonfeld, S., Drozdovitch, V., Akimzhanov, K., Aldyngurov, D., Bouville, A., Land, C., Luckyanov, N., Mabuchi, K., Semenova, Y., Simon, S., Tokaeva, A., Zhumadilov, Z. and Potischman, N. (2010). The utility of focus group interviews to capture dietary consumption data in the distant past: dairy consumption in Kazakhstan villages 50 years ago. *Journal of Developmental Origins of Health and Disease*, 1(4): 280–280.

SEMI-NUC (2015). Prospective cohort study of residents near the Semipalatinsk nuclear test site – feasibility. Available at http://cordis.europa.eu/projects/rcn/108459_en.html.

Shoikhet, Y. N., Kiselev, V. I., Algazin, A. I., Kolyado, I. B., Bauer, S. and Grosche, B. (2002). Fallout from nuclear tests: health effects in the Altai region. *Radiation and Environmental Biophysics*, 41(1): 69–73.

Sigurdson, A. J., Land, C. E., Bhatti, P., Pineda, M., Brenner, A., Carr, Z., Gusev, B. I., Zhumadilov, Z., Simon, S. L., Bouville, A., Rutter, L., Ron, E. and Struewing, J. P.

(2009). Thyroid nodules, polymorphic variants in DNA repair and RET-related genes, and interaction with ionizing radiation exposure from nuclear tests in Kazakhstan. *Radiation Research*, 171(1): 77–88.

Simon, S., Baverstock, K. F. and Lindholm, C. (2003). A summary of evidence on radiation exposures received near to the Semipalatinsk nuclear weapons test site in Kazakhstan. *Health Physics*, 84(6): 718–725.

Simon, S. L., Hoffman, F. O. and Hofer, E. (2015). The two-dimensional Monte Carlo: a new methodologic paradigm for dose reconstruction for epidemiological studies. *Radiation Research*, 183(1): 27–41.

Simon, S. L., Beck, H. L., Gordeev, K., Bouville, A., Anspaugh, L. R., Land, C. E., Luckyanov, N. and Shinkarev, S. (2006). External dose estimates for Dolon village: application of the U.S./Russian joint methodology. *Journal of Radiation Research (Tokyo)*, 47 Supplement A: A143–147.

Stegnar, P., Shishkov, I., Burkitbayev, M., Tolongutov, B., Yunuso, M., Radyuk, R. and Salbu, B. (2013). Assessment of the radiological impact of gamma and radon dose rates at former U mining sites in Central Asia. *Journal of Environmental Radioactivity*, 123: 3–13.

Stepanenko, V.F., Hoshi, M., Bailiff, I. K., Ivannikov, A. I., Toyoda, S., Yamamoto, M., Simon, S. L., Matsuo, M., Kawano, N., Zhumadilov, Z., Sasaki, M. S., Rosenson, R. I. and Apsalikov, K. N. (2006). Around Semipalatinsk nuclear test site: progress of dose estimations relevant to the consequences of nuclear tests (a summary of 3rd Dosimetry Workshop on the Semipalatinsk nuclear test site area, RIRBM, Hiroshima University, Hiroshima, 9–11 March, 2005). *Journal of Radiation Research (Tokyo)*, 47 Supplement A: A1–13.

Stephan, G., Pressl, S., Koshpessova, G. and Gusev, B. I. (2001). Analysis of FISH-painted chromosomes in individuals living near the Semipalatinsk nuclear test site. *Radiation Research*, 155(6): 796–800.

STORE database (2015). Available at http://rbstore.org.

Tanaka, K., Iida, S., Takeichi, N., Chaizhunusova, N. J., Gusev, B. I., Apsalikov, K. N., Inaba, T. and Hoshi, M. (2006). Unstable-type chromosome aberrations in lymphocytes from individuals living near Semipalatinsk nuclear test site. *Journal of Radiation Research (Tokyo)*, 47 Supplement A: A159–164.

Zaridze, D. G., Li, N., Men, T. and Duffy, S. W. (1994). Childhood cancer incidence in relation to distance from the former nuclear testing site in Semipalatinsk, Kazakhstan. *International Journal of Cancer*, 59(4): 471–475.

Part VI
Ecology

11 Kazakhstan's Northern Aral Sea today
Partial ecosystem restoration and economic recovery

Kristopher D. White

Introduction

Occasional popular press headlines over the past decade that lauded the "return" of the Aral Sea (for example, Conant, 2006; Fletcher, 2007; Wester, 2014) are wholly inaccurate and misleading. This becomes abundantly clear once one considers a number of realities confronting the region that was once home to the world's fourth-largest lake in surface area. First, the Aral does not exist and hasn't been a single contiguous body since the late 1980s. Second, far from returning, what was once the Aral continues its recession and desiccation. Third, environmental and socio-economic crisis conditions that led many observers to proclaim the Aral a "disaster" or "catastrophe" continue to prevail throughout most of the region today, particularly in Uzbekistan's autonomous region of Karakalpakstan.

While these are unmistakable realities, there is some basis for the optimistic contemporary headlines. Kazakhstan's Northern Aral Sea (NAS) has stabilized following the 2005 completion of the nearly $86 million Kok-Aral dam and dike complex (The World Bank partially funded the project). In conjunction with related rechanneling and regulation of the Syr Darya's river inflow, this human intervention of a dam and dike ensures that precious positive additions to the NAS water balance are not lost to the south.

Encouraging results appeared much faster than most experts predicted. A modest increase in water level, volume, and surface area has accompanied dramatic reductions in water salinity. Partial ecological restoration has had positive impacts on the river delta, deltaic lakes, migratory bird habitat, biodiversity stocks, and overall ecosystem functioning. With water salinity dropping back to pre-crisis levels and with spawning habitat restored, native fish species have returned to the open lake. For the regional economy, this has resulted in a cautiously modest return of harvesting, processing, and economic export activity. The resulting employment, income, improved socio-economic wellbeing, and greater expenditures in other economic sectors such as retail and construction all represent welcome developments for the regional economy.

Though nowhere near the scale or scope of the fishing industry at its height of the 1950s and early 1960s, these recent improvements have engendered tangible hope and optimism among regional residents, including those not directly involved in fishing. Much of this hope stems from planned future human intervention, further ecological improvements, and expected increases in fish harvests.

This chapter explores recent incremental improvements in Kazakhstan's NAS regional ecological and economic conditions since completion of the Kok-Aral dam and dike complex. An ideal vantage point from which to view these developments is via fish and the fishing industry: harvest, processing, and export. For the region, fish have a uniquely vital combination of both ecological – ecosystem niche-occupying fauna species – and economic – exploitable natural resource, source of employment, income, and export revenue – value. Their return signals a potential reversal of environmental and socio-economic hardships associated with the crisis. Next, the chapter briefly reviews the Aral and its post-1960 desiccation and resultant crisis. The chapter pays particular attention to fishing and this industry's eventual collapse as the crisis worsened. Focus then shifts to the NAS by reviewing sequential restoration efforts between 1992 and 2005 and then discussing post-2005 improvements. The primary focus here is the partial return of the fishing industry and tangible regional benefits from increased harvest, processing, and export of fish. While incorporating recent studies concerning the NAS fishery, this section draws heavily on the author's own observations, discussions, fieldwork, and interviews during visits to the region in 2006, 2008, 2011, and 2014.[1] Furthermore, this chapter discusses likely near-future trajectories for the NAS, highlighting optimism for the region's ecological and socio-economic future.

The Aral Sea crisis and fishery

The post-1960 recession and desiccation of the Aral, once among the world's greatest lakes and spanning the border between southwestern Kazakhstan and northwestern Uzbekistan, has been thoroughly chronicled (for example, see Micklin, 2007; Glantz, 1999; Micklin and Aladin, 2008; Spoor, 1998). So too have the largely anthropogenic causes of this crisis (for example, see Micklin, 1988; Saiko and Zonn, 2000; Levintanus, 1992; Glazovskiy, 1991), disastrous ecological consequences (Kotlyakov, 1991; Aladin and Potts, 1992; Micklin, 1991), and a caustic blend of socio-economic ills associated with economic collapse and poor human health (for example, Small et al., 2001; Ataniyazova et al., 2001; Whish-Wilson, 2002; Crighton et al., 2011; Feshbach and Friendly, 1992). The crisis, with its dire ecological and societal repercussions, is routinely described as among the world's worst environmental disasters. The desiccation of the former seabed, now a new desert named Aralkum (Breckle and Wucherer, 2010) continues nearly unabated (Figure 11.1). This continued anthropogenic desertification process is most recently exemplified by the complete drying of the eastern basin of the southern, Large Aral for the first time in more than six centuries (Kiger, 2014).

Prior to its recession and associated crisis, the Aral once supported a thriving fishing industry that became of great importance to this region's economy by its

Figure 11.1 Continued twenty-first century desiccation and shrinkage of the Aral Sea, 2000 and 2014. Both are moderate resolution imaging spectroradiometer (MODIS) images captured aboard NASA's Terra satellite. The image on the left was captured on 25 August 2000. The image on the right was captured on 19 August 2014.

Source: NASA Earth Observatory, 2014.

peak in the mid-twentieth century. Even prior to the Soviet-era development of an industrial-scale production system that exploited a commodity for harvest, processing, and extra-regional export, fish were important for local residents for millennia. Early Neolithic settlements clustered around the Aral have yielded small spear and harpoon tips hypothesized to have been used for fishing (Boroffka et al., 2005), while more direct evidence of fish skeletal remains have been found in human settlements dating to the third century A.D. (Zonn et al., 2009). Fish from the Aral were clearly important elements of local dietary consumption as a valuable source of protein and as an economic resource for local barter and small-scale trade.

By the nineteenth century with Russian expansion into the Aral Sea basin and construction of a rail line connecting to Moscow, fish could be effectively exported from the region. In a historic lake-wide survey expedition, the first of its kind, Alexei Butakoff spent the winter of 1848–1849 at a fort constructed to safeguard an Orenburg company's fishing operations at the mouth of the Syr Darya (Butakoff, 1853). Extra-regional fish exports featured prominently in a 1921 event that remains a source of pride in Aralsk, Kazakhstan. Facing famine in civil war-ravaged Russian territory, Vladimir I. Lenin composed a letter requesting assistance from Aral fishers. The response of fourteen rail wagons of fish sent to impacted areas is still depicted in a large mural in the waiting hall of the Aralsk train station. The text of Lenin's letter is also inscribed in stone in the city's main square. Aral fishers were also called upon for assistance during the

Second World War – the Great Patriotic War – when canned fish went to Soviet military personnel under the slogan "More fish to the front and to the country" (Landsforeningen, 2003, p. 5).

By the mid-20th century, the Aral fishery accounted for 7 percent of the U.S.S.R.'s total inland fish harvests and represented 13 percent of Soviet commercial fish stocks (Zholdasova, 1999). While arguably not of major importance to the Soviet Union overall, this fishery was vital to the immediate regional economy, to Aral fishers, and to the two main processing centers of Aralsk, Kazakhstan, and Muynak, Uzbekistan. In Aralsk, the Aralrybprom fish processing plant supported a workforce of 3,000, and processed more than 20,000 tons annually (Thorpe and Van Anrooy, 2009). In Muynak, the Muynak Fish Canning Factory produced nearly 22 million cans of fish at its peak in 1958 and was then "one of the largest enterprises in the Soviet Union" (Zonn, 2010, p. 69). Fish harvests peaked in 1957, when 48,000 tons were caught across the entire lake (Micklin, 1988).

The well-documented demise of the Aral after 1960 with its shrinking surface area, declining volume, and dramatic increases in salinity corresponded with a decline and eventual collapse of its commercial fishery. With 1957 representing the height of harvests (48,000 tons), the total dropped by more than half in just a decade (less than 22,000 tons harvested in 1967). By 1977, just over 6,000 tons were harvested, and by 1984 commercial harvests reached zero. Incredibly, the fishery experienced its historical peak and complete collapse in a period of fewer than thirty years (White, 2014). Prior to the start of its modern desiccation in 1960, the Aral was home to twenty native species of fish, including twelve species (representing 60 percent of all fish biomass) of carp (*Cyprinidae*).

Through the 1980s, fourteen additional species were introduced into the Aral but the only one able to acclimate, survive, and reproduce in the then-high-salinity open lake was the Black Sea flounder (*Platichthys flesus*) brought from the Sea of Azov (Ermakhanov et al., 2012). As salinity levels continued to rise, southern portions of the sea became unfit habitat even for the salt-tolerant flounder. By then, all other species had either become extinct, such as the Aral salmon (*Salmo trutta aralensis*) or had vacated the lake for the deltas, deltaic lakes, or courses of the Aral's feeder rivers, Syr Darya in the north and Amu Darya in the south.

The Northern Aral Sea restoration efforts

By 1989, the plummeting volume and receding shoreline had produced a smaller detached "exclave" in the north. The resulting NAS became – and remains – a separate, distinct lake fed primarily by the Syr Darya and located entirely in Kazakhstan. Groundwater and precipitation on its surface also contribute to a much lesser extent. Compared to 1960, this part of the lake represents only about 9 percent of surface area and 7 percent of volume of the entire Aral. As a result of its relative size, the NAS is often referred to as the "Little" or "Small" Aral (White, 2013). Efforts to preserve the integrity of the NAS began in earnest not long after the 1991 dissolution of the U.S.S.R. The distinct possibility of a narrow seasonal channel flowing north to south between NAS and the southern Aral, eroding its way closer to the mouth of the Syr Darya, was of primary concern at the time. Eventually Syr Darya water flow could then be turned south, robbing the NAS of its primary water source (Aladin et al., 2008). To combat this possibility, in 1992 local residents built a dike mostly of sand across Berg Strait, but it quickly washed away.

A second attempt in 1996 was more successful because it was constructed with more solid materials, although without a spillway to release spring floodwaters. In April 1999, a breach of the structure killed two workers and swept twenty-seven others away, prompting the use of boats and helicopters for their rescue (Aladin et al., 2008). Although ultimately a failure, this second dike showed positive results in increased water volume and decreased salinity levels. These largely grassroots efforts (Foster, 2010) showed that a properly constructed and more structurally sound dike could improve the ecological condition of the NAS and potentially bring a return of fish – especially if it included a spillway to release high water. Recognizing the resulting likelihood of ecological and economic benefits shown by the previous dikes – and certainly influenced by the desperate need for positive developments in the region – final approval of what is officially known as the Syr Darya Control and Northern Aral Sea Phase 1 project was signed in June 2001 (World Bank, 2010).

The nearly $86 million project included construction of the dam, a connecting 8-mile dike across Berg Strait, and additional hydrologic infrastructure, including the Ak-lak spillway in the lower reaches of the Syr Darya. Designed to raise the lake level by about 2 meters (6.5 feet), the dam and dike portions of the project were completed in 2005.

Partial ecological restoration and economic recovery

Completion of the dam and dike complex brought the lake level to the project's design height in less than a year – much earlier than most experts expected. However, another fallacy concerning the NAS deserves mention here, in addition to the three common misconceptions regarding the former Aral Sea that opened this chapter. As with the larger Aral, the NAS is also not "returning." This smaller lake's level rose by about 2 meters (6.5 feet) fairly quickly and stabilized at 42 meters (138 feet), where it remains. Incidentally, the current level is a full 11 meters (36 feet) below where it was in 1960 (Micklin, 2010). Barring any water losses from an unlikely failure of the dam or drastic, sustained reductions in Syr Darya river inflow, the NAS will remain at its present level until planned and rather contentious future rehabilitation efforts are completed. The next section of this chapter discusses this possible future artificial intervention, or Phase 2. However, its successful completion, not to mention the precise form it would take, is far from certain.

Partial ecological restoration of the NAS since 2005 has been largely driven by the greater retention of freshwater inflow from the Syr Darya feeder river.

With the 2-meter (6.5-foot) rise in lake level, its surface area increased by approximately 18 percent (Micklin and Aladin, 2008). Wetland areas have been restored, and reed beds and other plant life again provide cover for both resident and migratory bird species. Shorebirds, ducks, swans, and flamingos appear in large numbers (Pala, 2011a).

A sharp decrease in salinity is important for aquatic biota, especially fish. At a likely historical high in 1989 – around the time of the NAS split from the larger Aral – average salinity was just over 30,000 parts per million (ppm). Today, while salinity levels vary somewhat across the NAS, the average stands at about 8,000 ppm. That is about or perhaps slightly below its 1960 level (Micklin, 2014). With dropping salinity and restoration of spawning habitat, as many as two dozen fish species have returned to the open lake from the Syr Darya and this river's deltaic lakes. Since 2005, the total amount of fish biomass is estimated to have increased by a factor of six (Pala, 2011b).

By the mid-20th century, the harvest, processing, and export of fish had become this region's economic base, though by the 1980s the worsening crisis devastated the fishing industry and regional socio-economic conditions. The improving economic situation and outlook around the NAS following completion of the latest dam and dike project is a direct result of the modest return of fish and the revitalization of fishing-related economic activity. Since 2005, NAS fish harvests have increased dramatically in metric tonnage and fairly substantially in number of species harvested (Table 11.1). Total fish harvests nearly doubled from 2005 to 2006 and increased more than seven times from 2005 to 2013. The top species harvested expanded from flounder (*Platichthys flesus luscus*), carp (*Cyprinus carpio aralensis*), bream (*Abramis brama orientalis*), and pike-perch (*Stizostedion lucioperca*) in 2005 to include roach (*Rutilus aralensis*), asp (*Aspius iblioides*), saberfish (*Pelecus cultratus*), and rudd (*Scardinius erythropthalmus*) by 2013.

Today there are approximately 1,000 fishermen harvesting fish on the NAS, a figure that includes about 600 part-timers who also work in other sectors like construction. The word "fishermen" is appropriate here as no women are engaged in the harvest of fish.[2]

As harvests have risen on the NAS, so have the number of processing plants and number of employees in this economic sector. Today there are three processing plants in Aralsk, two of which have started operations in the last five years. The oldest of them, Kambala Balyk, is in a former Soviet-era bread factory and began operations in the early 2000s to process flounder – at the time the only remaining fish harvested on the NAS. Earlier, the small amount of flounder brought to this plant was simply frozen and sold. Today, it specializes in smoking, drying, and salting catfish, bream, roach, and pike, filleting pike-perch, and producing vacuum-packed dried fish snacks from many species. Employment has increased at this plant from five workers when it opened to thirty by 2014.[3]

The Aral Fresh Fish Processing Plant occupies a large modern facility that began operations in 2009. It started with thirty employees and today employs seventy-five.[4] The Aral Service Center plant is on the grounds of the old Soviet-era Aralrybprom and began its operations in 2010. This factory's main activity

Table 11.1 Northern Aral Sea fish harvests, 2005–2013

Year	Total harvest (tons)	Individual species harvested (tons)								
		Flounder	Carp	Bream	Pike–perch	Roach	Asp	Saberfish	Rudd
2005	695	303	181	57	30	–	–	–	–
2006	1,360	700	190	120	70	250	30	–	–
2007	1,910	640	260	410	260	370	80	40	–
2008	1,490	410	170	360	170	340	90	–	–
2009	1,885	615	125	470	185	410	80	–	–
2010	2,810	715	115	835	245	765	70	65	–
2011	3,520	710	70	1,210	365	1,040	65	60	–
2012	4,189	720	117	1,639	416	1,100	96	101	–
2013	4,908	720	104	1,639	648	1,100	162	156	123

Source: Unpublished, Kazakhstan Research Institute of Fisheries, Aralsk branch

is processing and freezing pike-perch fillets, and in February 2012 it became the only officially licensed facility in Aralsk to export fish to the European Union (EU). Employment grew from twelve in 2010 to thirty in 2014.[5] Although Aral Service Center is currently Aralsk's only processing facility licensed to export to the EU, each of Aralsk's factories does export – both internationally and to other parts of Kazakhstan. For international exports, the main destinations are Russia and Georgia, followed by Azerbaijan, Turkey, Poland, Denmark, and Germany. Within Kazakhstan, fish and fish products are shipped mainly to Almaty, Astana, Aktobe, and nearby Kyzylorda.[6]

Despite these promising developments, the size of the NAS fishery and economic sector today is just a fraction of what existed in the mid-twentieth century. Present annual harvests may be about one-fourth of pre-1960 annual totals, and today's total processing factory employment (135) pales in comparison to the peak of Aralrybprom operations. Still, recent expansion in harvests, processing, and export economic activity has brought much-needed economic stimulus to the region. In discussing recent positive developments in the fishing sector here, Akshabak Batimova, deputy director at the Aral Fresh Fish Processing Plant, said that "people have begun to build new houses, and to paint and repair existing houses. In general, the fishermen are now the wealthiest people in the villages. They are building houses, buying boats and cars. Earlier fishermen transported fish by camel and cart. Now they use UAZ [a Russian off-road vehicle]. This is a very big development."

A future for the Northern Aral Sea

Much of the hopeful optimism derived from the 2005 dam and dike completion is clearly a result of the quick success – in ecological and economic terms – of this rehabilitation project. Much of today's optimism also seems to anticipate possible future success of the second phase, called officially the Syr Darya Control and Northern Aral Sea Project, Phase 2. In general, activities of this second phase can be categorized into: flood protection and increasing river flow along the course of the Syr Darya in tandem with increasing water diversion from the river to its delta lakes; and direct intervention on the NAS. Direct intervention could mean raising the existing dike and bring the water level from 42 meters to 48 meters (138 feet to 158 feet). Alternatively, direct intervention could mean building another dike across the southern extent of Saryshaganak Bay, bringing that bay's level to 53 meters (174 feet) and potentially restoring NAS water to the former port of Aralsk. Contentious debate continues, primarily over the form of direct intervention, delaying implementation. As of December 2014, it appeared that the Syr Darya flood mitigation and diversion to delta lakes work will proceed (2015–2021) followed by a yet-undetermined direct intervention on the NAS itself (2017–2022) (Abdel Ghany, 2014).

Notwithstanding uncertainties about the form and timing of further restoration projects, residents of the NAS region can, for the first time in decades, realistically envision a more prosperous future. Annual harvests, having already increased dramatically since 2005, are expected to plateau by 2020 at around 10,000 metric tons, or just more than double the current annual total.[7] If the current NAS fish management philosophy continues, long-term sustainability of fish stocks might also be realistically expected. Doubling of harvests and continued maintenance of that yield into the future could also double the expansion of processing and export activities. All of these, of course, have residents anticipating a long-awaited positive future.

In discussing improvements around the NAS, Zauresh Alimbetova, a long-time Aralsk resident and director of the Barsa-kelmes Nature Reserve, emphasized that the recent restoration and revival has "improved our socio-economic conditions, particularly for people who once were left without work, without the sea, without hope. With the sea having come back and the development of fisheries, our people have started to earn money, build houses, buy cars, educate their children, and believe in the future."

Conclusion

The recent stabilization of Kazakhstan's Northern Aral Sea has initiated a regional ecological and economic recovery process. This recovery results directly from human intervention, ironically taking similar form to the Soviet-era infrastructure and irrigation diversion projects often blamed for the demise of the sea.

As a vital ecological and economic resource, fish stocks are returning. The industry has brought much-needed jobs, income, as well as spending and investments to the local economy. With annual harvests expected to level off at about double the current amount, the processing and export sectors will also correspondingly grow. The related partial ecological restoration and economic recovery has also brought hope and optimism to a population and an environment long under assault from the largely human-induced Aral Sea crisis.

Notes

1 In particular as part of an international expedition to the NAS in 2011 and a more recent visit in 2014. For details of the 2011 expedition, see Micklin et al., 2014. Interviews for this chapter took place 8–12 September 2014, in Aralsk, Kazakhstan.
2 Interview with Zaulkhan Ermakhanov, director of the Aralsk branch of the Kazakhstan Research Institute of Fisheries. 12 September 2014, in Aralsk, Kazakhstan. Rigid gender roles generally prevail here. Just as only men fish, only women cut and clean fish in the factories.
3 As expressed by Garifulla Iskakov, chief technological consultant at the Kambala Balyk fish processing factory on 9 September 2014. *Kambala* in Russian translates to "flounder" in English. *Balyk* in Kazakh language translates to "fish" in English.
4 According to Akshabak Batimova, deputy director, on 11 September 2014. Modern equipment and a modern glass exterior make this plant a showcase for Aralsk's revival. Across town, images of this building can be seen in bus stops.
5 As told by Adilbek Aiymbetov, owner of Aral Service Center, on 8 September 2014.
6 As expressed by all the interviewees at Aralsk's fish processing plants. Almaty is Kazakhstan's former capital and largest city. Astana is the capital and third-largest

city (behind Shymkent). Kyzylorda (to the southeast) and Aktobe (to the northwest) are the closest Kazakhstan cities to Aralsk.

7   Interview with Zaulkhan Ermakhanov, director of the Aralsk branch of the Kazakhstan Research Institute of Fisheries. 12 September 2014, in Aralsk, Kazakhstan.

References

Abdel Ghany, A.S.M. (2014) Project Information Document (Concept Stage) – Syr Darya Control and Northern Aral Sea Project, Phase 2 – P152001. Washington, DC: World Bank. Available at http://documents.worldbank.org/curated/en/2014/09/20234171/project-information-document-concept-stage-syr-darya-control-northern-aral-sea-project-phase-2-p152001.

Aladin, N., Plotnikov, I., Ballatore, T. and Micklin, P. (2008) Review of technical interventions to restore the Northern Aral Sea. *Japan International Cooperation Agency Country and Regional Study Reports: Central Asia and Caucasus*, 4: 1–12.

Aladin, N.V. and Potts, T.W. (1992) Changes in the Aral Sea ecosystems during the period 1960–1990. *Hydrobiologia*, 237(2): 67–79.

Ataniyazova, O., Adrian, S., Mazhitova, Z., Moshammer, H., Prindull, G. and Zetterström, R. (2001) Continuing progressive deterioration of the environment in the Aral Sea region: disastrous effects on mother and child health. *Acta Paediatrica*, 90(5): 589–591.

Boroffka, N.G.O., Obernhänsli, H., Achatov, G.A., Aladin, N.V., Baipakov, K.M., Erzhanova, A., Hornig, A., Krivonogov, S., Lobas, D.A., Savel'eva, T.V. and Wunnemann, B. (2005) Human settlements on the northern shores of Lake Aral and water level changes. *Mitigation and Adaptation Strategies for Global Change*, 10(1): 71–85.

Breckle, S.W. and Wucherer, W. (2012) The Aralkum, a man-made desert on the desiccated floor of the Aral Sea (Central Asia): General introduction and aims of the book. In Breckle, S.W., Wucherer, W., Dimeyeva, L.A. and Ogar, N.P. (eds) *Aralkum – a Man-made Desert*. Springer-Verlag, Berlin, pp. 1–9.

Butakoff, A. (1853) Survey of the Sea of Aral. *Journal of the Royal Geographical Society of London*, 23: 93–101.

Conant, E. (2006) Return of the Aral Sea. *Discover Magazine*. September 1. Available at http://discovermagazine.com/2006/sep/returnaralsea.

Crighton, E.J., Barwin, L., Small, I. and Upshur, R. (2011) What have we learned? A review of the literature on children's health and the environment in the Aral Sea area. *International Journal of Public Health*, 56(2): 125–138.

Ermakhanov, Z.K., Plotnikov, I.S., Aladin, N.V. and Micklin, P. (2012) Changes in the Aral Sea ichthyofauna and fishery during the period of ecological crisis. *Lakes & Reservoirs: Research and Management*, 17(1): 3–9.

Feshbach, M. and Friendly Jr., A. (1992) *Ecocide in the USSR: Health and Nature Under Siege* (New York: Basic Books).

Fletcher, M. (2007) The return of the sea. *The Times*. 23 June. Available at http://www.timesonline.co.uk/tol/news/world/europe/article1975079ece.

Foster, H. (2010) Local villagers' efforts led to the saving of the North Aral Sea. *Central Asia Newswire*. 14 September. http://centralasianewswire.com/Local-villagersrsquo-efforts-led-to-the-saving-of-the-North-Aral-Sea/viewstory.aspx?id=1684.

Glantz, M.H. (1999) Sustainable development and creeping environmental problems in the Aral Sea region. In Glantz, M.H. (ed.) *Creeping Environmental Problems and Sustainable Development in the Aral Sea Basin* (Cambridge: Cambridge University Press) pp. 1–25.

Glazovskiy, N.F. (1991) Ideas on an escape from the "Aral Crisis." *Soviet Geography*, 32(2): 73–89.

Kiger, P.J. (2014) Lakes around the world are rapidly disappearing. *Discovery News*. 29 September. Available at http://news.discovery.com/earth/global-warming/lakes-around-the-world-are-rapidly-disappearing-140930.htm.

Kotlyakov, V.M. (1991) The Aral Sea basin: a critical environmental zone. *Environment: Science and Policy for Sustainable Development*, 33(1): 4–38.

Landsforeningen, L.H. (2003) *Masterplan: Setting the Course for the Northern Aral Sea Fishery*. Danish Society for a Living Sea, Lemvig, Denmark.

Levintanus, A. (1992) Saving the Aral Sea. *Journal of Environmental Management*, 36(3): 193–199.

Micklin, P. (1988) Desiccation of the Aral Sea: a water management disaster in the Soviet Union. *Science*, 241(4870): 1170–1176.

Micklin, P. (1991) Touring the Aral: visit to an ecological disaster zone. *Soviet Geography*, 32(2): 90–105.

Micklin, P. (2007) The Aral sea disaster. *Annual Review of Earth and Planetary Sciences*, (35): 47–72.

Micklin, P. (2010) The past, present, and future Aral Sea. *Lakes & Reservoirs: Research and Management*, 15(3): 193–213.

Micklin, P. and Aladin, N.V. (2008) Reclaiming the Aral Sea. *Scientific American*, 298(4): 64–71

Micklin, P., Aladin, N.V. and Plotnikov, I.S. (2014) An expedition to the northern part of the small Aral Sea (August 29 to September 16, 2011). In Micklin, P., Aladin, N. and Plotnikov, I.S. (eds) *The Aral Sea, The Devastation and Partial Rehabilitation of a Great Lake* (Berlin: Springer-Verlag), pp. 337–351.

Pala, C. (2011a) Kazakhstan: sea reclaimed as lake. *IPS News Agency*. 2 November. Available at http://www.ipsnews.net/2011/11/kazakhstan-sea-reclaimed-as-lake.

Pala, C. (2011b) In northern Aral Sea, rebound comes with a big catch. *Science*, 334(6054): 303.

Saiko, T.A. and Zonn, I.S. (2000) Irrigation expansion and dynamics of desertification in the Circum-Aral region of Central Asia. *Applied Geography*, 20(4): 349–367.

Small, I., Van der Meer, J. and Upshur, R.E. (2001) Acting on an environmental health disaster: the case of the Aral Sea. *Environmental Health Perspectives*, 109(6): 547–549.

Spoor, M. (1998) The Aral Sea basin crisis: transition and environment in former Soviet Central Asia. *Development and Change*, 29(3): 409–435.

Thorpe, A. and Van Anrooy, R. (2009) *Inland fisheries livelihoods in Central Asia: Policy interventions and opportunities*. Food and Agriculture Organization of the United Nations, Rome.

Wester, T. (2014) Symphony for the return of the Aral Sea. *Moscow Times*. 31 March. Available at http://www.themoscowtimes.com/news/article/feature-symphony-for-the-return-of-the-aral-sea/497088.html.

Whish-Wilson, P. (2002) The Aral Sea environmental health crisis. *Journal of Rural and Remote Environmental Health*, 1(2): 29–34.

White, K.D. (2013) Nature-society linkages in the Aral Sea region. *Journal of Eurasian Studies*, 4(1): 18–33.

White, K.D. (2014) Nature and economy in the Aral Sea Basin. In Micklin, P., Aladin, N.V. and Plotnikov, I. (eds) *The Aral Sea, the Devastation and Partial Rehabilitation of a Great Lake* (Berlin: Springer-Verlag), pp. 301–335.

World Bank (2010) *Kazakhstan – Syr Darya Control and Northern Aral Sea Project.* Washington, DC: World Bank. Available at http://documents.worldbank.org/curated/en/2010/05/12284611/kazakhstan-syr-darya-control-northern-aral-sea-project.

Zholdasova, I. (1999) Fish population as an ecosystem component and economic object in the Aral Sea basin. In Glantz, M.H. (ed.) *Creeping Environmental Problems and Sustainable Development in the Aral Sea Basin* (Cambridge, U.K.: Cambridge University Press), pp. 204–224.

Zonn, I., Glantz, M., Kostianoy, A. and Kosarev, A. (2009) *The Aral Sea Encyclopedia* (Berlin: Springer-Verlag).

Zonn, I.S. (2010) Socio-economic conditions of the Aral Sea region before 1960. In Kostianoy, A.G. and Kosarev, A.N. (eds) *The Aral Sea Environment* (Berlin: Springer-Verlag), pp. 65–73.

12 Conservation and multipurpose management of the unique walnut-fruit forests of southern Kyrgyzstan

Jean-Pierre Sorg and Maik Rehnus

Introduction

With only 6.97 percent forest cover, Kyrgyzstan is one of the most sparsely forested countries in Asia (Grisa et al., 2008). Unique forests of walnut (*Juglans regia* L.) and other fruit-bearing species, mainly in the *Rosaceae* family, grow in the southern part of Kyrgyzstan (Figure 12.1), primarily in the Ferghana and Chatkal regions. Walnut-fruit forests (WFF) occupy about 47,000 hectares (116,100 acres) (Grisa et al., 2008). This ecosystem is characterized by a high species diversity, a high rate of endemism (meaning that ecologically a species is unique to a defined location), and naturally growing wild walnut. WFF are therefore considered biodiversity hotspots (Fisher and Christopher, 2007) and belong to the designated Mountains of Central Asia hotspot (Critical Ecosystem Partnership Fund, 2014).

These regions have international significance as genetic pools for many tree species (Mamadjanov, 2006; Vavilov, 1931; Venglovsky, 2006). The WFF also are important for local livelihoods because people from surrounding villages depend on them for food, fodder, and fuel. However, the forest is endangered by uncontrolled cattle grazing, rapid urbanization, and overexploitation. The history of management in the WFF has been marked by changing government and economic regimes (Musuraliev, 1998; Venglovsky, 2006).

Current state and importance of walnut-fruit forests

WFF occur on mountain slopes and play an important role in protecting water resources and soil against erosion (Matveev, 1979). Most stands of walnut trees (81.2 percent) occur naturally in the mountain zone at around 1,400 to 1,800 meters (4,600 to 5,900 feet) above sea level. More than half of the WFF are on hillsides with northern slopes (58.6 percent), while 83 percent occur on slopes of between 11 and 35 degrees (Müller and Sorg, 2001; Venglovsky, 2006). Walnut is a fairly drought-tolerant species but, given its preference for somewhat high elevations, it is surprising to note that walnut is quite sensitive to frost and low winter temperatures. A decline in the area of WFF would make the region more prone to erosion and could negatively impact water regulation at a regional level.

Figure 12.1 Distribution of the walnut-fruit forests in Kyrgyzstan and the study area of the ORECH-LES research project

The study areas are in the Ferghana region. Map adapted from Grisa et al. (2008).

The WFF have great economic importance as a significant source of fruits and timber. On average, some 800 to 1,000 tons of walnuts (up to 3,000 tons), 800 tons of apples (up to 4,000 tons), and 20 to 30 tons of pistachios (up to 200 tons) are collected annually in the WFF (Venglovsky, 2006). The timber is also widely used as a valuable raw material for furniture, but its current use is limited by the trees' protected status in Kyrgyzstan (Venglovsky, 2006). However, large areas of the WFF are no longer productive, so the actual potential of the WFF is greater than these numbers indicate (Müller and Sorg, 2001; Scheuber, Köhl and Traub, 2000; Venglovsky, 2006).

In the past, natural WFF were thinned to a great degree, mainly due to tree felling, livestock grazing, and open aging stands. Today, stands with high crown densities account for just 9.2 percent of the total area of walnut forests. In contrast, stands with low crown densities) occupy 42.6 percent of the total area (Venglovsky, 2006). Stands with low crown densities tend to have lower fruit productivity. Moreover, these forests have largely lost their protective function against erosion. According to harvest records from 1930 to 1997, no collection of walnuts ever reached the estimated potential annual yield (Venglovsky, 2006). In many cases, yield is limited by adverse site or climatic conditions. For example, late spring frosts, dry summers, and early autumn frosts frequently destroy the entire crop. Over the past fifty years, bountiful harvests exceeding 1,000 tons were recorded nine times; average harvests of between 501 and 1,000 tons, sixteen times; poor harvests between 150 and 500 tons, fourteen times; and complete yield failures were recorded seven times (Venglovsky, 2006). These figures suggest that nut production is typically low and irregular in the WFF.

The intensive harvesting of walnut timber and burls (knotty growths used in furniture and veneers) during the past 100 to 150 years seriously damaged the forests. Tree felling negatively affected both the structure of walnut stands and the dynamics of the forest ecosystem as a whole. At present, the trees are in critical condition. More than half of the stands are of secondary growth or coppice origin, and many are root- or mold-damaged. Today, most stands are also quite thin, and in many areas, less valuable tree and shrub species have replaced valuable walnut species (Venglovsky, 2006). Apart from haymaking and firewood harvesting, the productivity of such damaged forest stands is low and of little economic importance.

The Ferghana–Chatkal WFF region is now characterized largely by sparsely forested areas as well as by deforested areas that have failed to regenerate (Venglovsky, 2006; Venglovsky et al., 2010). Natural regeneration has mostly failed on account of unrestricted cattle grazing, intensive haymaking, and the virtually complete harvesting of fruits. Walnut trees have high light requirements; if they are unable to reach sunlight, seedlings and even saplings cannot compete and quickly die. Without a forest management plan that accounts for the needs of the trees, self-sown young shoots that survive the perils of haymaking and grazing are generally doomed by lack of sunlight under the forest canopy.

The lack of natural regeneration and the low productivity of existing stands have led to reforestation and plantation efforts. In addition, great attempts have been made to identify new varieties, and researchers have worked in particular on the qualitative and quantitative production of fruits (see Mamadjanov, 2007, for a review). The first walnut cultures were planted in 1930 in a limited area (Dyachenko, 1934). Since 1950, the State Forest Service has created artificial stands on a fairly large scale. However, these forest cultures are often planted under walnut forest canopies with high crown densities, so many seedlings fail due to lack of light (Venglovsky, 2006). As a side effect, such plantations—if they are fenced—have promoted natural regeneration. However in most cases, poorly maintained fences, haymaking, and cattle grazing adversely affect the establishment and preservation of young trees. Nevertheless, good results have occurred in some locations where young trees were planted in sparsely forested plots or open clearings (Venglovsky, 2006).

Thus, it is clear that the natural distribution of the WFF is strongly affected by anthropogenic pressures and artificial reforestation and plantation efforts. Apart from naturally occurring stands on the northern slopes in the mountain zone, a small proportion of stands are still found on more accessible slopes. Today, there are many areas where trees once grew naturally, but these have since been cleared for agricultural purposes. Mature stands now account for 41.2 percent of the total forested WFF area, stands nearing maturity account for 23.9 percent, and young stands for only 15 percent (Venglovsky, 2006).

After Kyrgyzstan gained independence in 1991, much of the country's Soviet-era infrastructure broke down, including industry, public services, and parts of the governmental administration. An exception, the State Forest Service, survived this difficult period, although it now operates with limited

Figure 12.2 Natural conditions in the walnut-fruit forest (photo: Maik Rehnus)

Stands contain trees of different diameter classes, and regeneration occurs naturally.

resources. During this period, the forest became an essential source of walnuts, other fruits, fuel, hay, pastureland, and other non-timber products for villagers in the surrounding area (Messerli, 2002; Rehnus et al., 2013a; Scheuber, Köhl and Traub, 2000; Schmidt, 2005, 2007). Not surprisingly, the needs of local communities conflicted with established conservation-oriented forest policy (Schmidt, 2007; Carter et al., 2003). Today, as in the past, continuing and ever-increasing pressure on these forests is not sustainable (Venglovsky et al., 2010). Multifunctional management approaches that involve local communities are urgently needed (Jalilova, 2013; Müller and Sorg, 2001; Rehnus and Sorg, 2010).

Scientific basis for the conservation and sustainable, multifunctional management of walnut-fruit forests

In recognition of its importance, in 1945 the WFF were declared a state forest fruit reserve, meaning that tree felling for timber production was prohibited and only sanitary cuttings to remove dead and diseased trees were allowed. The overall objectives of the protected area include multipurpose forest management, improvement of forest productivity, and preservation and enhancement of the protective functions of the WFF (Venglovsky, 2006). However, forest management, in terms of adequate conservation and thinning practices, has hardly achieved health and sustainable productivity of both trees and stands (Venglovsky, 2006; Venglovsky et al., 2010; Sorg et al., in review).

Figure 12.3 A walnut-fruit forest altered anthropogenically, meaning by human activity (photo: Maik Rehnus)

Note the evenly aged stand and the complete lack of understory due to overgrazing.

Although a number of researchers have contributed significantly to our understanding of the biology and ecology of walnuts, for example, their findings were largely ignored during the Soviet era. Forest administrators concentrated primarily on planting new forests and largely ignored existing and aging stands. Today, the productive and protective value of aged and untended stands is quite low as a result of that long-term focus on new plantings. Furthermore, many plantations are unsuitable for achieving high yields due to conditions under the forest canopy. Unfortunately, the overall impact of these interventions on the diversity of the WFF is difficult to record because no monitoring protocol was established.

The ORECH-LES[1] research project began in 1999 to provide a better understanding of the current state of WFF and to identify ways to improve the productive and protective functions of these forests. The project ran from 1999 until 2013 under the auspices of the Swiss Development Cooperation and investigated forestry and agroforestry and promoting implementation of research results in the management of Kyrgyzstan's walnut-fruit forests.

ORECH-LES investigated silviculture (creating forest cultures for timber or fruit-bearing production and tending cuttings), agroforestry (multifunctional use), firewood consumption, selection of the best walnut forms and varieties, natural regeneration, and biodiversity of WFF. It used an existing network of 34 trial plots in Arslanbop, Kaba, Ortok, and Uzgen, with experimental and control plots (Figure 12.1). In addition, institutional aspects of the human-forest interface were the subject of extended research activity.

Drawing on results from previous Soviet and Kyrgyz research (Beyeler et al., 2011), researchers carried out several case studies. This chapter presents highlights of these studies. We also discuss the resulting recommendations at the end of this chapter.

Silvicultural research

The history of research in the WFF covers a relatively long period (see Musuraliev, 1998; Venglovsky, 2006). However, little is known about the long-term influence of thinning on natural and planted WFF in Kyrgyzstan. In particular, knowledge is lacking about how thinning affects fruit production, especially in older stands (> 30 years). A better understanding of how silvicultural interventions affect less productive stands will play a major role in determining sustainable ways to manage the WFF.

Continuous inventories and harvest measurements were carried out on eighteen trial and control plots over thirteen years. Results show that: (1) thinning has a positive influence on diameter at breast height (dbh); (2) dbh growth and crown projection increases are strongly and positively correlated; (3) large crowns enhance the production of fruits; and (4) temperature conditions have a major influence on production of fruits (Sorg et al., in review). These points are particularly relevant for young plantations but are also valid for relatively old ones (> 50 years). We conclude that regular thinning substantially improves fruit production and forest stability in both young stands and older walnut-fruit forests.

Agroforestry research

Agroforestry practices in the WFF and their profitability, including interactions between trees and livestock and, sometimes, even trees and agricultural products, are not well described in the literature. It is clear, however, that the multipurpose production of WFF in southern Kyrgyzstan suffers from a lack of management (Messerli, 2002; Rehnus and Sorg, 2010; Schmidt, 2005). Different people often use the same plot to collect various timber and non-timber forest products. The multipurpose use of the forest often results in conflicts, overexploitation, and forest degradation. A better understanding of current agroforestry activities and conflicts will play a major role in shaping future sustainable agroforestry practices.

We therefore analyzed current agroforestry practices using interviews with farmers, and reviewed five years of input–output data for hay and walnut production for three case studies. The results showed that: (1) haymaking and walnut collection are the primary agroforestry practices in the WFF and have clear economic importance; (2) walnut fruits in particular are a source of additional income for farmers; (3) haymaking activities are strongly influenced by the need to feed cattle during the winter; and (4) walnut production is difficult to estimate because it is highly dependent on weather conditions and cropping practices within the stands (Rehnus et al., 2013a). Finally, this case study highlights the

Figure 12.4 Demand for fuel from the walnut forest has increased since Soviet times, causing some parts of the forest to be overused for firewood collection (photo: Jean-Pierre Sorg)

need for improved agroforestry technologies and identifies potential means for a sustainable, multipurpose management that focuses on income generation.

Demand for firewood

During Soviet times, the state provided local residents with electricity and charcoal for heating and gas for cooking, although many households continued to use wood, especially for baking bread. However, after independence in 1991, electricity and charcoal were no longer available, so people were forced to use wood for all their energy needs. By the early twenty-first century, firewood was again by far the most important energy source for residents in the vicinity of the WFF (Schmidt, 2007). As the population in the region has expanded, demand for firewood has increased (Colfer and Schmidt, 2005), and the availability of deadwood correspondingly decreased (Gottschling, Amatov and Lazkov, 2005). This led to a discussion about the sustainability of current firewood use, including granting of official permits for firewood collection (Müller and Sorg, 2001).

We investigated firewood collection and use in three villages and analyzed differences between the annual increment of woody biomass and firewood consumption during the winter. The calculated individual firewood consumption averages 9 pounds per capita per heating day. The difference between increment and consumption shows that the surrounding forests are overused for firewood collection (Rehnus et al., 2013b). Pressure on the forest and overuse of preferred species for firewood will decrease the genetic diversity of these species and of the forest as a whole (Figure 12.4).

Selection and cultivation

WFF are characterized by extreme diversity of walnut forms, which makes it possible to carry out continuous selection work (Mamadjanov, 2001). According to Mamadjanov (2001, 2006), the variety of forms is especially apparent in the size, mass, form, and other properties of its fruit. The fruit varies in shape from round to oblong and in color from straw-yellow to dark brown. Some nuts are extremely oily, and taste ranges from bitter to sweet. Extracting the nut may be easy or difficult, and the mass of the nut varies from big to small fruits. Biologically, walnuts can be subdivided into: those that blossom early in the season and those that blossom late; those with immunity to diseases and those without; those that bear fruits on a regular basis and those that fruit irregularly; and those that are high-yielding and those that are low-yielding. Moreover, there are walnut forms characterized by self-fertilization and forms that bear fruits without pollination. The goal of this research was to select the most promising forms of walnuts from natural and cultivated stands and to introduce them to industrial cultures to increase productivity.

Some varieties and forms differ in yielding capacity, depending on their degree of adjustment to local climatic conditions (Mamadjanov, 2006). However, the mountain climate conditions of the WFF—which may include challenges like spring frosts, high precipitation during the flowering period, and early summer droughts—clearly influence annual yield (Mamadjanov, 2006). For good harvests, cultivation of high-yielding species in nurseries is recommended; their subsequent introduction to stands in the WFF will increase the overall productivity of the forest (Mamadjanov, 2006).

Natural regeneration

The WFF of the early twenty-first century are strongly affected by a lack of natural regeneration. To assess how human activities impact regeneration patterns, we conducted detailed regeneration analyses on fenced plots after tending cuttings. Our results showed that the natural potential for self-restoration of WFF species is high. Despite the intensive collection of walnuts, the number of new shoots following a good yield year can exceed 400 per hectare (162 per acre) (Venglovsky et al., 2010). Typically, a plot contains a considerable number of two- and three-year-old self-seedlings. However, the number of seedlings four years and older drops off sharply. The reasons for this drop-off are manifold (Venglovsky et al., 2010). First, walnuts have high light requirements; after two years, their light requirement increases sharply, and seedlings that cannot reach sunlight cannot compete and die. Second, self-seedlings are particularly vulnerable to dry conditions and often die during dry years. In addition, attrition occurs due to competition with grassy vegetation for moisture and nutrients. Nevertheless, our results indicate that the regeneration process is successful under natural conditions. Anthropogenic activities such as haymaking are more often the cause of regeneration failure and must be better managed before natural generation can occur.

Ornithological studies

Recent studies underscore the value of the WFF for bird diversity. Up to 107 bird species are closely associated with the WFF (Herold, 2005; Jalilova, 2007). Their habitat needs, however, are poorly understood. The white-winged woodpecker, for example, is endemic to Central Asia and selects trees with described parameters for cavity activities. It is one of the least-studied woodpecker species in the world.

We investigated this species' habitat selection and cavity tree selection in southern Kyrgyzstan. Using birdsong playbacks on circular plots, we systematically searched for woodpeckers and then examined the relationship between woodpecker occurrence and habitat factors. Results revealed a preference for walnut forests, with occupancy rates declining with altitude. In addition, results showed that cavity trees, which are positively associated with walnut forests and the occurrence of damaged trees with broken and/or dead limbs, had larger diameters at breast height and were more likely damaged than other available trees (Rehnus et al., 2011). Future management plans should consider the habitat requirements of the white-winged woodpecker because it is an indicator species for other bird species (Herold, 2005; Jalilova, 2007; Rehnus et al., 2011).

Socioeconomic aspects

Since the breakup of the Soviet Union in 1991, Kyrgyzstan has undergone a difficult process of economic, political, and social transition. All levels and segments of society are impacted, including the forestry sector (Colfer and Schmidt, 2005). We conducted an extended research project to examine the human-forest interface and its relation to institutional aspects of the state-owned WFF (Schmidt, 2007). The economic difficulties of the transition process prompted the question: "How can these forests be sustainably managed in a partnership involving the State Forest Service, local people, and other relevant stakeholders?"

The research used a combination of qualitative and quantitative methods at four sites in the WFF belt, each with different forest management conditions. It identified opportunities and constraints for involving local residents in forest management and assessed the potential for those who lease a forest plot to contribute their skills, knowledge, and experience to forest management. Results indicated that: (1) generally, area residents have solid skills and relevant technical and marketing knowledge and are, under certain circumstances, increasingly innovative; (2) applied ecological knowledge is less widespread; (3) forest use is not as multifunctional as expected, given the range of non-timber and agricultural products available in these forests; and (4) the WFF are a key subsistence resource and a welcome, if rather unreliable, source of income (Schmidt, 2007). Finally, this study confirms that local people can, with the professional assistance of foresters, contribute to the sustainable management of the WFF if clear agreements between the state and local people exist. Active forest management by local people is particularly likely under conditions of secure, long-term forest tenure.

Table 12.1 Recommendations of the First International Conference on the Sustainability in Kyrgyzstan's Walnut-fruit Forests: State, Conservation and Management

Forest management

- As a first step, existing knowledge must be incorporated into multipurpose and sustainable management plans.
- Clear agreements between the state and local people should be set up. For example, one farmer should be allowed to use all products from a single plot.
- To guarantee the sustainability of forest management in different regions, an overarching management plan should be set up at the national level, including mechanisms independent of state control.
- To reduce pressure on the existing WFF, reforestation should be promoted on state and municipal lands. Initially, state subsidies will be necessary and should be incorporated into the national management plan.
- Given the multipurpose management of the WFF, key management goals should be based on an agroforestry approach and implemented by the State Forest Service in close collaboration with local residents.
- Strong forest management depends on a motivated, well-educated forestry staff. At present, forestry staffs receive minimal pay and no social benefits. This should be rectified, ensuring that they receive adequate salaries and benefits as well as training opportunities and the potential to earn bonuses.
- Introduction of new varieties of walnut and pistachio should be promoted. Ample research is available to facilitate this process and should be used.

Education of local people and forestry staff

- Local people should be able to exchange experiences and access information about current agroforestry best practices, available technologies, and other training and education opportunities.
- Training programs for forestry staff should be revised because they do not reflect the current state of knowledge. At the same time, training programs for forest owners, farmers, local councillors, and other interest groups should be organized at the local level in collaboration with local branches of the State Forest Service.
- State institutions should promote continuing education for all forest staff. As some NGOs have in-depth knowledge and extensive experience in forestry, agroforestry, and renewable resource management, their participation should be requested.
- Schools should promote a healthy appreciation for the natural environment. Adequate school materials and teaching tools should be developed to assist teachers.

Participatory land-use planning

- Local stakeholders need to be involved in land-use planning to ensure that new forest management policies reflect a balance among environmental and socioeconomic interests. Management policies and concrete management measures must be explained and negotiated with local residents.
- Alternative sources of energy should be made available to reduce pressure on the forest from firewood collection.
- Agricultural productivity must be improved to reduce farmers' use of forest land to meet their basic needs.
- Harvesting and processing of non-timber forest products should be reorganized in the frame of multipurpose and sustainable resource management, including all stakeholders. Thus new sources of income can be opened.
- Cattle grazing must be managed to ensure that the forests are not negatively impacted. This will require reducing the number of animals allowed in the forest and shortening the length of their stay.
- To facilitate natural regeneration of the forest, it may be necessary to control access. For example, periodic cattle lockouts and periodic suspension of haymaking activities will improve the survival rates of young walnut shoots.

Research needs

- A new strategy must be developed to promote investments in forest research.
- Cooperation with research institutions in other countries should be promoted. New methods and technologies should be developed to improve the productivity of the WFF.
- Considerable gaps remain in understanding the biodiversity of WFF. In particular, little is known about the birds, mammals and insects there, and how declining WFF health affects them. These gaps must be addressed in future management plans.
- The relationship between science and industry should be strengthened to ensure that new forest management methods and technologies are developed and implemented.

Practical implementation of scientific results

Today, the knowledge necessary for guiding the conservation, restoration, and long-term improvement of the WFF is available. To contribute scientific results to WFF stakeholders, ORECH-LES organized seminars with State Forest Service staff, tenants, students, and village elders. These seminars focused mainly on sustainable and multipurpose resource management, for example through silviculture or agroforestry. ORECH-LES also helped organize the "First International Conference on the Sustainability in Kyrgyzstan's Walnut-fruit Forests: State, Conservation and Management" held in Arslanbob on 14–18 September 2011. About sixty walnut specialists from eleven countries (Russia, Kazakhstan, Tajikistan, Azerbaijan, United States, New Zealand, Germany, Switzerland, Austria, Great Britain, and Kyrgyzstan) attended. Participants presented new research developments and identified gaps in knowledge about sustainable WFF management. In particular, these two goals were identified as key steps toward ensuring sustainable and multifunctional management:

1   A reduction in human pressures on WFF resources is necessary to conserve and strengthen the global production capacity of the WFF; and
2   The health and productivity of WFF depend on sufficient, informed forest management interventions. At present, thinning practices are urgently required and therefore must be legalized.

To achieve these goals, conference participants prepared a detailed list of recommendations for improving forest management, local education, and participatory landscape management planning, as well as further research. Table 12.1 reformulates and summarizes the recommendations.

Acknowledgements

We thank the Swiss National Science Foundation, the Velux Foundation, the Karl Popper Foundation, and the Vontobel Foundation for their financial support. All referenced studies were conducted within the framework of the ORECH-LES project. We thank numerous colleagues and students for their work within ORECH-LES, especially Bronislav I. Venglovsky, Davlet Mamadjanov,

---

Zakir Sarymsakov, Bakhtiyar Abdykakharov, Ennio Grisa, and Kaspar Schmidt. Eric Freedman, Mark Neuzil, Erin Gleeson, and Florian Zellweger provided constructive and insightful comments on the chapter.

Note

1 ORECH-LES is a research project designed to provide better understanding of the current state of WWF and to identify ways to improve the productive and protective functions of these forests.

References

Beyeler, S., Rehnus, M., Venglovskaya, G. A., Sorg, J.-P. and Venglovsky, B. I. (2011). *Bibliography on the Walnut-Fruit Forests of Southern Kyrgyzstan*. ORECH-LES, Zurich and Bishkek.

Carter, J., Steenhof, B., Haldimann, E. and Akenshaev, N. (2003). Collaborative forest management in Kyrgyzstan: moving from top-down to bottom-up decision-making. *The Gatekeeper Series*, no. 108. International Institute for Environment and Development (IIED).

Colfer, C. J. P. and Schmidt, K. (2005). Case 8: Kyrgyzstan. In *The Complex Forest: Communities, Uncertainty, and Adaptive Collaborative Management*, ed. C. J. P. Colfer.. Resources for the Future, Washington D.C., pp. 272–282.

Critical Ecosystem Partnership Fund (2014). Critical Ecosystem Partnership Fund. Available at: http://www.cepf.net/resources/hotspots/Europe-and-Central-Asia/Pages/default.aspx.

Dyachenko, A. E. (1934). Walnut forests in southern Kyrgyzstan. *Collection of Works Walnut: Biology, Culture and Economy* (Lestekhizdat Publishing House: Moscow), pp. 154–221.

Fisher, B. and Christopher, T. (2007). Poverty and biodiversity: measuring the overlap of human poverty and the biodiversity hotspots. *Ecological Economics*, 62(1): 93–101.

Gottschling, H., Amatov, I. and Lazkov, G. (2005). Zur Ökologie und Flora der Walnuss-Wildobst-Wälder in Süd-Kirgistan. In *Archiv für Landschaftsforschung und Naturschutz*, 44: 85–130.

Grisa, E., Venglovsky, B. I., Sarymsakov, Z. and Carraro, G. (2008). *Forest Typology of the Kyrgyz Republic*. Intercooperation, Bishkek.

Herold, B. (2005). *The Avian Communities and Their Habitat Associations of the Walnut Fruit Forests of Southern Kyrgyzstan*. Master thesis, Ernst-Moritz-Arndt University Greifswald.

Jalilova, G. (2007). *Effects of Different Types of Forest Management Activities on Diversity of Birds in the Walnut Fruit Forests in Kyrgyzstan*. Master's thesis, University of Natural Resources and Life Sciences, Vienna.

Jalilova, G. (2013). *Evaluating Management Strategies for Maintaining Forest Biodiversity in the Walnut Fruit Forests in Kyrgyzstan*. PhD thesis, University of Natural Resources and Life Sciences, Vienna.

Mamadjanov, D. (2001). An assessment of the local and foreign varieties and forms of the walnut according to their economically valuable and biological features. In *Silviculture and Forest Culture Research in Kyrgyzstan*, pp. 9–15.

Mamadjanov, D. (2006). Study of varieties and diversity of walnut forms in Kyrgyzstan. *Schweizerische Zeitschrift für Forstwesen*, 157(11): 499–506.

Mamadjanov, D. (2007). *Study and Selection of Promising Varieties and Forms of Circassian Walnut for Use in Industrial Plantations in the Walnut-Fruit Forests Zones of Kyrgyzstan.* PhD thesis, Institute for Forest and Walnut Research National Academy of Sciences of the Kyrgyz Republic, Bishkek.

Matveev, P. N. (1979). Hydrological and protective properties of walnut-fruit forests of southern Kyrgyzstan. In *Bioecological Research in the Walnut-Fruit Forests of Southern Kyrgyzstan* (Frunze: Ilim Publishing House), pp. 117–133.

Messerli, S. (2002). Agroforestry: a way forward to the sustainable management of the walnut fruit forests in Kyrgyzstan. *Schweizerische Zeitschrift für Forstwesen*, 153(10): 392–396.

Müller, U. and Sorg, J.-P. (2001). Gestion multifonctionnelle des forêts de noyer du sud du Kyrgyzstan: tradition, problèmes actuels, perspectives. *Schweizerische Zeitschrift für Forstwesen*, 152(4): 138–144.

Musuraliev, T. M. (1998). Forest management and policy for the walnut-fruit forests of the Kyrgyz Republic. In *Biodiversity and Sustainable Use of Kyrgyzstan's Walnut-Fruit Forests*, eds J. Blaser, J. Carter and D. Gilmour. IUCN, Gland, Switzerland and Cambridge, UK and Intercooperation, Berne, Switzerland. pp. 3–17.

Rehnus, M. and Sorg, J.-P. (2010). Sustainable management of unique natural walnut-fruit forests in southern Kyrgyzstan. Available at http://www.tropentag.de/2010/abstracts/full/306.pdf.

Rehnus, M., Sorg, J.-P. and Pasinelli, G. (2011). Habitat selection and attributes of potential cavity trees of the white-winged woodpecker (Dendrocopos leucopterus) in the walnut-fruit forest in Kyrgyzstan. *Acta Ornithologica*, 46(1): 83–95.

Rehnus, M., Mamadzhanov, D., Venglovsky, B. I. and Sorg, J.-P. (2013a). The importance of agroforestry hay and walnut production in the walnut-fruit forests of southern Kyrgyzstan. *Agroforestry Systems*, 87(1): 1–12.

Rehnus, M., Nazarek, A., Mamadzhanov, D., Venglovsky, B. I. and Sorg, J.-P. (2013b). High demand for firewood leads to overuse of walnut-fruit forests in Kyrgyzstan. *Journal of Forestry Research*, 24(4): 797–800.

Scheuber, M., Köhl, M. and Traub, B. (2000). Forstliche Inventur als Planungsgrundlage für die Forstwirtschaft Kirgistans. *Schweizerische Zeitschrift für Forstwesen*, 151(3): 75–79.

Schmidt, K. (2007). *Livelihoods and Forest Management in Transition – Knowledge and Strategies of Local People in the Walnut-Fruit Forests of Kyrgyzstan.* PhD thesis, University of Reading.

Schmidt, M. (2005). Utilisation and management changes in south Kyrgyzstan's mountain forests. *Journal of Mountain Science*, 2(2): 91–104.

Sorg, J.-P., Urech, Z. L., Mamadzhanov, D. and Rehnus, M. (in review). Thinning effects on walnut stem and crown diameter growth and fruiting in the walnut-fruit forests of Kyrgyzstan.

Vavilov, N. I. (1931). Wild relatives of fruit trees in the Asian part of the USSR and the origin of fruit trees. *Trudy po prikladnoi botanike, genetike i selektsii (Works on Applied Botany, Genetics, Artificial Selection)*, 26(3): 343–360 (in Russian).

Venglovsky, B. I. (2009). Bioecological peculiarities of renewal and development of walnut forests in Kyrgyzstan, National Academy of Science of the Kyrgyz Republic. Institute for Forest and Walnut Research, Bishkek.

Venglovsky, B. I., Mamadjanov, D., Sorg, J.-P., Rehnus, M., Sarymsakov, Z. and Abdukakharov, B. A. (2010). Bioecological bases for forestry management in walnut forests of Kyrgyzstan and their multifunctional uses (Southern Branch, Bishkek: Institute of Walnut and Fruit Cultures).

13 Ecologically based Integrated Pest Management programs for food security crops in Central Asia

Karim Maredia, George Bird, Doug Landis, Frank Zalom, Joy Landis, Megan Kennelly, Mustapha El-Bouhssini, Nurali Saidov and Murat Aitmatov

Introduction

The unexpected consequences of the post-World War II chemo-technology era resulted in the evolution of the technologies eventually called Integrated Pest Management (IPM). During this period, there were only limited direct contacts between Central Asian and Western agricultural scientists. An exception was a bilateral IPM meeting at Michigan State University (MSU) in 1975. After the break-up of the Soviet Union in 1991, the national governments of the newly independent states and international development agencies initiated agricultural research and development programs to enhance local food security and livelihoods. In the late 1990s, the Consultative Group on International Agricultural Research (CGIAR) in collaboration with national agricultural research systems established a regional program for agricultural research and development in Central Asia and the Caucasus to enhance the institutional capacity of public research organizations. Many initiatives were launched to break through the isolation and improve food self-sufficiency and livelihood (Babu and Tashmatov, 1999; Babu and Pinstrup-Andersen, 2000). This work comes in the context of challenges to the region's food security posed by climate change (Sommer et al., 2013) and concerns about the need for increased agro-biodiversity (Giuliani et al., 2011).

This chapter recounts the experience of international and domestic scientists who designed a collaborative IPM research and capacity-building program for three key food security crops – wheat, potato, and tomato – in Kyrgyzstan, Tajikistan, and Uzbekistan.

Statement of the problem

In Soviet times and continuing into independence, farmers in Central Asia have faced a number of issues related to use, availability, quality, and affordability of chemical pesticides. The intensive use and misuse of chemical pesticides can be costly both environmentally and financially. The negative impacts of pesticides on the environment and human health have been well documented worldwide (Pingali and Roger, 1995; Pingali, 1995). The challenge for scientists and practitioners was to build on prior research and collaboratively develop practical and cost-effective best practices that are ecologically sound to manage pests that damage and reduce yields in food crops. However, the institutional capacity and human resources to develop and implement ecologically based approaches to pest management were limited in Central Asia.

A regional approach

Prior studies have explored the potential benefits of IPM to improve the region's crop yield and farm income while reducing environmental and health risks. For example, Chermenskaya et al. (2010) assessed 139 extracts from 123 plant species for their behavior-modifying and insectoacaricidal activities against three species of phytophagous pests in Kyrgyzstan. Other relevant research has examined health risks posed by agricultural pollutants in groundwater and surface water systems. One such study in the Aral Sea Drainage Basin that encompasses parts or all of the region's five former Soviet republics noted "intensive agriculture … associated with extensive use of fertilizers and pesticides … has polluted water and soils." That study investigated health hazards "related to water-borne, basin-scale spreading of multiple persistent pollutants, including pesticides and toxic metals." It found cumulative health hazards that exceeded guideline values in downstream surface water commonly used without treatment for human consumption (Törnqvist et al., 2011).

Responding to Central Asia's pest management and food security needs and to expand the region's IPM capacity, the U.S. Agency for International Development provided a planning grant to MSU and the University of California-Davis (UC-Davis) to assess needs and identify local priorities. This grant was awarded through the Global IPM Collaborative Research Support Program (CRSP) (now referred to as the IPM Innovation Lab) managed by Virginia Tech University. A team of agricultural scientists representing MSU and UC-Davis visited Uzbekistan in May 2005 and interacted with institutions and stakeholders involved in IPM.

During this visit, a Regional IPM Stakeholders Forum in Tashkent assessed the needs and identified key partners for initiating a collaborative research support program. More than fifty stakeholders from Uzbekistan, Tajikistan, Kyrgyzstan, and international agricultural research centers attended. The stakeholders represented government agencies, nongovernmental organizations (NGOs), universities, international agricultural research centers, and inter-governmental organizations. During the forum, breakout sessions helped identify needs, constraints, and priorities for research and capacity-building.

At the forum, wheat, potato, and tomato were selected as priority crops for research and outreach. The U.S. team also visited research institutes, universities, and bio-laboratories (producers of biological control agents) and met with farmers in Uzbekistan. The participants identified an urgent need for a regional program and expressed a strong willingness to work together to set up an IPM network in Central Asia. The key findings of this assessment concurred with a similar assessment by Gerd Walter-Echols (2005) in Tajikistan in May 2005.

Building the foundation for ecologically based IPM programs

Based on the needs identified at the stakeholders' forum and during the institutional visits, the research team designed and launched a regional project referred to as Central Asia IPM project Phase I. Phase I (2005–2009) was implemented by MSU in collaboration with UC-Davis, the International Center for Agricultural Research in Dry Areas (ICARDA), and a number of governmental and non-governmental organizations and local universities. The project began in October 2005 and included Kyrgyzstan, Tajikistan, and Uzbekistan. It focused on three key components highlighted at the Tashkent stakeholders' forum:

- A collaborative research program to enhance the efficiency and product lines of bio-laboratories;
- A collaborative research program to enhance biological control of pests through landscape ecology and habitat management; and
- Strengthened outreach and educational programs in ecologically based IPM.

Using participatory and team-building approaches, three research associates from the region were recruited and posted in Tajikistan, Kyrgyzstan, and Uzbekistan to implement the project. They worked collaboratively with the ICARDA regional program and with U.S.-based project team members at MSU and UC-Davis.

During the Soviet era, hundreds of bio-laboratories were established in Central Asia to produce entomophages – organisms that feed mainly on insects – for field release to provide biological control of key pests. After the collapse of the Soviet Union, many of these laboratories shut down and others experienced significant reductions in efficiency. Local capacity needed to be enhanced. The first component, collaborative research to enhance efficiency and product lines of bio-laboratories, focused on predatory mites (Tashpulatova and Zalom, 2007). This research tested colonization and acclimatization of the predatory mite *Amblyseius sp* on bran mites, spider mites (family Tetranychidae), and other prey species in bio-laboratories in Uzbekistan and Kyrgyzstan. The results revealed that predatory mites can be potentially successful biological agents against the spider mite, *Tetranychus urticae*, in vegetable fields and against the whitefly, *Trialeurodes vaporariorum*, in tomato fields. New methodologies to maintain and rear predatory mite stock cultures during winter were developed.

In addition, this research determined effective predator–prey ratios. In addition to managing spider mites, *A. mckenziei* was found to be effective in controlling *Thrips tabaci* in onion crops in Uzbekistan and Kyrgyzstan. *Thrips tabaci* causes direct damage and also is known as a vector of the serious onion disease iris yellow spot virus.

The second component, collaborative research on landscape ecology and biological control, took place in Tajikistan (Saidov et al., 2007). There is increasing recognition among biological control researchers and IPM practitioners worldwide that conservation of natural enemies via landscape management is a key to ecologically based IPM systems (Landis et al., 2000). Carefully selected native plants that provide benefits to natural enemies including pollen, nectar, and other resources can be incorporated into agricultural landscapes to attract natural enemies that will enhance biological control of crop pests in agricultural production systems.

In collaboration with the Tajik Academy of Agricultural Sciences, the project developed a database on native flowering plants. Available seeds were collected for field testing. The team evaluated sixty native and locally adapted species for their attractiveness to natural enemies of pests. Among twelve native species most attractive to natural enemies, eight showed potential usefulness in agricultural landscapes for improving biological control of pests. The project tested them in fields of maize, cotton, wheat, and vegetable crops. To disseminate the concept of landscape ecology in the region, research results were presented through workshops and publications, as well as a television documentary produced and broadcasted in Tajikistan.

The third component, outreach and education, focused on both academic and non-academic stakeholders. It provided training and outreach through student field schools and farmers' field schools in collaboration with local NGOs, government institutes, and universities in all three countries (Aitmatov et al., 2007). To foster networking, team members actively participated in national, regional, and international meetings.

The activities implemented in Phase I produced significant beneficial impacts, particularly in breaking down isolation between host countries and the international community, creating awareness on IPM issues, and introducing concepts of ecologically based IPM in crop management programs. A three-member team of post-doctoral research associates trained in ecologically based approaches worked to increase awareness and use of ecologically based IPM at multiple levels: farmers, agricultural advisors and educators, university educators, and national research institutes.

The collaborative research, training, and outreach programs implemented during Phase I created networks and raised awareness of ecologically based IPM throughout the region (Maredia and Baributsa, 2007). Research focusing on bio-laboratories and application of landscape ecology laid a strong groundwork for integrating biological control components. Outreach programs implemented through the farmers' field schools provided a platform for delivering information and technologies to farmers and to AgroLead, a new NGO in Kyrgyzstan. In addition, student field schools served as a source of practical training for university students.

Development and delivery of IPM packages for food security crops

Building on the foundation established during Phase I, a consortium of universities and organizations initiated Phase II in October 2009. The objective was to develop and deliver ecologically based packages for wheat, tomato, and potato cropping systems. Phase II (2009–2014) was implemented by MSU in collaboration with UC-Davis, Kansas State University (KSU), and ICARDA, as well as governmental and non-governmental organizations and local universities. Figure 13.1 presents the resulting conceptual framework for development and delivery of ecologically based packages throughout Central Asia.

This approach allowed use of Phase I results and provided opportunities to involve existing technologies and to introduce new knowledge and technologies from other regions.

IPM packages consist of multiple tactics for managing pests affecting a specific crop or cropping system. A package may include components from cultural, biological, behavioral, mechanical, host plant resistance, regulatory, chemical, and biotechnological approaches. The packages for wheat, tomato, and potato targeted pest management problems in these three key food security crops in Tajikistan, Kyrgyzstan, and Uzbekistan. These crops were identified through consultations and recommendations of stakeholders at a regional forum in Bishkek in June 2009.

Wheat IPM

Wheat is the main staple crop in Central Asia, and the focus of the wheat IPM research and outreach activities has been in Tajikistan. A team of scientists[1] established two applied research and demonstration sites in the southern and northern regions of the country. Key pest and disease problems there include yellow rust (caused by the fungus *Puccinia striiformis*), Sunn pest (*Eurygaster integriceps*) – which also damages barley – and cereal leaf beetle (*Oulema melanopus*).

The package (see Appendix 13A) for wheat includes:

- Resistant varieties – the yellow rust-resistant variety 'Ormon' from ICARDA;
- Introduction of flowering nectar plants such as coriander (*Coriandrum sativum*), sweet basil (*Ocimum basilicum*), marigold, and mint (*Mentha* spp.) to attract parasites and predators;
- Biological control – cereal leaf beetle and Sunn pest parasitoids;
- Cultural control (hand-picking) of Sunn pest; and
- Planting and harvest date considerations.

There were substantial yield benefits in research plots that followed the IPM package compared with farmer practices. The data from three years indicate an average yield increase of 38 percent in IPM plots.

Potato IPM

Potato is an important food security crop in Central Asia, where it is considered a "second bread." These research and outreach activities focused in Kyrgyzstan and

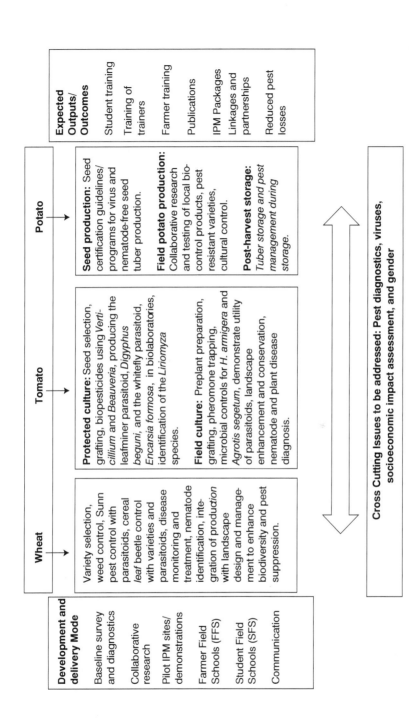

Development and delivery Mode	Wheat	Tomato	Potato	Expected Outputs/ Outcomes
Baseline survey and diagnostics	Variety selection, weed control, Sunn pest control with parasitoids, cereal *leaf* beetle control with varieties and parasitoids, disease monitoring and treatment, nematode identification, integration of production with landscape design and management to enhance biodiversity and pest suppression.	**Protected culture:** Seed selection, grafting, biopesticides using *Verti-cillium* and *Beauveria*, producing the leafminer parasitoid, *Digyphus beguni*, and the whitefly parasitoid, *Encarsia formosa*, in biolaboratories, identification of the *Liriomyza* species.	**Seed production:** Seed certification guidelines/ programs for virus and nematode-free seed tuber production.	Student training
Collaborative research				Training of trainers
Pilot IPM sites/ demonstrations			**Field potato production:** Collaborative research and testing of local bio-control products, pest resistant varieties, cultural control.	Farmer training
Farmer Field Schools (FFS)		**Field culture:** Preplant preparation, grafting, pheromone trapping, microbial controls for *H. armigera* and *Agrotis segetum*, demonstrate utility of parasitoids, landscape enhancement and conservation, nematode and plant disease diagnosis.		Publications
Student Field Schools (SFS)			**Post-harvest storage:** *Tuber storage and pest management during storage.*	IPM Packages
Communication				Linkages and partnerships
				Reduced pest losses

Cross Cutting Issues to be addressed: Pest diagnostics, viruses, socioeconomic impact assessment, and gender

Figure 13.1 Conceptual framework for development and delivery of ecologically based IPM packages in Central Asia

Table 13.1 Performance of potato varieties in Tajikistan in 2013 and 2014

Variety/Line	Total kilograms harvested in 2013	Total kilograms harvested in 2014
Boulder	10	21
Missaukee	13	25.5
Dakota Diamond	22	43
Kalkaska	24	49.4
MSP270-1	16	31.5
MSQ176-5	3	5
MSL268D	18	33
MSM182-1	9	16
Cardinal – Taj-1 (local check)	7	12
Picasso – Taj-2 (local check)	4.5	7.5

Tajikistan. The team established potato applied research and demonstration sites in both countries. Key pest problems there include the Colorado potato beetle (*Leptinotarsa decemlineata*), potato late blight (caused by *Phytophthora infestans*), potato scab (caused by the bacterium *Streptomyces scabies*), viruses (several), and potato cyst nematode (*Globodera* spp.).

The package (see Appendix 13B) for potato includes:

- Certified seeds – virus-free clean seed tubers;
- Soil or seed treatment to reduce fungal pathogens – *Trichoderma* species;
- Resistant varieties – potato cyst nematodes, Colorado potato beetles, and late blight;
- Biological and cultural control;
- Roguing infested plants in the field;
- Bio-pesticides – e.g. neem oil (derived from the plant *Azadirachta indica*).

The screening of improved varieties in Tajikistan in 2013 and 2014 in small plots found a threefold to fourfold yield gain in improved varieties compared to local ones. This shows great potential for improved varieties that can be integrated into IPM packages.

Tomato IPM

Tomato is an important food security crop used in daily diets. Tomato is cultivated both in greenhouses and open fields. Tomato research and outreach activities focused on Uzbekistan, where the project team[2] developed IPM packages (see Appendices C and D) for greenhouse cultivation and open fields. The crop's key pest problems are various species of white flies, mites, leaf miners, boll worms, aphids, Fusarium wilt, and viruses.

The package for tomato cultivation (Appendix 13C) in greenhouses includes:

- Soil or seed treatments: (e.g. *Trichoderma* species);
- Grafting on resistant root stock – Southern root-knot nematode, white flies, aphids, and Fusarium wilt;
- Rouging in the nursery to remove infected plants;
- Yellow sticky traps to aid in monitoring pests and making decisions;
- Bacterial formulations (*Bacillus subtilis*);
- Biological control (parasitoid release for insect control).

The IPM package for tomato cultivation in open fields (Appendix 13D) includes:

- Soil or seed treatments – *Trichoderma* species;
- Grafting on resistant root stock – Southern root-knot nematodes, aphids, and fusarium;
- Biological control;
- Mulching for disease control and moisture conservation;
- Rouging in the nursery;
- Screening of resistant varieties;
- Pheromone traps;
- Yellow sticky traps;
- Bio-pesticides.

The tomato IPM packages need to be field tested in local farming situations for further recommendations.

Communication and dissemination of research results

Over a period of ten years, the project team prepared more than 100 publications and extension materials such as leaflets, brochures, proceedings, scientific papers, and books on aspects of IPM in tomato, wheat, and potato crops. The materials were distributed widely to more than 5,000 Central Asian stakeholders (researchers, students, extension specialists, and farmers) during extension and outreach programs such as farmers' field schools, student field schools, farmer field days, workshops, and five regional IPM forums. The majority of publications were made available in Russian and local languages. More information on the project is available at www.ipm.msu.edu/international/central_asia_ipm.

A decade's key accomplishments, 2005–2014

- *Broken isolation from the global IPM community*: For more than seven decades during the Soviet era, scientists and farmers in Central Asia were isolated from cutting-edge Western agricultural research and pest control best practices, and technologies. The project helped reconnect IPM specialists in region with the U.S. and global IPM community.

- *Ecologically based packages for food security crops*: The research initiated development of ecologically based packages for wheat, potato, and tomato systems in countries where these are traditional food security crops.
- *Training of local farmers, scientists, and students*: The project trained more than 1,500 participants through farmers' field schools. More than fifteen students underwent training at research sites through collaboration with local universities. Three students from Tajikistan, Kyrgyzstan, and Uzbekistan received opportunities to earn graduate degrees at MSU. Sixteen regional scientists attended International Agroecology, IPM, and Sustainable Agriculture short courses at MSU.
- *Publications and sharing of information with stakeholders*: This includes dissemination of bulletins, flyers, posters, crop calendars, and research papers in local languages to farmers and other stakeholders.
- *Recognition*: The consortium received the CGIAR King Baudouin Science Award in 2008 for Outstanding Partnership for Sustainable Agriculture in Central Asia.

Sharing of results and recommendations for future collaboration to continue capacity-building

The project organized a regional workshop in Tajikistan in August 2014 to share its results and achievements with stakeholders and seek their input for future collaboration. The workshop produced these recommendations:

Areas for future collaborations, new projects, and activities

- Conduct additional research and provide extension services on IPM for other horticultural crops, with a special emphasis on apricots, grapes, melons, and apples;
- Enhance extension education services for farmers, including use of cellphones;
- Establish pest diagnostic labs and centers in various regions, possibly including mobile diagnostic units;
- Strengthen breeding programs for good-quality seed and enhance national seed systems;
- Assess the impact of climate on agricultural pests and develop IPM programs to adapt to and mitigate impacts of climate change;
- Collect, publish, and disseminate information on traditional pest control practices and knowledge.

Publications and dissemination of research results, information, and experiences

- Publish a book capturing ten years' experiences and achievements of the project;

- Publish easy-to-understand, user-friendly booklets in local languages on nematodes, viruses, and landscape ecology;
- Publish booklets on IPM for each of the three focus crops;
- Publish special bulletins on landscape ecology and agro-landscape enhancing, and the experience and approaches of farmers' field schools;
- Develop a roster of IPM/plant protection specialists in Central Asia and post it on the ICARDA website;
- Post project photos on the website.

Conclusion

IPM is only a part of the efforts to enhance food security in Kyrgyzstan, Tajikistan, and Uzbekistan, but a crucial part. Adoption of best practices in IPM should complement and reinforce research about and implementation of other environmentally sustainable initiatives by farmers, government ministries, international funders, researchers, and NGOs to diversify crops, to cope with the effects of climate change, and to enhance the economic status of rural communities. With an excellent network and institutional capacity now established, there are potential opportunities for strengthening and expanding collaborative research and outreach programs to further enhance IPM programs. These opportunities include cross-cutting topics such as gender equality and other socioeconomic aspects for greater adoption of IPM by local communities. Ultimately, the greater impacts of IPM programs can be achieved only if they are integrated into the overall agricultural R&D agenda of the countries and the region.

Acknowledgements

Financial support for the Central Asia IPM CRSP Innovation Lab project was provided by the U.S. Agency for International Development under Cooperative Agreement No: EPP-A-00-0400016-00, and by Michigan State University.

Notes

1 Dr. Doug Landis (Michigan State University); Dr. Megan Kennelly (Kansas State University); Dr. Mustapha Bohssini (ICARDA); Dr. Nurali Saidov (Tajikistan); Dr. Anwar Jalilov (Tajikistan); and Shahlo Safarzoda (graduate student from Tajikistan at Michigan State University).
2 Dr. Frank Zalom (UC-Davis); Dr. Barno Tashpulatova (Uzbekistan); Dr. Ravza Mavlyanova (Uzbekistan); and Bahodir Eshchanov (graduate student from Uzbekistan at Michigan State University).

Ecologically-based IPM Package for wheat

Central Asia Integrated Pest Management Collaborative Research Support Program: Dr. Nurali Saidov, IPM CRSP Coordinator/Research Fellow, Tajikistan; Dr. Doug Landis, Michigan State University; Dr. Mustapha El-Bouhssini,

IPM packages deliver food security

For the past 5 years IPM CRSP researchers have been developing sets of agricultural practices for wheat and vegetable production in Central Asia. The anticipated outcome is improved plant health, reduced pesticide use, and a resulting increase in production and food security along with farmer income.

By partnering with scientists, educators, outreach specialists, and farmers in the region, the IPM CRSP is working to improve the livelihood and food security of people living in poverty in Tajikistan, Uzbekistan, Kyrgyzstan and the surrounding area.

An IPM package is a set of practices and technologies that can be used in production of a crop to increase yield and reduce pesticide use. The key pest problems for wheat production in Tajikistan are yellow rust (stripe rust), Sunn pest and cereal leaf beetles. Potential IPM components to reduce these problems include:

Disease resistant varieties

Collaborating international and local wheat breeders have identified several wheat varieties resistant to yellow rust. These have been released for use by Central Asian farmers.

For more information: www.ipm.msu.edu/central-asia.htm

production in Tajikistan

ICARDA, Aleppo, Syria; Dr. Megan Kennelly,
Kansas State University; Dr. Anvar Jalilov,
Tajik Academy of Agricultural Sciences,
Tajikistan.

Seeding rates
Seeding rates are being studied to
fine-tune the optimum rates for best
yields.

Planting and harvest dates
Research indicates that planting
wheat earlier in northern Tajikistan
can help avoid infestation by the
Sunn pest, a group of insects
that damages plants and reduces
yields and quality by feeding
on leaves, stems, and grains.
Harvesting wheat immediately after
physiological maturity also reduces
the effects of these pests.

Biological control
Native parasitoids exist for Sunn
pest and cereal leaf beetle.
Planting local native plants such
as coriander and dill near wheat
fields could provide a nectar source
for the beneficial species that can
reduce pest insect populations.

Fertilizer rate and timing
Delivering fertilizer to the plants
at the right time and amount will
enhance plant health and yields.

Weed control
Controlling weeds early before they
can compete will improve wheat
yields.

This research was supported by the Integrated Pest Management Collaborative Research
Support Program (IPM CRSP), which was made possible by the United States Agency
for International Development and the generous support of the American people through
USAID Cooperative Agreement No. EPP-A-00-04-00016-00.

Ecologically-based IPM Package for potato

 Central Asia Integrated Pest Management Collabora- tive Research Support Program: Dr. Murat Aitmatov, IPM CRSP Coordinator/Research Fellow, Kyrgyzstan;

IPM packages deliver food security
For the past 5 years IPM CRSP researchers have been developing sets of agricultural practices for wheat and vegetable production in Central Asia. The anticipated outcome is improved plant health, reduced pesticide use, and a result- ing increase in production and food security along with farmer income.

By partnering with scientists, educators, outreach specialists, and farmers in the region, the IPM CRSP is working to improve the livelihood and food security of people living in poverty in Tajikistan, Uzbekistan, Kyrgyzstan and the surrounding area.

An IPM package is a set of practices and technologies that can be used in production of a crop to increase yield and reduce pesticide use. The key pest problems for potato produc- tion in Kyrgyzstan are Colorado potato beetles, late blight, and potato cyst nematodes. Potential IPM practices to reduce these problems include:

Disease-free certified seed
Use of certified seed will ensure growers have clean, disease-free seed material to plant.

Resistant varieties
Collaborating international

For more information   www.ipm.msu.edu/central-asia.htm

production in Kyrgyzstan

Drs. George Bird, Walter Pett, and David Douches, Michigan State University.

and local potato breeders are identifying varieties with the traits best able to resist late blight as well as insect pests and nematodes (*Globodera* spp.).

Biological control
Potato seed is being inoculated with the biopesticide *Thrichoderma* to gain biological control of potato fungal pathogens. Other available biopesticides include neem, nucleopolyhedrosis virus, *Verticillium*, *Beauveria bassiana*, *Metarhizium,*and others.

Cultural control
Mulching in the field conserves moisture and helps with disease control.

Removing disease-infected plants culls weaker plants before they affect the desirable seed.

Monitoring pests
Placing yellow sticky traps in the field helps monitor for whiteflies and aphids and assists in control decisions.

This research was supported by the Integrated Pest Management Collaborative Research Support Program (IPM CRSP), which was made possible by the United States Agency for International Development and the generous support of the American people through USAID Cooperative Agreement No. EPP-A-00-04-00016-00.

Ecologically-based IPM Package for greenhouse

Central Asia Integrated Pest Management Collaborative Research Support Program: Dr. Barno Tashpulatova, IPM CRSP Coordinator/Research Fellow, Uzbekistan; .

IPM packages deliver food security

For the past 5 years IPM CRSP researchers have been developing sets of agricultural practices for wheat and vegetable production in Central Asia. The anticipated outcome is improved plant health, reduced pesticide use, and a result-ing increase in production and food security along with farmer income.

By partnering with scientists, educators, outreach specialists, and farmers in the region, the IPM CRSP is working to improve the livelihood and food security of people living in poverty in Tajikistan, Uzbekistan, Kyrgyzstan, and the surrounding area.

An IPM package is a set of practices and technologies that can be used in production to increase yield and reduce pesticide use. Key pests in protected culture are greenhouse whitefly, tomato russet mite, leafminers, spider mites, aphids, nematodes, bacterial spot, early blight, macrosporium leaf spot, late blight, damping-off, top rot of fruit, septoria blight, tobacco mosaic virus, potato virus–X, mild mosaic, cucumber mosaic virus I, single virus streak, stripe, and tospoviruses. Potential IPM practices to reduce these pest problems include:

tomato production
in Uzbekistan

Dr. Frank Zalom, University of California-Davis; Dr. Ravza Mavlyanova, AVRD-C/World Vegetable Center.

Soil or seed treatments
Soil or seed treatments with *Trichoderma* spp., *Pseudomonas fluorescens* or *Bacillus subtilis* help control soil borne fungal and bacterial diseases.

Grafting on resistant root stock
Grafting on resistant root stock offers Fusarium disease control.

Biological control
Parasitoids can be released in the **greenhouse to control whiteflies,** caterpillar pests and others. *Bacillus subtillis* is a good biological agent because of its stabiity to CA conditions.

Cultural control
Mulching in the crop conserves moisture and helps with disease control. Removing disease-infected plants stops further spread.

Monitoring for pests
Placing yellow sticky traps in the production area helps monitor for **whiteflies and aphids and assist in** control decisions. Pheromone traps can be used to monitor for tomato fruitworm.

For more information
www.ipm.msu.edu/central-asia.htm

This research was supported by the Integrated Pest Management Collaborative Research Support Program (IPM CRSP), which was made possible by the United States Agency for International Development and the generous support of the American people through USAID Cooperative Agreement No. EPP-A-00-04-00016-00.

Ecologically-based IPM Package for open field

Central Asia Integrated Pest Management Collaborative
Research Support Program: Dr. Barno Tashpulatova, IPM
CRSP Coordinator/Research Fellow, Uzbekistan;

IPM packages deliver food security

For the past 5 years IPM CRSP researchers have been developing sets of agricultural practices for wheat and vegetable production in Central Asia. The anticipated outcome is improved plant health, reduced pesticide use, and a resulting increase in production and food security along with farmer income.

By partnering with scientists, educators, outreach specialists, and farmers in the region, the IPM CRSP is working to improve the livelihood and food security of people living in poverty in Tajikistan, Uzbekistan, Kyrgyzstan, and the surrounding area.

An IPM package is a set of practices and technologies that can be used in production to increase yield and reduce pesticide use. Key pests in open fields are fruitworms, cutworms, tomato russet mites, leafminers, aphids, nematodes, bacterial spot, early blight, macrosporium leaf spot, late blight, damping-off, top rot of fruit, septoria blight, tobacco mosaic virus, potato virus–X, mild mosaic, cucumber mosaic virus I, single virus streak, stripe, and tospoviruses. Potential IPM practices to reduce these pest problems include:

tomato production in Uzbekistan

Dr. Frank Zalom, University of California-Davis; Dr. Ravza Mavlyanova, AVRDC/World Vegetable Center.

Soil or seed treatments
Trichoderma lignorum can be released on the soil before planting to help control soil borne fungal and bacterial diseases.

Grafting on resistant root stock
Grafting on resistant root stock offers Fusarium disease control.

Biological control
Encarsia can be released for **biological control of whiteflies,** and *Trichogramma* and *Bracon* for biocontrol of fruitworms. Biopesticide options are neem, nucleopolyhedrosis virus, *Verticillium, Beauveria bassiana, Metarhizium*, and others.

Cultural control
Mulching in the crop conserves moisture and helps with disease control. Removing disease-infected plants stops further spread.

Monitoring for pests
Placing yellow sticky traps in the **field helps monitor for whiteflies** and aphids and assist in control decisions. Pheromone traps can be used to monitor for tomato fruit worm, and blue sticky traps for thrips.

For more information
www.ipm.msu.edu/central-asia.htm

This research was supported by the Integrated Pest Management Collaborative Research Support Program (IPM CRSP), which was made possible by the United States Agency for International Development and the generous support of the American people through USAID Cooperative Agreement No. EPP-A-00-04-00016-00.

References

Aitmatov, M., Bird, G. and Pett, W. (2007) Development and dissemination of IPM knowledge through outreach and university education program in Central Asia. *Proceedings of the Central Asia Regional IPM stakeholders Forum, Dushanbe, Tajikistan*, 27–29 May 2007.

Babu, S. and Pinstrup-Andersen, P. (2000) Achieving food security in Central Asia: Current challenges and policy research needs. *Food Policy*, 25(6): 629–635.

Babu, S. and Tashmatov, A. (1999). Attaining food security in Central Asia: Emerging issues and challenges for policy research. *Food Policy*, 24(4): 357–362.

Chermenskaya, T.D., Stepanycheva, E.A., Shchebikova, A.V. and Chakaeva, A.S. (2010) Insectoacaricidal and deterrent activities of extracts of Kyrgyzstan plants against three agricultural pests. *Industrial Crops and Products*, 21: 157–163.

Giuliani, A., van Oudenhoven, F. and Mubalieva, S. (2011) Agricultural biodiversity in the Tajik Pamirs. *Mountain Research and Development*, 31(1): 16–26.

Landis, D.A., Wratten, S.D. and Gurr, G.M. (2000) Habitat management to conserve natural enemies of arthropod pests in agriculture. *Annual Review of Entomology*, 45: 175–201.

Maredia, K.M. and Baributsa, D.N. (2007) Integrated Pest Management in Central Asia. Proceedings of the Central Asia Region Integrated Pest Management Stakeholders Forum, Dushanbe, Tajikistan, 27–29 May 2007.

Pingali, P.L. (1995) Impact of pesticides on farmer health and the rice environment: an overview of results from a multidisciplinary study in the Philippines. In Pingali, P. and Roger, P. (eds), *Impact of Pesticides on Farmer Health and the Rice Environment*. Boston, MA: Kluwer Academic Publishers.

Pingali, P.L. and Roger, P.A. (1995) *Impact of Pesticides on Farmer Health and the Rice Eco-System*. Boston, MA: Kluwer Academic Publishers.

Saidov, N., Landis, D. and Bohssini, M. (2007) A history of habitat management in the former USSR and Commonwealth of Independent States and current research in Central Asia. Proceedings of the Central Asia Regional IPM Stakeholders Forum, Dushanbe, Tajikistan, 27–29 May 2007.

Sommer, R., Glazirina, M., Yuldashev, T., Otarov, A., Ibraeva, M., Martynova, L., Bekenov, M., Kholov, B., Ibragimov, N., Kobilov, R., Karaev, S., Sultonov, M., Khasanova, F., Esanbekov, M., Mavlyanov, D., Isaev, S., Abdurahimov, S., Ikramov, R., Shezdyukova, L. and de Pauw, E. (2013) Impact of climate change on wheat productivity in Central Asia. *Agriculture, Ecosystems and Environment*, 178: 78–99.

Tashpulatova, B. and Zalom, F. (2007) Enhancing the efficiency and product lines of bio-laboratories in Central Asia. Proceedings of the Central Asia Regional IPM Stakeholders Forum, Dushanbe, Tajikistan, 27–29 May 2007.

Törnqvist, R., Jarsjö, J. and Karimov, B. (2011) Health risks from large-scale water pollution: trends in Central Asia. *Environment International*, 37: 435–442.

Walter-Echols, G. (2005) Opportunities for Integrated Pest Management in Tajikistan. Unpublished Consultancy Report. FAO/TCIE.

14 A treasure in the desert?

Carbon stock estimates for *Haloxylon aphyllum* in the northeastern Karakum Desert

Allan Buras, Niels Thevs, Stefan Zerbe, Walter Wucherer and Martin Wilmking

Introduction

Among the earth's terrestrial ecosystems, deserts and other dryland ecosystems are the least productive and thus exhibit the lowest vegetation carbon densities, or mass of carbon per area [t C ha^{-1}] (for example, Cao and Woodward, 1998; Townsend et al., 2008). Despite their low carbon densities, dryland ecosystems may contribute significantly to global carbon stocks as they cover an area of approximately 28.1 million square kilometers (10.8 million square miles) and thus represent the largest of all terrestrial biomes (Trumper et al., 2009; Epple, 2012). However, detailed studies of the contribution of particular desert ecosystem components to global carbon stocks are rarely available (Cao and Woodward, 1998; Lal, 2002; Trumper et al., 2008, 2009; Epple, 2012).

In contrast to the hot deserts of the low latitudes that are mainly bare of higher vegetation, the winter-cold Karakum, Kysylkum and Muyunkum deserts of Central Asia are sparsely vegetated in general (Walter and Breckle, 1986; Rachkovskaya, 1995). However, within these deserts – and in particular in the Northeastern Karakum – comparably dense, forest-like stands of *Haloxylon aphyllum*, also known as black saxaul, are found where groundwater conditions provide suitable living conditions (Rotov, 1969; Netchayeva et al., 1973; Rachkovskaya, 1995). These stands protrude from the surrounding desert due to an above-average water supply and thus an above-average plant cover – and therefore, carbon stock. The value of these stands may relate to different ecosystem services:

1   Provisioning service: The local population has long used saxaul wood as firewood and is still preferred for preparing *shashlik*, a traditional food, due to its high content of essential oils.
2   Regulating (and possibly economic) service: sequestration of carbon dioxide. If this sequestration is accounted for financially – for example, in terms of the REDD+ program (Reduced Emissions from Deforestation and forest Degradation), CDM (Clean Development Mechanism), or the UNCCD (United Nations Convention to Combat Desertification), the stands may be a factor in the low income of local residents because they are not logged (UNFCCC, 2002a, 2002b; Parker et al., 2009).

3   Supporting service: shelter and habitat for a large variety of desert animals, such as the saxaul sparrow (*Passer ammodendri*), the Pander's hog (*Podoces panderi*), turtles, and mice.

The absolute carbon stock values of these stands are mandatory information for estimating the quantity of I and II. Their spatial distribution and extent is relevant information for III. However, within the literature, there is little relevant and up-to-date data available (Kurochkina, 1966; Walter and Breckle, 1986; Buras et al., 2012; Thevs et al., 2012), and none of these references estimate in detail the total carbon stock of *H. aphyllum* on a larger scale. This information may be useful to stakeholders, such as:

- Ecologists, with respect to the contribution of Central Asian desert ecosystems to the global carbon cycle;
- Foresters, in monitoring and managing *H. aphyllum* stands;
- Policymakers and nature conservationists, in climate change mitigation activities, combating desertification, and nature conservation.

Research question

To provide a first step in filling these knowledge gaps, we address the following questons:

- How to derive remotely sensed carbon stock estimates for *H. aphyllum* stands in the northeastern Karakum?
- What is the recent carbon stock of *H. aphyllian* in the northeastern Karakum?

Material and methods

Study object: mono-specific Haloxylon aphyllum stands

Haloxylon aphyllum is more salt-tolerant and expresses a higher affinity to groundwater than other frequently occurring woody plant species (e.g. *Calygonum* spec., *Haloxylon persicum*) in the Northeastern Karakum (Rotov, 1969; Netchayeva, 1973). This affinity limits its distribution to dune depressions with an above-regional-average groundwater supply where it is a dominant woody species and, thus, forms mono-specific forest-like stands with *Carex physodes* as the dominant grass understory (Kurochkina, 1966; Rotov, 1969; Netchayeva et al., 1973; Rachkovskaya, 1995). Single individuals of *Calygonum* may occur but will likely not contribute substantially to the carbon stock of these stands due to their local rarity and comparably low carbon stock contribution (Buras et al., 2012).

Figure 14.1 Map of Turkmenistan with study area in the Northeastern Karakum Desert

Training area for GIS calibration

The training area for calibration of the satellite images was in Charlak – the core area of the biosphere state reserve Repetek (38.4° North, 63.3° East) in the Northeastern Karakum Desert (Figure 14.1). We chose Charlak because it has been a nature reserve since 1927, was recognized by UNESCO as a Biosphere Reserve in 1978, and contains an undisturbed mono-specific stand of *H. aphyllum.* We recorded the GPS coordinates, height, canopy area, and basal area of sixty *H. aphyllum* individuals according to the Point Centered Quarter method (Mueller-Dombois and Ellenberg, 1974). By applying an allometric formula and average carbon contents (Buras et al., 2012), we estimated the total above- and below-ground carbon stock for each specimen.

To create a basis for remote sensing of *Haloxylon* carbon stock, we calculated a root-root regression (Model I) between the estimated carbon stock and the in-situ measured canopy area. This allowed us to estimate carbon stock based on a high resolution QUICKBIRD (QB) satellite image (pixel size: 0.6 m x 0.6 m, recorded 9 June 2010). For the complete QB image, we defined canopy areas using a manual classification based on specific spectral properties of *Haloxylon* vegetation in the RED and NIR channels, as well as considering the NDVI (Normalized Differenced Vegetation Index – see Lillesand et al., 2004, and Buras, 2013 for details).

To validate this approach, we defined a rectangular area whose boundaries correspond with the GPS coordinates of the four individuals for each of the fifteen sampling points shown in Figure 14.2. We calculated the sum of the corresponding test areas' carbon stock and tested it for correlation with the remotely sensed carbon stock derived from Model I.

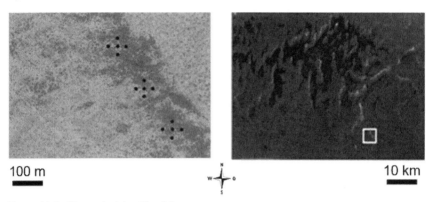

100 m

10 km

Figure 14.2 Channel of the Charlak training site

Upscaling to the LS-scale

In the next step, we used LANDSAT (LS; Enhanced Thematic Mapper) satellite images to upscale Model I to a larger scale. To do so, 1,100 coordinates in the mono-specific *H. aphyllum* stand of Charlak and corresponding with the pixels centers of a LS scene (Path 157, Row 33, recorded 16 June 2009) were chosen as training plots. For each plot (30 m x 30 m, i.e. one LS pixel or 2,500 i.e. 50 x 50 QB pixels), we calculated the average NDVI. To test for their similarity, we calculated Spearman's rank between both NDVI (QB vs. LANDSAT) values. Further, the resulting average QB-NDVI was tested for correlation with the sum of QB remotely sensed carbon stock estimates derived from Model I for the same areas, thus summed over 2,500 pixels). Finally, we modeled the observed relationship. As linear models revealed to overestimate the carbon stock of pixels with low NDVI and high NDVI, we computed a two-parameter logistic function (Model II), which better explains the variance of carbon stock estimates using NDVI as indicated by a higher explained variance of the model (r^2). We computed Model II to test whether it is possible to upscale the canopy area–carbon stock relationship to the LS-scale by averaging NDVI, which is a good proxy for biomass (Lillesand et al., 2004; Buras et al., 2013). To create a basis for scaling up the carbon stock estimates, we carried out the same modeling (as with Model II) procedure for the LS scene (Model III). This allowed us to compare the LS NDVI with QB-based remotely sensed carbon stock estimates for the same area. However, the relationship between LS NDVI and QB carbon stock showed more noise (a lower r^2). Therefore, the carbon stock estimates were square-root transformed to stabilize the variance of count data (Crawley, 2007) as carbon stock estimates were based on counts of pixels classified as *H. aphyllum*. Here, a two parameter Michaelis–Menten model expressed the best explanation of carbon stock estimates by LS NDVI.

Finally, we manually classified the whole Landsat scene to determine the mono-specific stands in the specific part of the Northeastern Karakum where they occur naturally. Here, the NDVI turned out to be a very sensitive channel because these stands exhibited comparably high NDVI values (Figure 14.2, right). However, RED, GREEN, and BLUE channels were also included in the manual classification to improve the matching of classified pixels with visually determined *H. aphyllum* pixels (RGB image). Based on Model III, we estimated the standing carbon of *H. aphyllum* from the NDVI for all LS pixels classified as *H. aphyllum* stands. We carried out all GIS programming and statistical analyses with Q-GIS (Version 1.6.0; Open Source Geospatial Foundation), GRASS GIS (Version 6.4.0; Open Source Geospatial Foundation) and 'R' (Version 3.0.1, R Foundation for Statistical Computing, Vienna, Austria; extended with the 'rgdal' package).

Findings

The canopy areas of the sixty measured specimens had a high explanatory power on the respective carbon stock estimates (Model I: $r^2 = 0.78$, $p < 0.001$, Figure 14.3 left). Remotely sensed biomass estimates for the fifteen point-based areas showed a higher explanatory power on the carbon stock sums of the four specimens (validation of Model I: $r^2 = 0.91$, $p < 0.001$; Figure 14.3 right). Based on Model I and the classified QB image, the total standing carbon stock of Charlak was estimated at 755 t C in an area of 99 hectares (245 acres), meaning average carbon density of 7.6 t C ha^{-1}).

QB and LS NDVI values for the 1,100 training plots showed a significant high correlation ($r = 0.88$, $p < 0.001$). The best-fit two parameter logistic regression among QB NDVI and remotely sensed carbon stock of the training plots had a high explained variance (Model II: $r^2 = 0.88$, p < 0.001, compared to $r^2 = 0.81$, $p < 0.001$ for the linear model, Figure 14.4).

Carbon stock estimates for Charlak based on model II were 785 t C with carbon densities ranging from 0.2 to 16.7 t C ha^{-1} (mean: 8.0 t C ha^{-1} ± sd: 4.4 t C ha^{-1}).

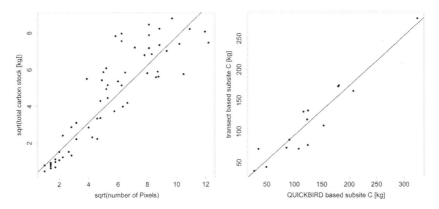

Figure 14.3 The square-roots of canopy area and total carbon stock of *H. aphyllum*

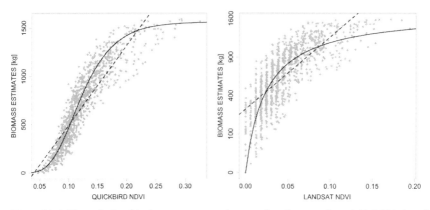

Figure 14.4 The relationship between remotely sensed carbon stock and Quickbird and Landsat NDVI models

The relationship between LS NDVI and remotely sensed carbon stock for the same training plots was comparably lower (Model III: r^2 = 0.67, p < 0.001, compared to r^2 = 0.59, p <0.001 for the linear model, Figure 14.4). From Model III the total carbon stock of Charlak was estimated at 735 kt C with carbon densities ranging from 0.1 to 15.4 t C ha^{-1} (mean 7.7 ± 3.6 t C ha^{-1}).

According to the manual classification of the LS scene, altogether 45 square kilometers (17.4 square miles) of mono-specific *H. aphyllum* stands were located in the Northeastern Karakum. Based on Model III, the total carbon stock of these stands was estimated at 31 kt C with an average carbon density of 7.0 ± 2.8 t C ha^{-1} (range 2.5–15.6 t C ha^{-1}).

Discussion and conclusion

Given the average proportional contribution of aboveground biomass of *H. aphyllum* to its total biomass (53 percent), the above-ground biomass here related to *H. aphyllum* is 15.5 kilotons. Compared to Thevs et al. (2012), who estimated the total above-ground carbon stock of the Northeastern Karakum at 341 kt over an area of roughly 10,000 square kilometers (38,600 square miles), the large contribution of carbon stocks related to *H. aphyllum* stands (4.5 percent of the total carbon stock on roughly 0.5 percent of the total area – thus nine times higher carbon density as an average) to the total ecosystems' carbon stock clearly becomes visible.

Our estimates are supported by prior studies. Kurochkina (1966) reported a range of 1.5–4.8 t C ha^{-1}, for the corresponding ecotype. To make it easier to compare with our data, we calculated carbon stocks from Kurochkina' s results. As our estimates also include below-ground carbon, and the ratio of above- and below-ground carbon stocks according to the literature ranges from 0.9 to 1.7 (Prichodko and Prichodko, 1968; Miroshnichenko, 1975; Gunin and Dedkov, 1978), values of up to 10 t C ha^{-1} would still be within the range of data mentioned by Kurochkina (1966). These values are comparable to the average C densities in our study, which were estimated at roughly 8 t C ha⁻¹. However, Kurochkina (1966) reports values of up to 9.6 t C ha⁻¹ for above-ground carbon stock for *H. aphyllum* growing with a better water supply (that is, at most 20.1 t C ha⁻¹ if belowground carbon is included). Therfore, theoretically, it seems possible that a partition (17 percent, according to our estimates) of mono-specific *H. aphyllum* stands in dune depressions, but under comparably good conditions, could express higher-standing carbon stock values than the range of data Kurochkina (1966) cited. In the context of previous research, the results from our remote sensing approach seems realistic. Comparison of Models I, II, and III and their rather similar estimates of the carbon stock of the training area supports confidence in our approach.

To our knowledge, there has been no other investigation dealing in detail with such large-scale estimates related to *H. aphyllum* either in the Northeastern Karakum or elsewhere in its distribution area. A comparison to *Populus euphratica* – the dominant tree species of the most productive Central Asian ecosystems along rivers – which express carbon densities between 3.0 and 22.5 t C ha⁻¹ further highlights the important contribution of *H. aphyllum* stands to the region's carbon stock (Thevs et al., 2011; Buras et al., 2013).

Our results may provide useful information for ecologists, foresters, and policymakers. Due to their relatively high carbon stock compared to surrounding deserts, monospecific *H. aphyllum* stands in the Northeastern Karakum represent an important ecosystem component for dependent species. In particular, mapping these stands may prove valuable in monitoring *Passer ammodendri* and *Podoces panderi*, both of which depend on *H. aphyllum* stands. It may allow estimates of the stands' connectivity with the birds' area of influence and, in this context, the effects on population genetics through eased or hampered exchange by lower or higher distances.

In another context, the results can serve as a baseline in any kind of carbon trade mechanism and nature conservation program. Here, mechanisms such as REDD+, UNCCD, and CDM could determine an economic value of carbon stock values. In this context, conservation of *H. aphyllum* stands could be accounted for economically to increase the often-marginal financial income of local residents.

Furthermore, an ongoing or retrospective longitudinal monitoring of these stands by remote sensing could reveal ecological changes in the Karakum Desert. These changes may originate from groundwater withdrawal in the Southern Karakum for irrigation or changes in temporary precipitation patterns – on which the study species depend – related to global climate change. Both variables may lower the groundwater level. Knowledge about the vegetation carbon stock and its changes over time could deepen the understanding of vegetation responses to global climate change (e.g. Kirilenko and Solomon, 1998; Cramer et al., 2002; Eisfelder et al., 2010, 2012).

Our results extend the data available in the literature to a larger scale and record the actual distribution and carbon stock of mono-specific *H. aphyllum* stands in the Northeastern Karakum Desert. The findings can be applied in the context of climate change mitigation and ecosystem monitoring. However, further investigation is necessary to expand our results to all of Central Asia and to cover other ecotypes. To do so, specific calibration of satellite images on ground-truth data will be required to achieve verifiable results to estimate carbon stock related to *H. aphyllum* elsewhere in the region.

References

Buras, A. (2013) Assessing the carbon sequestration potential of *Populus euphratica* and *Haloxylon spec.* in Central Asian Desert ecosystems. PhD thesis, University Greifswald.

Buras, A., Thevs, N., Zerbe, S. and Wilmking, M. (2013) Productivity and carbon sequestration of *Populus euphratica* at the Amu Darya, Turkmenistan. *Forestry*. Available at http://forestry.oxfordjournals.org/content/early/2013/06/10/forestry.cpt014.full.

Buras, A., Wucherer, W., Zerbe, S., Noviskiy, Z., Muchitdinov, N., Shimshikov, B., Zverev, N., Schmidt, S., Wilkming, M. and Thevs, N. (2012) Allometric variability of Haloxylon species in Central Asia. *Forest Ecology and Management*, 274: 1–9.

Cao, M. and Woodward, F. I. (1998) Net primary and ecosystem production and carbon stocks of terrestrial ecosystems and their responses to climate change. *Global Change Biology*, 4: 185–198.

Cramer, W., Bondeau, A., Woodward, I., Prentice, C., Betts, R. A., Brovkin, V., Cox, P. M., Fisher, V., Foley, J. A., Friend, A. D., Kucharik, C., Lomas, M. R., Ramankutty, N., Sitch, S., Smith, B., White, A. and Young-Molling, C. (2002) Global response of terrestrial ecosystem structure and function to CO_2 and climate change: results from six dynamic global vegetation models. *Global Change Biology*, 7: 357–373.

Crawley, M. J. (2007) *The R-book* (Chichester, UK: John Wiley and Sons).

Eisfelder, C., Keunzer, C. and Dech, S. (2010) A review on derivation of biomass information in semi-arid regions based on remote sensing data. *Proceedings of SPIE*, Volume 7831.

Eisfelder, C., Kuenzer, C. and Dech, S. (2012) Derivation of biomass information for semi-arid areas using remote-sensing data. *International Journal of Remote Sensing*, 33(9): 2937–2984.

Epple, C. (2012) The climate relevance of ecosystems beyond forests and peatlands: Aareview of current knowledge and recommendations for action – BfN-Skripten 312 Bonn (German Federal Agency for Nature Conservation).

Gunin, I. D. and Dedkov, W. P. (1978) *Ekologichetskie Rezhim pustennyh biogeotsenozov* (Moscow: Izdvo Nauka) (in Russian).

Kirilenko, A. P. and Solomon, A. M. (1998) Modeling dynamic vegetation response to rapid climate change using bioclimatic classification. *Climatic Change*, 38: 15–49.

Kurochkina, L. J. (1966) in B. A. Bykow. *Rastiteljnijj pokrow Kasachstana Nauka Kasachstanskoj SSR Alma-Ata* (in Russian).

Lal, R. (2002) Carbon sequestration in dryland ecosystems of West Asia and North Africa. *Land Degradation and Development*, 13(1): 45–59.

Lillesand, T. M., Kiefer, R. W. and Chipman, J. W. (2004) *Remote Sensing and Image Interpretation* (5th edition) (New York: Wiley & Sons).

Miroshnichenko, Y. M. (1975) Root systems of trees and bushes and their ecology in the eastern Karakum. *Botanicheskii Zhurnal*, 60: 1176–1196 (in Russian).

Mueller-Dombois, D. and Ellenberg, H. (1974) *Aims and Methods of Vegetation Ecology* (1st edition) (New York: Wiley & Sons).

Netchayeva, N. T., Vasilevskaya, V. K. and Antonova, K. G. (1973) *Life Forms of Plants of Karakum Desert* (Moscow: Nauka) (in Russian).

Parker, C., Mitchell, A., Trivedi, M., Mardas, N. and Sosis, K. (2009) *The Little REDD+ Book*. Global Canopy Foundation.

Prichodko, S. and Prichodko, N. (1968) Rost i razvitie kornevyh system belogo i tsernogo saksaulob Isv Turkmen SSR, serija boil Nauka: pp. 37–45 (in Russian).

Rachkovskaya, E. I. (1995) Vegetation of Kazakhstan and Middle Asia (Desert region), Scale 1: 2 500 000, Komarov Botanic Institute, Russian Academy of Sciences, Saint Petersburg.

Rotov, R. A. (1969) Biological-Morphological Features of Perennial Desert Plants (Moscow: Nauka) (in Russian).

Thevs, N., Wucherer, W. and Buras, A. (2012) Spatial distribution and carbon stock of the Saxaul vegetation of the winter-cold deserts of Middle Asia. *Journal of Arid Environments*, 90: 29–35.

Thevs, N., Zerbe, S., Buras, A., Kühnel, E., Abdusalih, N. and Ovezberdyyeva, A. (2011) Structure and wood biomass of near-natural floodplain forests along the Central Asian rivers Tarim and Amu Darya. *Forestry*, 85(2): 193–202.

Townsend, C. R., Begon, M. E. and Harper, J. L. (2008) *Essentials of Ecology* (3rd edition) (New York: Wiley & Sons).

Trumper, K., Ravilious, C. and Dickson, B. (2008) Carbon in drylands: desertification climate change and carbon finance. A UNEP-UNDP-UNCCD technical note for discussions at CRIS 7, Istanbul, Turkey, 3–14 November 2008.

Trumper, K., Bertzky, M., Dickson, B., Van der Heijden, G., Jenkins, M. and Manning, P. (2009) The Natural Fix? The role of ecosystems in climate mitigation. A UNEP rapid response assessment. United Nations Environment Programme UNEPWCMC, Cambridge UK.

United Nations Framework Convention on Climate Change (2002a) Report of the Conference of the Parties on its Seventh Session held in Marrakech from 29 October –10 November 2001. Addendum Part Two: Action Taken by the Conference of the Parties, Volume I (FCCC/CP/2001/13/Add 1). United Nations Framework Convention on Climate Change Secretariat, Bonn, Germany.

United Nations Framework Convention on Climate Change (2002b) Report of the Conference of the Parties on its Seventh Session held in Marrakech from October 29–November 10, 2001. Addendum Part Two: Action Taken by the Conference of the Parties, Volume II (FCCC/CP/2001/13/Add 2). United Nations Framework Convention on Climate Change Secretariat, Bonn, Germany.

Walter, H. and Breckle, S. M. (1986) *Ecology of the Earth – Specific Ecology of Temperate and Boreal Zones of Eurasia* (Stuttgart: Gustav Fischer Verlag) (in German).

15 Through the crystal ball

Mark Neuzil and Eric Freedman

Emil Shukurov remembers what the great walnut forest of Central Asia was like. His first memory came in the decade after World War II ended and when the centralized economic expansion plans of the Soviet empire had only barely touched the remote valleys in southern Kyrgyzstan where tens of thousands of acres of *Juglans regia* grew. It was—and is—a complex ecosystem that also hosts apple, pear, and plum trees—130 species overall—and wild boars, deer, bears, owls, hawks, white woodpeckers, and other wildlife, as well as farmers, herders, and nomads descended from the tribes that roamed the region for centuries.

"It was a paradise," Shukurov, now in his 80s, recalled in an interview in late 2014.[1] And he has more than a passing interest in the forests—a highly trained biologist, the tall, lean scientist has kept a critical eye on the area for almost sixty years. (The Soviets supported an experimental research station nearby in 1945 to start commercializing the timber and fruit.) He ticked off a list of environmental problems affecting the world's largest walnut grove (150,000 acres, in several sections): poaching of fruit and lumber, overgrazing, climate change, corrupt officials, poor resource management, and more.

The Aral Sea is the media darling of Central Asia environmental problems. As we have seen, it gets rock-star attention, fueled in no small part by the arresting visual images of rusting, stranded fishing boats and a lake bottom-turned-desert. But as the contributors in this volume have ably demonstrated, the list of environmental concerns in Central Asia is a long one, with difficult and multifaceted causes.

The walnut forest, the largest patch of which is known as Arslanbob (27,000 acres), in Chapter 11 is a case in point. The trees hold a deep cultural significance among the local population. Most local schoolchildren know the story of Alexander the Great, the Macedonian king and military genius (356–323 BC) who conquered Persia, Egypt, Syria, Mesopotamia, Bactria, and the Punjab but met his match on the plains of the mountains and steppes of Central and South Asia against its herders, tribespeople, and nomads as he marched to India. Battered, hungry, and facing a revolt in his ranks after outstripping his supply lines, the general and his army holed up in the walnut forest, nursing themselves back to life by eating its high-fat, high-protein nuts and hunting its game.

Alexander figures prominently in the mythology of the Middle East and Central and South Asia. An alternative version of the walnut story has him planting the original trees in the region. Another tree story, mentioned by Marco Polo in his journal, has Alexander defeating Darius at the *Arbre Sec* ("dry tree" or "solitary tree"), the only tree within hundreds of miles, perhaps in north Persia near the present Turkmenistan border.[2]

It is likely Alexander returned home with walnut plantings, perhaps from the genetic stock in the Sogdiana region between the Amu Darya and Syr Darya rivers, to begin plantations in Europe. And in a bit of hubris/marketing, he named them "Greek" walnuts. Some etymological evidence for the tale exists in the Russian word for walnuts: *gretski*, meaning Greek, and a common local nickname for walnuts, "Greek nuts."

Apocryphal or not, these stories are a source of pride in both their telling of native resistance to Alexander's army and the life-giving nature of the woods. Their cultural importance makes the threats to the groves even more worrisome to scientists and government officials. And the threats are not new. Some conservation efforts were taken in the 1970s, notably the establishment of the Dashman Forest Reserve of 12,000 acres in 1975 in the Jalal-Abad province in Kyrgyzstan. But matters took a sharp downward turn in the 1980s as the Soviet system started to totter and the forest faced its greatest threat from illegal logging and overgrazing, according to Shukurov. After independence, jurisdiction over the forest passed to the local communities, with the reasoning that the fledgling national government lacked the resources to manage it. Neighbors, many deprived of their Soviet-supplied coal and electricity, were allowed to harvest dead trees for firewood and lumber.

Alexander Temirbekov, a technical adviser for the Kyrgyz Association of Forest and Land Users in Bishkek, noted that 200,000 people live in or near the forest and many have depended on the wood and fruit their entire lives.[3]

Policing the uses of the forest proved difficult, and continued corruption at the local level, both before and after independence, did not help. Trees were girdled (gouged with an axe to kill them) and then cut down as "legal" dead harvests. A moratorium on logging was put in place. An export ban on lumber and nuts was established.

Cattle continue to graze in the timberlands, eating or stomping on young trees, sometimes crowding out native deer. "The greatest threat is that the natural ecosystem of the forest will be destroyed because of a lack of diversity of the grasses and young trees after the grazing," Shukurov told us.

Walnut burls—large knotty growths on the trees cut for highly figured furniture, veneer, bowls, gunstocks, and other uses—are a valuable target for poachers. Some are as large as automobiles and worth hundreds of thousands of dollars each. "The sad thing is that most experts look at the forest not as an ecosystem, but as an industrial system," Shukurov said.

Climate change brings another set of agricultural and silvicultural problems, including the proliferation of invasive species such as the gypsy moth. "The [cutting] moratorium stopped illegal fellings," Temirbekov said. "But felling is a major tool for management to control pests and diseases."

Adylbek Ormonov, director of the Kyrgyzstan State Agency on Environmental Protection and Forestry, is concerned about the age of the forest as the lack of young trees adversely affects its health. Cattle ruin the saplings, he said, and are difficult to fence out, although "in some parts there are fences and the forest is very healthy there."[4] Some of the 200- to 300-year-old trees need to be culled. He held up some of the fruits of the Arslanbob. The lighter nuts received more water during their growth, he explained, while the darker ones come from drier regions. "And the black ones taste better," he said with a smile.

A workshop in 1995, put together by the World Conservation Union, drew attention to the plight of the forest.[5] Shukurov favors a combination of artificial planting and natural regeneration to revive the groves, but he carries with him the pessimism of a lifetime of battling for the forest. "In many places it will be impossible anyway," he predicted.

The challenges, noted in Chapter 11, faced by those in government, science, and NGOs at Arslanbob have distinct features, but also share elements with other environmental issues discussed in this book. At least the walnut forest is contained within the borders of Kyrgyzstan. A significant factor in many of the other problems illuminated by our contributors is the geopolitical boundaries of Central Asia, a product of the early Soviet period (begun in 1924, mostly completed by 1937) in which the USSR leaders' strategy of divide-and-conquer among the native populations left a crazy-quilt map of distrust and worse. "Ethnic gerrymandering" is how journalist Philip Shishkin referred to it after Josef Stalin forcibly moved clans and ethnic groups into three new republics: Uzbekistan, Kyrgyzstan, and Tajikistan

Figure 15.1 Stone statue in a Bishkek park (photo: Mark Neuzil)

(Shishkin, 2013, pp. 73–74). Dissent was successfully suppressed most of the time, but after independence in 1991 the new nations were left with borders that often made little ethnic or geographic sense.[6] "The region's ethnic tapestry is so rich that just when you think you've encountered all possible ethnic groups and subgroups here, you find someone else," he wrote (Shishkin, p. 238).

The significant role of ethnic tensions, many of which have religious overtones with the rise of Islam and the outbursts of violence that accompany it, has often shoved environmental concerns into the backseat of regional social concerns. In the West, a common predictor of the rise and fall of environmental problems in a social system is the relative economic health of the system. The economic argument can be boiled down to "rich people are greener" because individuals don't examine environmental problems when they've got economic ones.[7] Some evidence exists that poorer *nations* have high environmental concerns, but those countries usually have difficulty paying for solutions. Outside of the economic argument, moderate evidence exists of a relationship between democratization and levels of environmental sustainability (Whitford and Wong, 2009).

Neither of these factors function in favor of the five countries we have examined in Central Asia. Tajikistan's estimated gross domestic product of $9.2 billion (USD) for 2014 places it near the bottom of the global rankings, and Kyrgyzstan's output of $7.6 billion is even lower. Using another measure, median per capita income, Kyrgyzstan ($828) and Tajikistan ($713) also fall in the lowest tier of global economic health. Kazakhstan has the most robust economy among the five countries (2013 GDP of $224.4 billion USD). None of this includes the amount of money lost to corruption (Gascoigne, 2014).

In terms of democratic processes, the measures are equally bleak. Kyrgyzstan graded out as "partially free" by the watchdog group Freedom House in 2015,[8] but Kazakhstan, Tajikistan, Uzbekistan, and Turkmenistan received "not free" rankings (Freedom House, 2015). Uzbekistan and Turkmenistan were in the bottom ten "Worst of the Worst 2011: The World's Most Repressive Societies," along with North Korea, Libya, and Somalia (Freedom House, 2011). Corruption measures also paint a bleak picture: Among 177 countries listed by the NGO Transparency International, Kazakhstan (140), Kyrgyzstan (150), Tajikistan (154), and Turkmenistan and Uzbekistan (tied for 168) point to the abuse of power, pervasive bribery, and secret deals that are common (Transparency International, 2013).

Wildlife management and international borders are less problematic than some other environmental issues because of the existence of treaties such as CITES (Convention on International Trade in Endangered Species of Wild Fauna and Flora). International trade in about 5,000 species of animals and nearly 30,000 species of plants are protected through CITES, which dates back to an international conference held in 1963. But treaties need signatories, and signatories need to live up to the terms of the document. In the case of CITES, for example, Kazakhstan, Kyrgyzstan, and Uzbekistan have signed it, but Tajikistan and Turkmenistan have not. In another example concerning the greenhouse gas emissions treaty known as the Kyoto Protocol, Kazakhstan, Kyrgyzstan, Tajikistan,

Turkmenistan, and Uzbekistan all are signatories, but none are included in the list of industrialized countries committed to reducing CO_2 emissions in the first target period. Thus little action has been taken on pollution reduction—and no real incentive exists to do so.

Water might be the most prevalent cross-border issue, as seen in several chapters. "Water, or lack of it, unifies inner Asia," wrote one historian (Adshead, 1993, p. 7). It is not that water resources are scarce, necessarily; water falls in the form of snow and collects in the region's many rivers and lakes. But rain tends to be rarer, and rainfall is more convenient for agriculture—it is usable water for irrigation and watering livestock. Environmental problems such as water use provide opportunities for cross-cultural and cross-boundary cooperation, but evidence that this has taken place is sparse. NGOs are attempting to help, but difficulties with government instability and corruption are roadblocks, and some NGOs themselves are not immune to corruption, favoritism, and mismanagement. Water and energy combine to make hydropower, as seen in Chapter 4, and its use can affect issues like irrigation and drinking water as well.

Feeding, clothing, and sheltering the population as cheaply and efficiently as possible are always high priorities for any society. Climate change, as discussed in Chapter 1, threatens those agricultural systems in ways that the Soviets—who attempted to turn Central Asia, in the words of one writer, into a cotton monoculture "megafarm"—could not have imagined (Soucek, 2000, p. 235).

Figure 15.2 The yurt, the traditional home for many Central Asian herding families (photo: Mark Neuzil)

Soviet Uzbekistan, under the corrupt and iron fist of Sharaf Rashidov (1959–1983) in particular, underwent a "catastrophic destruction of the country's environment and public health" to meet Soviet price and production goals for cotton (Soucek, pp. 254–255). Soviet disregard of environmental health is a well-known story and a problematic and dangerous legacy.

The views from the West, particularly as presented through Western-style or Western-sponsored media (Chapter 8), illustrate environmental problems that may not get much attention in the public arenas of Central Asia because of limitations on press freedom and free expression—many, if not most, political and intellectual freedoms, in sum. The openness of *glasnost* has not been realized in the media systems of these five countries, and, as in all sovereign states, propaganda apparatuses exist as a counter-narrative as the countries struggle with authoritarianism.

The fabled Silk Road, a network of trading routes, once traversed Central Asia, connecting East and West and transmitting cultures, religious faiths, goods, and ideas. In 2014, UNESCO designated 3,100 miles that cross Kazakhstan and Kyrgyzstan into China as a World Heritage Site under the formal title Silk Roads: the Routes Network of Chang'an-Tianshan Corridor. Historically, to survive their treacherous, uncertain missions, travelers along the Tianshan Corridor depended on the water, fruits, and wildlife they found along the way. In fact, many archeological sites along the corridor, as UNESCO notes, relate to the water and water management so essential for trade. Their journeys traversed the same steppes, deserts, and mountains beset by environmental crises today. The people of Central Asia continue to rely on the same imperiled resources.

It is the hope of the editors that this book will cast light on the pressing environmental issues of the day in this ancient yet rapidly modernizing region with its natural wealth and ecological challenges, and that it will continue or initiate discussions and research about possible solutions. Many of these challenges are unique to the region, so one assumes that the answers will be as well. That may make them more difficult to accomplish, but the people of Central Asia have persisted through difficult times in what may seem like most of their existence—a trait that should not be underestimated.

Notes

1 Interview with the authors, 29 November 2014, Bishkek, Kyrgyzstan.
2 From Polo's description, it appears the tree was a *Platanus*, possibly a sycamore.
3 Interview with the authors, 28 November 2014, Bishkek, Kyrgyzstan.
4 Interview with the authors, 28 November 2014, Bishkek, Kyrgyzstan.
5 The papers were collected and published as *Biodiversity and Sustainable Use of Kyrgyzstan's Walnut-fruit Forests*, J. Blaser et al., eds. IUCN (1998).
6 In reality, of course, all nations need to deal with minority populations within their borders, be they ethnic, linguistic, or religious.
7 See for example Malcolm Fairbrother (2013) Rich people, poor people, and environmental concerns: Evidence across nations and time, *European Sociological Review*, 29(5), pp. 910–922.
8 Although rated overall as partly free, Kyrgyzstan ranked as "not free" in Freedom House's separate *Freedom of the Press* report.

Bibliography

Adshead, S.A.M. (1993) *Central Asia in World History* (London: Macmillan).

Blaser, J., Carter, E.J., Gilmour, D.A., Venglovsky, B. and Yunossova, I., eds (1998) *Biodiversity and Sustainable Use of Kyrgyzstan's Walnut-fruit Forests* (Gland, Switzerland: IUCN).

Fairbrother, M. (2013) Rich people, poor people, and environmental concerns: Evidence across nations and time. *European Sociological Review*, 29(5), pp. 910–922.

Freedom House (2011) *Worst of the Worst 2011: The World's Most Repressive Societies.* Available at https://www.freedomhouse.org/sites/default/files/WorstOfTheWorst2011. pdf.

Freedom House (2015) *Freedom in the World 2015.* Available at https://freedomhouse.org/report/freedom-world/freedom-world-2015#.VQNC9eHMI-o.

Gascoigne, C. (2014) New study: Crime, corruption, tax evasion drained a record US$991.2bn in illicit financial flows from developing economies in 2012. Global Financial Integrity. Available at http://bit.ly/1uKm9OH.

Shishkin, P. (2013) *Restless Valley: Revolution, Murder and Intrigue in the Heart of Central Asia* (New Haven, CT: Yale University Press).

Soucek, S. (2000) *A History of Inner Asia* (Cambridge: Cambridge University Press).

Transparency International. (2013) *Corruption Perceptions Index 2013.* Available at http://www.transparency.org/cpi2013/results.

Whitford, A.B. and Wong, K. (2009) Political and social foundations for environmental sustainability. *Political Research Quarterly*, 62(1), pp. 190–204.

Index

Italic page numbers indicate tables; bold indicate figures.